The Little Magazine in Contemporary America

EDITED BY IAN MORRIS AND
JOANNE DIAZ

The University of Chicago Press   *Chicago and London*

IAN MORRIS has taught courses on literature, writing, and publishing at Lake Forest College in Illinois and Columbia College Chicago. He was managing editor of *TriQuarterly* magazine for over a decade and is the founding editor of Fifth Star Press and the author of the novel *When Bad Things Happen to Rich People.* JOANNE DIAZ is associate professor of English at Illinois Wesleyan University. She was an assistant editor at *TriQuarterly* and is the author of two collections of poetry, *The Lessons* and *My Favorite Tyrants.*

The University of Chicago Press, Chicago 60637
The University of Chicago Press, Ltd., London
© 2015 by The University of Chicago
All rights reserved. Published 2015.

Printed in the United States of America

24 23 22 21 20 19 18 17 16 15   1 2 3 4 5

ISBN-13: 978-0-226-24055-8 (cloth)
ISBN-13: 978-0-226-12049-2 (paper)
ISBN-13: 978-0-226-24069-5 (e-book)
DOI: 10.7208/chicago/9780226240695.001.0001

Library of Congress Cataloging-in-Publication Data
The little magazine in contemporary America / edited by Ian
    Morris and Joanne Diaz.
        pages cm
    Includes index.
    ISBN 978-0-226-24055-8 (cloth : alkaline paper) — ISBN
    978-0-226-12049-2 (paperback : alkaline paper) — ISBN
    978-0-226-24069-5 (e-book) 1. Little magazines—United
    States. 2. Periodical editors—United States. 3. Periodicals—
    Publishing—United States. I. Morris, Ian, 1961– editor.
    II. Diaz, Joanne, editor.
        PN4878.3.L54 2015
        051—dc23

                                    2014045144

♾ This paper meets the requirements of ANSI/NISO Z39.48-1992
(Permanence of Paper).

THE LITTLE MAGAZINE IN
CONTEMPORARY AMERICA

Contents

Preface

IAN MORRIS AND JOANNE DIAZ

We compiled this book in order to offer some insight into the experience of editing little magazines during the most radical paradigm shift since the invention of movable type. This undertaking draws its inspiration in large part from two influential texts of the last century. The first of these, *The Little Magazine in America: A Modern Documentary History* (published fall 1978 as an issue of *TriQuarterly*, and again in 1980 by the Pushcart Press), was a sprawling, 750-page compendium of essays and interviews detailing the state of little magazine publishing in the United States from roughly the end of the Second World War through the 1970s. The editors, Elliott Anderson and Mary Kinzie, were partly inspired in this project by an earlier book, *The Little Magazine: A History and Bibliography*, edited by Fredrick J. Hoffman, Charles Allen, and Carolyn Ulrich. The study was published by Princeton University Press in 1946 and surveyed magazines from the dawn of modernism and the founding of *Poetry* in 1911. These two books, which have established a cult following, feature the stories of editors with outsized personalities whose iconoclastic impulses have inspired many of today's best editors.

The moment seems right for another broad view. Not only has the advent of online platforms disrupted the prevailing order in every aspect of publishing, but the thirty-five-year interval since the publication of the Anderson/Kinzie anthology has the feel of a coherent epoch. New Criticism has been supplanted by theories of reading that are more attentive to gender, race, and issues of globalization. Enrollment in creative writing programs has risen exponentially across the country; even so, funding for many little magazines has been cut or omitted altogether from university budgets, while many other independent magazines struggle to survive. It has become increasingly apparent that the period between 1980 and 2015 will be seen as the end of the ascendancy of print periodicals.

With this new paradigm in mind, we began reaching out to editors of the leading little magazines of the past thirty years, asking them to contribute original essays on a topic of their choosing. The imposition of these requests became apparent to us as soon as we began sending out solicitations. Any little magazine editor has thousands, sometimes tens of thousands, of manuscripts pass before his or her eyes every year, along with review copies of hundreds of new books, e-mails from authors, and requests from subscribers. The advent of the Internet has added exponentially to the demands upon the editor's attention. In addition to time spent blogging, tweeting, editing Tumblr feeds, and posting on Facebook, editors now have access to an inexhaustible supply of information pertaining to the field, including other magazines, the works of authors whom the editor may wish to publish, and endless links leading to matters current in the field, both high and low. Add to this unceasing textual blur the fact that many little magazine editors are college instructors or are supporting themselves with better-paying editorial work, and most are writers themselves, facing deadlines for articles, while the cursors on their home computers blink on page 307 of a five-hundred-page novel in progress.

We were therefore gratified that most of the editors we approached were enthusiastic about the project and eager to contribute. Some of them cited a desire to continue the discussion begun by Hoffman, Allen, and Ulrich; and Anderson and Kinzie. Others were motivated by the state of the debate over the effects of online publishing on print magazines. The prevailing sentiment, however, was that a revisiting of the subject was overdue.

Much to our delight, each submission we received provided fresh insight into the state of little magazines today. For months we had worked in solitude, outlining the structure for this book and, in doing so, developing a sense of the history of publishing over the past thirty years. Now, all at once, a dialogue was forming. From the first we could see why the individual stories of magazine editors dominated not only the first-person recollections in Anderson and Kinzie, but also the ostensibly scholarly Hoffman et al. Above all, little magazine editors value the ways in which literary conversations evolve in their pages and on their websites. It is this conversation that inspires, challenges, and sustains them, regardless of changes in technology, medium, or financial constraint.

There are many compelling creation myths in this volume, as editors tell of the experience of waiting for the shipment of the first issue to arrive, all of them anxious, all of them, it would turn out, with good reason. Lee Gutkind wakes in the middle of the night and rechecks the first issue of *Creative Nonfiction* to find a large chunk of the first essay missing. Keith Gessen recounts nearly losing his rent-controlled sublet when the first shipment of *n+1* arrived early. Greg Johnson describes the moment that Joyce Carol Oates and Ray Smith opened a box containing the first issues of the *Ontario Review* only to find many of them smeared with blood.

A few of the editors we invited were unable to contribute. One or two others initially committed but had to drop out owing to time constraints. Because this anthology begins with the 1980s, we wrote to Gordon Lish—to many the father of 1980s minimalist fiction—to contribute a piece on his *Quarterly* (1987–1995). What we received in return was a blank postcard, with the handwritten message:

Sorry, the thing
was the thing it was, and now
it's not. Nothing
to add, save
Kind regards,
Gordon Lish[1]

We felt this was an elegant articulation of how little magazines burn brightly for a time and then extinguish themselves. As Jeffrey Lependorf observes in this volume, literary magazines are usually quite short-lived: "I regularly describe starting a literary magazine as akin to starting a restaurant: some open and close, some have a few good years, and a few seem to be around as long as anyone can remember."[2] In fact, many scholars of the little magazine would argue that such impermanence actually defines the format. T. S. Eliot believed that a magazine should have "a single editor, a small circulation, and a short life span, rarely exceeding that of the founding editorship."[3] In the second and third decades of the twentieth century many magazines appeared spontaneously in support of a flurry of new movements, including Futurism, Surrealism, and Vorticism. Their editors would turn out a few numbers at odd intervals and then move on to new projects or movements. However, as the century progressed, editors sought and perfected more sustainable approaches to publishing. Longevity was in. Indeed, *Poetry*, one of the first modernist magazines, thrives to this day (after nine or so decades of hand-to-mouth existence). In our book, current *Poetry* editor Don Share offers a vision at the end of the next century of the magazine's operations.

Once we recognize that the general profile of the little magazine editor allows for an intrinsic idiosyncrasy, the history of little magazines (for all their characteristic eclecticism) aligns along a relatively narrow range of tendencies. Editors characteristically establish new magazines in reaction to—and usually out of dissatisfaction with—the literary status quo or their respective eras. For example, Harriet Monroe founded *Poetry* to pro-

1. Personal correspondence with Ian Morris, October 30, 2010.
2. "Introduction: A Decade or So of Little Magazines; One Reader's Perspective," 5.
3. T. S. Eliot, quoted in *The Little Magazine in America: A Modern Documentary History*, ed. Elliott Anderson and Mary Kinzie (Yonkers, NY: Pushcart Press, 1978), 217.

mote a prosody stripped of "eloquence, grandiloquence, poetic diction—
all the frills and furbelows, which had overdraped, over-ornamented its
beauty."[4] In this volume, Charles Henry Rowell, founding editor of *Callaloo*,
describes the urgent need that he saw in the 1970s for a magazine devoted to Black writers of the South. In his essay on *Exquisite Corpse*, Andrei
Codrescu lambastes the conservatism of little magazines, and the culture
as a whole, in the 1980s, and notes how the *Corpse* served as antidote to
that tendency. Bruce Andrews, founding coeditor of *L=A=N=G=U=A=G=E*,
describes the theoretical and cultural interventions that that magazine
made for just a few short years in the 1980s.

In keeping with the approach of our predecessors, we maintain the de-
scriptor "little" rather than "literary." While many, perhaps most, of the
little magazines of the past century featured poetry and fiction, many did
not. We have chosen "little" to allow for nonliterary content.[5] The earliest modernist magazines, such as the *Little Review* (1914–22) and the *Seven
Arts* (1916–17), were preoccupied with the full scope of the arts, as were the
post-WWII magazines *Kulchur* (1960–66) and *Yugen* (1958–62), and some
in this volume, including BOMB, *n+1*, and *Bitch*, which was born out of the
zine scene, and *Women's Review of Books*.

Penury is integral to the definition of the little magazine. Hoffman
characterized the little magazine as a vehicle for "artistic work which for
reasons of commercial expediency is not acceptable to the money-minded
periodicals or presses."[6] Three decades later, Anderson and Kinzie agreed
with this characterization: "Little magazines generally put experiment
before ease, and art before comment. They can afford to do so because
they can barely afford to do anything; as a rule they do not, and cannot,
expect to make money."[7] While several of the magazines featured in this
book—including *McSweeney's*, *Bitch*, BOMB, and *Poetry*—have thrived, at
least in terms of circulation and longevity, these characterizations remain
true for the majority of magazines. And the editors of these magazines
would all agree that making money has never been a primary goal.

The ingenuity with which editors have responded to financial con-

4. *Poetry* 33 (October 1928), 34.
5. Robert Scholes and Clifford Wulfman acknowledge the difficulty of assigning small
magazines to one category or another in their book *Modernism in the Magazines: An Introduction* (New Haven, CT: Yale University Press, 2010); and George Plimpton bristles at
the diminutive connotations of the phrase "little magazine" in his essay "Enterprise in
the Service of Art," in *The Little Magazine in America: A Modern Documentary History*. Even
so, many editors use the phrase "little magazine" with no difficulty.
6. Frederick J. Hoffman, Charles Allen, and Carolyn F. Ulrich, eds., *The Little Magazine: A
History and a Bibliography* (Princeton, NJ: Princeton University Press, 1947), 2.
7. "Prefatory Note," *The Little Magazine in America: A Modern Documentary History*, 3.

straints has been a significant part of the legends of the magazines themselves. In the early twentieth century, members of the American literary
avant-garde traveled to Europe in search of a more stimulating intellectual and cultural discourse and, coincidentally, favorable exchange rates.
A celebrated example of this last phenomenon was *Broom* (1921–24), a
magazine that began its brief but eventful run as a full-color affair, published in a Roman palace and ended in New York, "greatly reduced in size"
and done in by censorship and a lack of financing.[8] Daisy Aldan, editor of
the New York School magazine *Folder* (1953–56), describes how she put together the first issue, along with Grace Hartigan, Frank O'Hara, and John
Ashbery: "They all came to this little studio and we all walked around a
table putting the pages together like a smorgasbord." Later in the same interview she said, "Certainly being poor never deterred a truly gifted person
from creating art," which might serve as a motto for the little magazine.[9]

Editors have traditionally found ways of getting by, including in many
cases editors paying considerable amounts of money out of pocket. And
in this book, Rebecca Wolff, founding editor of *Fence*, vividly captures the
demands and pressures a self-financed magazine places upon its editor.
In general, little magazines are founded and run with a highly specialized
readership in mind. The idea of altering their content to attract more subscribers would strike most little magazine editors as precisely beside the
point. What these editors seek is influence within the larger community
of the arts. Major figures such as James Joyce, e. e. cummings, T. S. Eliot,
Ezra Pound, H. D., Amiri Baraka, and others have had their most celebrated
and widely read works published in little magazines. For example, T. S. Eliot's "The Love Song of J. Alfred Prufrock," "The Waste Land," and "Tradition and the Individual Talent" were all first published in magazines with
subscriptions under a thousand. These days, printing costs have made the
independent print magazine almost a thing of the past. And the editors
of university magazines, who once could boast of the prominent writers
they published between their subsidized covers as rationale for their existence, now attend panels and workshops at academic conferences on how
to increase subscriptions. In his essay on the *Alaska Quarterly Review*, Ronald Spatz acknowledges that it is no longer sufficient for well-established
magazines to tout their list of accomplished authors. Instead, editors must
find new ways to create literary communities, whether it be online or in
person via reading series and other public forums.

In the 1960s and 1970s, as magazine editors were confronted with sharp

8. Hoffman, Allen, and Ulrich, *The Little Magazine: A History and a Bibliography*, 101–7.
9. *The Little Magazine in America: A Modern Documentary History*, ed. Anderson and Kinzie,
274, 278.

increases in offset printing costs, many of them relied on the mimeograph machine as a less expensive method of publication. While the technology seems almost ostentatiously obsolete today, mimeo machines were commonplace as recently as two decades ago. Cranked by hand and later electrically, they were unwieldy and unforgiving in their design and operation. A generation of American writers, editors, and artists mastered this means of production. From Berkeley to Greenwich Village, editors of American avant-garde magazines were able to produce and distribute magazines and handmade anthologies at extremely low cost. Perhaps the prototypical example of the intersection between this technology and the little magazine scene was the story of *Blue Suede Shoes*, which was born when editor Keith Abbott pilfered a box of mimeograph paper at Washington State University, where he was a graduate student. He went on to borrow his friend's A. B. Dick mimeograph machine to publish four issues of *Blue Suede Shoes* and four books of poetry in his first year as editor.[10]

Though Beats and Black Mountain poets generally kept each other at arm's length, both favored an asceticism that was well suited to the do-it-yourself aesthetic of the materials at hand. The appearance of magazines like the *Black Mountain Review* (1954–57) and the *Neon* (1956–60) coincided with the rise of the counterculture movement of the 1950s and 1960s. The handmade, low-budget look of these magazines suggested an outlaw aesthetic that was also reflected in the magazines' contents. Ed Sanders's *Fuck You: A Magazine of the Arts* (1962–65) provides an example of this aesthetic.

Mimeographed and creatively bound with staples, *Fuck You* (1962–65) was the manifestation of Sanders's "message of Ghandian pacifism, great sharing, social change, the expansion of personal freedom (including the legalization of marijuana, and the then-stirring messages of sexual liberation)."[11] Steven Clay and Rodney Phillips remember the mimeo revolution with some nostalgia: "Looking back at them now, the books and magazines of the mimeo revolution appear imbued with a vivid purity of intention that seems impossible in today's publications."[12] The mimeograph was a tool for creating an oppositional aesthetic among a whole generation of influential iconoclastic editors. It was not merely a means of communication; it transformed that communication as well.

The mimeo revolution has captured the imagination of young scholars and aficionados in the digital era. Decades after the Xerox machine

---

10. "*Blue Suede Shoes*, Issue 379 (The Babe Ruth Essay)," in *The Little Magazine in America: A Modern Documentary History*, 474.
11. Steve Clay and Rodney Phillips, *A Secret Location on the Lower East Side: Adventures in Writing, 1960–1980* (New York: Granary Books, 1998), 167.
12. Ibid., 15.

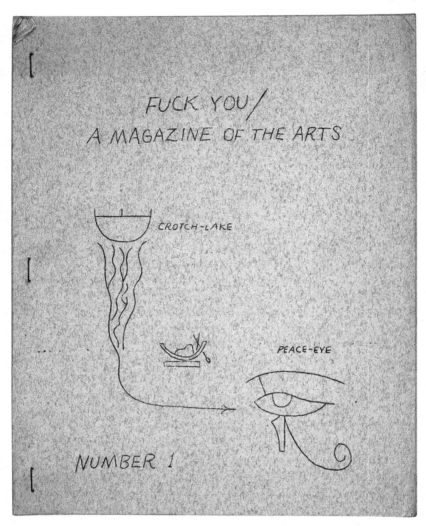

FIGURE 1. Front cover of *Fuck You: A Magazine of the Arts*, no. 1 (1962). Source: Edward Sanders.

drove the mimeograph into obsolescence, Facebook pages, blogs, and websites exist to archive high-resolution photos of old mimeo magazines.[13] Once the mimeo machine fell by the wayside, zine editors of the 1980s and 1990s took advantage of the technology of the photocopier to mass pro-

13. For an excellent example, see the Mimeo Mimeo website: http://mimeomimeo.blogspot.com.

duce printed material. Not only was the technology superior to that of the mimeograph, but one no longer needed to own the machine or have access through school, just a Kinko's card. In their interview for this volume, Andi Zeisler and Lisa Jervis, founding editors of *Bitch* magazine, recollect their early experiences with such machines before their magazine developed into the popular four-color magazine that it is today.

The most significant development in little magazines in the second half of the twentieth century was that journals and magazines produced in universities, with institutional support, began to challenge the independent, movement-driven magazines of the prewar era. Certainly, there were some editors—and readers—who preferred the intellectual cache that came with university-sponsored magazines; in his essay "Academia and the Little Magazine," Charles Robinson privileges the high-quality production of university magazines over the DIY aesthetic of the mimeo revolution: "The psychological value of a tidy periodical of ninety-six or more pages, replete with drawings, engravings—often vari-colored printing—is devastating. The majority of independent magazines are handset or mimeographed (often from incomplete or mixed fonts) and shoddy by comparison."[14] The university has been integral to the evolution of the modern little magazine, from *Hound and Horn* (1927–34) at Harvard to *The Kenyon Review* at Kenyon College (1939–present). The GI bill and a rapid expansion of the state universities turned out a generation of graduate students who were contemporary and cosmopolitan in their interests. The tradition of the university professors of the time was to exclude work from the canon that had not had a century or more to establish its position in the canon. The reading of contemporary fiction and poetry, or worse, the writing of it, was best left to leisure hours. Suddenly, iconoclastic work from the States or abroad became an obsession with young women and men of letters. Certainly, the relationship between universities and their magazines can be fraught. As Carolyn Kuebler observes in her essay for this volume, universities hold the purse strings of these literary enterprises, and they can ultimately determine the fate of a little magazine in tough financial times. Still, the relationship between universities and the little magazines can also be a mutually beneficial one: it is an inexpensive investment that yields cultural capital in the form of Pushcart Prizes, *Best American* selections, and other accolades.

A primary contention of this book is that the role of the little magazine is to promote the avant-garde—that is, little magazines function as a "front

14. "Academia and the Little Magazine," in *The Little Magazine in America: A Modern Documentary History*, 28.

guard" that anticipates the newest movements in literature, politics, and art.[15] Indeed, Hoffman contends that this notion is so integral to the mission of the little magazine that they should be called "advance-guard" magazines, and we tend to agree.[16] Robie Macauley, editor of the *Kenyon Review* from 1959 to 1977, said "that a good literary magazine ought to be ten years ahead of general acceptance.... This is what avant-garde really means, although the term is often confused, in the minds of editors, with pure experiment for experiment's sake."[17] Above all, it was Ezra Pound who most thoroughly grasped the values of the little magazine as a vehicle for the avant-garde:

Work is acceptable to the public when its underlying ideas have been accepted. The heavier the "overhead" in a publishing business the less that business can afford to deal in experiment. This purely sordid and eminently practical consideration will obviously affect all magazines save those that are either subsidized (as chemical research is subsidized) or very cheaply produced (as the penniless inventor produces in his barn or his attic).[18]

We also believe that in considering a magazine to be avant-garde one must also consider the means by which the magazine is produced—as was demonstrated by the influence of the mimeo machine. An innovative, problem-solving approach to producing and distributing a magazine on a very limited budget has been the mother of ingenuity since Harriet Monroe first began soliciting financing in 1911. Since then, whether featuring ads from the Topeka and Santa Fe Railway System or pioneering the use of blog technology to initiate and sustain literary conversations, little magazine editors have been by necessity innovators, operating outside of the prevailing modes of commercial publishing. In this volume, we provide examples of how online technology has become the latest means of low-budget production and how innovative editors have exploited this reality to make it about more than inexpensive server hosting. Rebecca Morgan Frank, founding editor of *Memorious*, describes her early desire for a simple aesthetic that would be accessible to the largest number of online readers. Jonathan Farmer, founding editor of *At Length*, considers how his online platform has allowed his magazine to thrive in ways that it wouldn't have as a printed magazine. Ander Monson, founding editor of *DIAGRAM*, remembers how the aesthetic for his online magazine was born out of his

15. For more on the broader cultural and literary significance of avant-garde literature, see Marjorie Perloff, *The Futurist Moment: Avant-Garde, Avant-Guerre, and the Language of Rupture* (Chicago: University of Chicago Press, 2003).
16. Hoffman et al., *The Little Magazine: A History and a Bibliography*, 3.
17. Anderson and Kinzie, *The Little Magazine in America: A Modern Documentary History*, 74.
18. "Small Magazines," *English Journal* 19, no. 9 (November 1930): 702.

fascination with old dictionaries and how-to manuals, thus hearkening back to the heyday of printed materials.

While the notion that a politically themed literature, specifically writing in which the content of a story or a poem progresses toward a political message, could be deemed good literature is not widely held today, political—generally leftist—magazines were important contributors to the role of little magazines in advancing the literary and cultural arguments before the Second World War. What kept these magazines relevant to the general literary and artist discussion was the tendency in the best of the magazine to favor quality of writing over purity of Marxist ideal. In our section "Politics, Culture, and the Little Magazine," our contributors trace the evolution of political discourse and its current influence over the past thirty years. For example, Lawrence-Minh Bùi Davis and Gerald Maa, founding editors of the *Asian American Literary Review*, provide historical context for understanding the political and aesthetic necessity of their new magazine.

The ultimate and most pressing charge of this book is to ask how the publication of little magazines changed over the past thirty years and what insight we can offer to those readers, writers, and editors who would enter into such an endeavor in a new era of little magazine publishing. Our book is divided into five thematic sections: "The Editor as Visionary"; "Politics, Culture, and the Little Magazine"; "Innovation and Experimentation: The Literary Avant-Garde"; "The University Magazine"; and "Today's Magazines and the Future." As we organized each of these sections, we paid careful attention to how each magazine both complies with and resists the modernist tendencies of magazines through much of the twentieth century. We observed that while defined movements or systems of theory are alive and well in literary and art criticism, editors no longer seem interested in aligning themselves with defined aesthetic movements.

Little magazine editors are always aware of the current state of little magazine publishing but are also deeply committed to adopting and exploiting new platforms for showcasing the best writing in America. Jane Friedman and Don Share, who represent two of the most venerable—and until the last decade—old-fashioned magazines, *Virginia Quarterly Review* and *Poetry*, are two of the most recognizable advocates for modernization.

A post on *Poetry*'s widely read Harriet Blog simultaneously suggests the direction that little magazines may be headed in and why anticipating future trends will become increasingly difficult. Craig Santos Perez begins his essay, "I've seen the best minds of my generation destroyed by Facebook," by recollecting that "once, blogging was king."[19] Perez describes his evolution from a blogger who scorned Facebook to a devotee of the social media site. The author is announcing that he is abandoning his blog, a medium unknown to the first online magazine editors, and recording this act on the blog of the website of the very little magazine recognized as the first of the modernist era. Online magazines that may have once seen themselves as serving the same function as a print magazine only in a different medium have added blogs, Facebook pages, Twitter accounts, and myriad other online tools, not only to draw attention to their content but also to create and maintain a dialogue within the literary community at large.

And yet, even as the little magazine adapts to the digital age, the passion and commitment of editors and writers refuse to wane. Certainly, some magazines will become online-only projects, but others will remain faithful to the power of the literary object. Each print issue of *McSweeney's* is still a collector's item, distinct from what precedes or follows it both in content and format. Other magazines will lift away from the page, and from written language, altogether. *The Drum*, a new online fiction magazine, provides free podcasts that feature the writer reading his or her work. *Tin House's* online feature "Tin House Reels" is dedicated to short films that foreground the relationship between word and image. In this way, readers can also become viewers of video content that stimulates and inspires, thus continuing the conversation that the magazine initiates. As Cara Blue Adams notes in her essay on *The Southern Review* for this volume, it is this conversation, regardless of medium, that is what's most thrilling about little magazines. Thanks to globalization, smartphones, and wireless technology, the actual location of a magazine and its editors is becoming increasingly irrelevant, and this might actually be a strength of the magazine in the twenty-first century. In their commitment to avant-garde aesthetics, their global engagement, and their eagerness to influence poets, critics, and scholars who might then influence a wider readership, these new little magazines are surprisingly similar to their modernist antecedents from the 1920s. One can imagine that thirty years from now, when little magazine editors come together to discuss the state of their various projects, they too will signal their debt to Harriet Monroe, Margaret Anderson, Eugene Jolas, and Gorham Munson.

19. "I saw the best minds of my generation destroyed by Facebook," Harriet Blog: http://www.poetryfoundation.org/harriet/2012/04/i-saw-the-best-minds-of-my-generation-destroyed-by-facebook/, accessed April 30, 2012.

Acknowledgments

Without librarians, this project would have not come together. In particular, we thank Beth Harris at Hollins University's Wyndham Robertson Library, Tony Heaton and Meg Miner at Illinois Wesleyan University's Ames Library, Sigrid Perry at Northwestern University's Special Collections, Randy Souther at the University of San Francisco's Gleeson Library, and the history staff at the United States Census Bureau. Marcy Dinius, Jenny Gavacs, Erik Gellman, Susan Hahn, Michele Rubin, Bill Henderson, and Gayle Rogers offered invaluable suggestions and historical knowledge during the early stages of this project. Thanks to Clara Sankey of *McSweeney's* for her cheerful assistance with our various queries. We are grateful for the support provided by the Andrew W. Mellon Center for Curricular and Faculty Development at Illinois Wesleyan University. We would like to give special thanks to Alaina Waterman, who skillfully handled a variety of tasks, including assistance with fact-checking, permissions, and manuscript preparation. We have been fortunate in our contributors, whose enthusiasm for this project—and patience for the time it took for it to come to fruition—have made the entire enterprise worthwhile. And, finally, thanks to Mary Zerkel, Joanne Zerkel, and Jason Reblando, who, in all things, showed the greatest of wisdom and insight.

Ian Morris
Joanne Diaz

Introduction

A Decade or So of Little Magazines: One Reader's Perspective

JEFFREY LEPENDORF

It is in the intimate form that works of art achieve their exact meaning.
WILLIAM CARLOS WILLIAMS (from "Author's Introduction to *The Wedge*")

"Do you know *McSweeney's*?" That was the first question I got, from a family friend, when I announced that I would soon be the next executive director of a nonprofit organization called the Council of Literary Magazines and Presses, or more commonly, CLMP. "Have you seen *McSweeney's*?" This was 2001 and I *hadn't*, but I soon became acquainted with it, and enamored of it, in addition to dozens, and ultimately, hundreds more over the next nearly decade and a half. I was familiar with a number of literary magazines before my time at CLMP, including the *Paris Review* (whose founder, George Plimpton, also helped found CLMP—then the Coordinating Council of Literary Magazines, or CCLM), and a number of other great journals still around today, most with the word "Review" in their names. But my life as a "lit mag junkie" started with *McSweeney's,* or as it's officially known, *Timothy McSweeney's Quarterly Concern.*

Dave Eggers started the more-or-less quarterly publication in 1998, but it really became a literary household name and achieved "insider," must-read status in 2000 when Eggers's memoir, *A Heartbreaking Work of Staggering Genius*, became a bestseller. The book features an extended series of pages literally of fine print, where, among others things, Eggers details the economics of publishing the very book the reader was holding in his or her hands. This refreshing level of self-awareness and reading meta-experience—not to mention the novelty of this kind of typesetting in a contemporary memoir—revealed a deep reverence for the beauty and potential of print. Combined with wonderful writing and the addressing of serious issues with a jaunty wink, this became the standard stuff of *McSweeney's.*

McSweeney's takes an almost obsessive-compulsive approach to typesetting and format, each issue appearing in a unique form—literary cabinets of wonder. Issues have been packaged as a boxed collection of chapbooks, an oblong hardback edition complete with CD play-along soundtrack, a hardcover book featuring any one of three different dust jackets, an assortment of separately bound short stories in a hardcover binding secured with a giant rubber band, a bundle of "mis-delivered" mail, even a "Sunday" newspaper. *McSweeney's* lavishly turns conventions of typesetting on their heads, delighting in placing emphasis on things like fine print and footnotes, antique scroll decoration and the like. Now often imitated, *McSweeney's* distinguished itself early on. Although the veneer of *McSweeney's* might at first suggest high academic pretension, closer examination reveals planned inconsistencies designed to attract a savvy readership in on the conceit. While the caliber and kinds of writing first published in *McSweeney's* aligned it with many other literary journals being published at the same time, the design element appealed to those seeking something outside of the mainstream, something for a select few clever enough to "get it," though also decidedly outside of academia.

For example, issue no. 4, the first issue of my own subscription, sports an image of a bird beneath a simple masthead, an image that at first glance appears, beyond the novelty of this journal's cover being in fact a box, much like the standard image on the cover of any number of perfect-bound academic reviews. A second look, however, reveals that uneven wooden planks replace this robin's feet, and that a tiny human arm protrudes from its left side.

Beneath the "McSweeney's" on the cover, small print appears where we might expect to find a subtitle such as "a special issue devoted to poetry in translation," but instead find the words, "trying, trying, trying, trying, trying." The back of the box features a simple table of contents surrounded by a border comprised of a ring of words in exceedingly fine print—almost too small to read. They appear to be transcribed lines from an unidentified writer's private notepad, including "cut out part in which Leslie Nielsen meets Trotsky—silly" and "egg on breakfast plate need not bloom into flowers." Asterisks follow two of the fiction pieces listed. Near the bottom of the box the tiniest of possible footnotes reads, "Includes story which stars or mentions monkeys." The entirety of one of the collection of booklets inside, titled "Notes and Background and Clarifying Charts and Some Complaining," takes the place of the traditional colophon and subscriptions/submissions guidelines page. In this case a "footnote" receives the same treatment as one of the literary works it shares space with and in fact functions as a work of literature in its own right.

McSweeney's elevates the "inessential" and overlooked to the level of literature. By holding a magnifying glass to the otherwise invisible design conceits of antique literary publishing, this journal invites readers to revel in the sheer delight of the arcane, while the design and format reflects an

FIGURE 2. Cover of *McSweeney's*, no. 4 (Late Winter 2000). Source: Dave Eggers. Photo by Jason Reblando.

urbane, cultured, inquisitive, and hip readership. Eggers started the journal with the idea that it would only publish pieces rejected by other magazines. It has abandoned this noble early mission, but remains a vibrant home for contemporary fiction and a living temple to the possibilities of print. By the way, those who wish to see a dazzling precursor will seek out archival early issues of *Cold Drill*, a magazine founded in 1970 by Anthony Thomas Trusky (who also cofounded Ahsahta Press) while teaching at the MFA department of Boise State University, and will there encounter something that consists of collections of everything from cassette tapes to notched, individually generated computer printouts—even scratch 'n sniff poetry—all loosely contained in corrugated cardboard box holders roughly the size of a large hardcover book.

I began by focusing on *McSweeney's*, but could easily have focused on any number of other literary magazines that have carved out a unique niche among readers. *McSweeney's* represents one of well over a thousand American literary magazines currently available. As far as I can tell, the Council of Literary Magazines and Presses began producing a "Catalog of Literary Magazines" (with several variations of that title appearing over the years) in 1975. That first directory, which I was able to peruse thanks to the exceptional magazine holdings of the New York Public Library, consists of a simple forty-page booklet (beautifully offset printed in black and red ink on luxurious cream-colored paper), dwarfed by the most recent (and last) printed edition of the book, sporting well over four hundred pages (including listings for more than 1,300 magazines). That 2009/2010 "CLMP Directory of Small Presses and Literary Magazines" also represents a marker in the history of literary magazines: users now access an even more comprehensive directory online that publishers can update any time. The idea of an "annual directory" has passed. But I'm getting ahead of myself. It's instructive to peruse that earliest "catalog" to see which magazines in it are still going strong while looking over the shelves of the CLMP library at some of the wonderful magazines that began and ended in the last fifteen years or so since I started at CLMP in 2001, along with a few long-standing and beloved journals that finished their runs during that period as well.

The "CCLM Catalog of Literary Magazines 1975" includes listings for *Antioch Review, Poetry, Prairie Schooner, Chicago Review, Greensboro Review, American Poetry Review, Café Solo, Shenendoah, Fiction, North American Review,* the *Southern Review,* the *Massachusetts Review,* and many more still publishing. Some have become even more active following recent redesigns and reinventions. There are also many more there I don't recall ever knowing (such as *Aisling, Blue Pig, Scree,* and *Pivot*) and others that have ceased publication since then that I greatly miss (including *Antaeus* and *Chelsea*). Over the past fifteen years a number of spectacular new magazines have come on the scene as well, a few of which I'll write more about here. Any number of others, though, made valiant efforts to launch, even publishing more than a couple of issues, but failed to become the institutions that readers who enjoyed them might have hoped. Any number of new magazines manage to put out a fine debut, but then cease publishing after a second issue, and for any number of reasons. A few that made a particular impression on me when they first appeared during my early years at CLMP but are no longer publishing include *Insurance, Both, Croonenberg's Fly*, and *Gumball Poetry*, the latter publishing each tiny issue in a plastic capsule wrapped around an actual, colorful gumball, and distributed to readers through capsule dispensing machines. I regularly describe starting a literary magazine as akin to starting a restaurant: some open and close, some have a few good years, and a few seem to be around as long as anyone can remember.

Are the short-lived journals failures? I don't think so. Folks in the literary magazine community routinely ponder if literary magazines have — or should have — a natural life span of not more than a few years. Do magazines have missions to fulfill that should take as long to accomplish as there are those to publish them? Or, should magazines do what they set out to do in as few issues as possible and leave it to a new generation to, say, "offer an alternative to what's already out there," or "discover fresh, new talent"? While many start-up journals aspire to the longevity of a *Sewanee Review* (started in 1892), the *Yale Review* (begun 1819), *Poetry* magazine (launched in 1912), or *Virginia Quarterly Review* (founded in 1925), some feel that a journal that publishes a handful of excellent issues and then quietly recedes into history may equally accomplish its mission. Certainly the dozen issues of *o-blék: a journal of language arts* constitute no less an important curation of contemporary poetry for having published only twelve issues. In fact, I credit this magazine (founded by Peter Gizzi and published from 1987 to 1993) for significantly shaping what continues to be my own taste in poetry. Similarly, another favorite, *Meatpaper*, started by Sasha Wizansky and Amy Strader in 2007, used the form of the literary magazine to explore the literary delights of "meat culture." They announced in 2013, with their twentieth issue, that they had concluded their current journey with the magazine, but asked readers to stay tuned for another form of the magazine in the future.

Literary magazines get started for a variety of reasons, sometimes simply because a group of writers wants to see the writing of its own circle of friends in print. In other cases they fulfill a perceived need to bring a kind of literature to readers hungry for writing not regularly published elsewhere. This could mean publishing the literature of specific communities, many of which have been (and frequently still are) neglected by mainstream publishing. These include culturally specific communities (such as Afro-Caribbean, LGBT, or Pacific-Islander), aesthetic communities (for example, those interested in experimental poetry, "flash fiction," long form essays, or literary ephemera) and more virtual communities of readers interested in less commercially viable forms (including short stories, literature in translation, or small press book reviews).

A program officer at a foundation that used to—but sadly no longer—grants to literary magazines once said to me, "Jeffrey, look, I've got a graduate degree in literature. I read the *New Yorker*. These magazines (she had asked me to speak to her about some of the magazines represented by CLMP that we were most impressed by) all look terrific. But, really, *who reads this stuff*?" That's a question I get a lot: "Who reads this stuff?" Another question I am asked a lot is, "Do we really need so many literary magazines?" Generally this is followed by something like, "Aren't they just Balkanizing each other's audiences? Don't many of these just publish the same people?" Part of the answer can be found in the title of this article. I used the somewhat old-fashioned term "little magazines" in the title of this piece rather than "literary magazines" or "literary journals" for a reason: "little" represents one of—for me at least—the most wonderful functions of a successful literary magazine. Every good literary magazine represents a distinct sensibility, generally initiated by its editor(s) and, by extension, defined by a community of writers and readers. I've often said that a book is a group activity carried out one person at a time. Because a literary magazine is in fact, by definition, a *serial* publication, each magazine, by nature of the repetition of its editorial viewpoint, can both represent a focused community as well as help forge one. I think the very best magazines help define a community, at least aesthetically, acting as a printed gathering place: a literary touchstone.

Occasionally literary magazines reach relatively large audiences, but most readerships of literary magazines—certainly in comparison to commercial magazines like *People* or *Sports Illustrated*—remain rather small. Even the most successful literary magazines generally count their subscriber bases in the single thousands, almost never the tens of thousands. Many work hard to build subscriber bases numbering even a few hundred. Online publishing changes this equation but, still, when compared to other forms of media (television, movies, YouTube), even these larger and growing readerships remain, relatively, "little." When we read "little" in the context of a literary magazine to in fact mean "focused," though, we understand that "little" here represents a great virtue. Little magazines are not one size fits all, and they are not for everybody—at least any one literary magazine isn't for everybody. I do believe there's a literary magazine out there for everyone who reads; it's just that for any one person it's more likely a different magazine than the same. This is not a function of snobbery; it's a function of connoisseurship and it ought to be encouraged and celebrated.

Those critical of literary magazines often question why some magazines publish the same authors, as if only one museum should show paintings by, say, Picasso. If the very same John Ashbery poem or Junot Díaz short story appeared in multiple magazines, of course that would be ridiculous; but each magazine publishing these writers (and any number of others) publishes only unique pieces by these authors. Most magazines exist largely to discover new talent, but publishing established writers along with lesser-known voices presents an effective way to both define the sensibility of the magazine and to attract new readers. At the same time, literary magazines provide places for writers whose work has proven commercially viable to publish more experimental work or to work outside of their comfort zones. Whatever the reason, readers may very well look at a magazine new to them because of a poem by Sonia Sanchez or a translation of an essay by Alain Badiou, but then they are likely to discover many writers they may have never heard of before. If this collection of writing then appeals to them—presto!—they have a new and expanding personal library to explore: a literary magazine they can call their own. This discovery also means they have joined a group of individuals (fellow readers and subscribers) who shares their sensibility. Because magazines publish serially—this sensibility will continue to be articulated over a period of time—they have also joined an active community of readers and writers reading right along with them.

I spend a lot of time at CLMP talking to those starting magazines about their mission statements—the stated expressions of their editorial sensibilities—and not just because they will likely need them for grant proposals. Too frequently people planning on publishing a new magazine announce that they will be featuring "the very best poetry, fiction and creative non-fiction" they can find. Now, one would be hard-pressed to identify a literary magazine set on publishing mediocre poetry, fiction or creative nonfiction, or even "second-best." Many of the editors of the very best literary magazines profess that they simply publish what they find excellent, free of aesthetic prejudice. But despite what they may claim, this clearly isn't the case. What one editor considers the very best is not the same as what another prefers, at least not in all cases. Through their specific selections they define and express a sensibility, and through the expression of this sensibility, not only the specific selection of what appears, but also the arrangement of an issue, the typesetting, and its overall look and format. This sensibility, defined sometimes only through the course of a magazine's own history, is what attracts certain kinds of readers—and certain kinds of submissions—as well.

This is the case even with a magazine like *Ploughshares* (founded in 1971), which features a different guest editor for every issue. One might assume that this would result in a magazine that has no coherence as a serial, but in fact *Ploughshares* does cohere. Though the novelty of having changing guest editors does certainly provide a great deal of change and freshness for each issue, *Ploughshares'* own history will always, at least to some extent, define its future. *Ploughshares* always seems like *Ploughshares* to its readers because certain kinds of writers imagining their work in its past pages will be most likely to submit work to the magazine for future publication. Similarly, in terms of how a magazine's sensibility will attract a certain kind of writer as well as reader, a magazine like *Fence* (founded in 1997) has the mission of not advocating for any one aesthetic position, remaining, aesthetically speaking, "on the fence." *Fence* welcomes a variety of viewpoints that might not normally appear in the same magazine, and the establishment of *Fence* as an exceptional magazine in a relatively short amount of time perhaps speaks to the success of this mission. Yet, clearly, many kinds of writing would be extremely unlikely to appear in the pages of *Fence*. I suspect that Rebecca Wolff, its founder and publisher, might protest that this simply isn't true, that as long as the work submitted were excellent it could absolutely be a candidate for *Fence*. While in theory this may be true, I've never seen examples of what would likely be described as "cowboy poetry" or "genre fiction," for example, appear in its pages, with the possible exception of pieces categorized as such that utilize these categories toward a different, perhaps more "avant-garde," goal.

Similarly, I've never seen a concrete poem or an example of *L=A=N=G=U=A=G=E* poetry in the pages of another highly regarded magazine, the *Hudson Review* (founded in 1947), which features a great deal of poetry (and in its history has published the likes of Sylvia Plath, Anne Sexton, William Carlos Williams, and Ezra Pound). Like Rebecca Wolff, Paula Deitz, the current editor of the *Hudson Review*, has expressed a genuine openness to publishing work that one might not assume would fit the established sensibility of its pages. The issue here, however, isn't what these editors would be willing to publish, but what might conceivably be submitted to them for consideration based on the sensibilities they have projected over a number of issues, regardless of how they may describe their aesthetic openness or flexibility. Magazines that try to appeal to "everyone" tend not to last very long. In terms of effective focus and a strong curatorial voice, "little" really is a virtue.

Tin House (founded in 1999), another magazine establishing itself around the time I began at CLMP, provides a wonderful example of a successful literary magazine that, though on the surface might appear to be trying to reach "all readers," has in fact done an excellent job of expressing a focused sensibility that has gained them a rather large readership. *Tin House* borrows the graphic-heavy approach of popular magazines to attract a different readership than that of a more traditional journal. While the actual literature contained within might in some ways be similar to magazines that look quite different, *Tin House* presents its poems, short stories, and essays amid multiple images, assorted typefaces, ghosted designs, colored inks, and pull quotes. For example, the first issue contains poems by Charles Simic and C. K. Williams, and fiction by Rick Moody and David Foster Wallace—writers whose work could be found in a number of other publications at the same time. The work of these writers seems somehow different in this new context, though. Win McCormick, who founded *Tin House* (along with New York editors Rob Spillman and Elissa Schappell, and managing editor Holly MacArthur), writes about his design choices in his introduction to the first issue: "I wanted to create a literary magazine for the many passionate readers who are not necessarily literary academics or publishing professionals. I wanted to offer a fresh design that is elegant, readable and inviting ... with this combination of ingredients, I was certain we could establish a literary magazine that is accessible to the public as well as intellectually accomplished."[1]

The pervasive use of oversized pull quotes, graphics, and photos provides readers of *Tin House* with an invitation to approach the magazine by thumbing through its pages as one might peruse a copy of *Vogue*, and the blocky shape, which takes two hands to hold, and perfect binding allow it to enter the realm of the coffee-table book: something to then be savored in bits and pieces over a period of time, to remain out on display when not being read. Each issue even contained a recipe, a novel surprise for a literary publication, tying it once again to more popular periodicals. *Tin House* has been successful in acquiring wide distribution and a sizable readership—with a current print circulation well over 12,000 and an online readership that includes more than 22,000 unique visitors each month—in a relatively short period of time, in part because of its hybridization of popular magazine and classic literary journal. This also means that *Tin House* might be less likely to appeal to those who *do* want a more sober (design-wise that is) reading experience, and this fact in no way constitutes a failing. *Tin House*'s strongly expressed sensibility, along with a now well-established history of exceptional literary curation, will likely contribute to its longevity. In the case of all of these magazines, a history of annually renewing subscribers proves that these magazines have successfully shaped communities of readers, regardless of the size of that readership.

Clearly I love the way that the design of literary magazines influences the reading experience. The literary magazines to which *Tin House* presents an alternative to still represent a healthy portion of the literary jour-

1. "Publisher's Note," *Tin House* 1, no. 1 (1999): 4.

nals out there, including many with long-standing and enthusiastically supportive readerships. These journals tend to be typeset in standard, serif fonts, using templates that remain fixed, more or less, from issue to issue. They are generally free from images aside from their covers or the occasional "portfolio" of artwork reproduced on glossy paper and placed right in the middle. The classic "review" design reflects the primacy of the written word and provides a promise of fine writing, nothing more. These designs, when most successful, become nearly invisible, except perhaps in the coding inherent in their intentional deflection of attention. The *Hudson Review*, for example, has maintained a virtually identical design during nearly all of its more than fifty venerable years. Except for a changing table of contents, each cover is distinguished only by a subtle color shift in a muted, matte ink band covering the top of each issue. Eschewing newer printing methods allowing for full color and full-image coverage, the Spartan design approach of the *Hudson Review* promises a "no-frills" read—one intended for an audience already initiated into the world of letters. Positioned as diametrically opposed to the image-heavy come-ons of commercial magazines, literary journals like this pledge one thing only: literature. The *Hudson Review*, in fact, did recently freshen its design, introducing its new look with a blazing orange image, but one carefully integrated into the simple decorative band that readers of the magazine had come to look forward to seeing in their mailboxes. Some issues since have included audio CDs and there are a few other "modern" touches, but the *Hudson Review* editors know its readers and the *Hudson Review* of today would still be easily recognizable to any reader of the older design. In contrast, when the *Virginia Quarterly Review* (publishing since 1925) introduced its arresting redesign several years ago, it did so to mirror a strong new editorial vision (forged by Ted Genoways, who took the helm from 2003 to 2010) that added graphic novels, investigative journalism, cultural reporting, and photography to its roster. With this makeover came a brand new and considerably larger readership to this already esteemed journal.

Desktop publishing starts around 1985 if we assume it to have begun with the advent of WYSIWYG ("wissy-wig" or, "what you see is what you get") by Macintosh. With this innovation, what appeared on the computer screen looked like what would be printed out. Combined with the introduction of Pagemaker layout software by Aldus and Adobe's Post-Script innovations, a new era of DIY—"do it yourself"—publishing began. Since then, WordPress, InDesign, Dreamweaver—and more recently, social media platforms such as Twitter and Tumblr—and any number of other relatively inexpensive, and sometimes even free, software available for online and/or home use has dramatically changed the literary magazine landscape. The current ubiquity of smartphones and e-readers, plus the phenomenon of social networking, has launched a new digital revolution. I remember subscribing around 1987 to a literary-travel magazine hybrid called *Monk: The Mobile Magazine*, published from 1986 to 1997 directly from a Macintosh laptop in a traveling mobile home, each issue uploaded to a printing house and mail shop through a satellite dish from a different city. Today, magazines can send digital layout files to the printer nearly as easily as anyone can send a simple e-mail, and online journals can publish directly and instantly to their readers. The result is that we now have more magazines than ever before, many with design standards of the highest order, and many produced from personal laptops and reaching readers around the globe. We appear to be in a second great age of DIY publishing, surpassing that of the 1960s when mimeographed literary zines helped define a new literary landscape.

Over the past decade, the availability of literary magazines in bookstores (known in the trade as "newsstand") has been shrinking. And concurrent with fewer print magazines visible in bookstores has come another significant development in little magazine history: the increasing acceptance—and now ubiquity—of online publishing. This sea change has come about with the introduction, rise, and now routine use of the Internet, tablet computers, and mobile devices for reading. A class of publisher membership at CLMP added since 2000—and still the fastest growing kind of little magazine—is "online-only" literary magazines. It's now rare that even magazines that started and remain in print don't have an online presence (the *Mississippi Review* was one of the first literary magazines to have substantial content online, starting in 1995). These can vary from a simple splash page, through which one can either subscribe or simply learn of a magazine, to online "sister versions" of print magazines offering unique content, from pieces not appearing in print at all, to additional information on authors and printed pieces, to author interviews and active blogs. Online-only publishers, however, have been a much more recently growing phenomenon (though some were indeed around before I started at CLMP. Ravi Shankar started one of my favorites, *Drunken Boat*, in 2000. From the start it presented multimedia along with the written word in a way not possible with a print publication). The growth of publications born and existing only on the Internet could at this point be considered epic. Work appearing in online-only journals now also and unquestionably has been published, another change since literature first started appearing online, when questions about whether or not appearing online indeed even counted as "really" having been published. I don't feel a need to question whether online literary blog sites such as *HTMLGiant* or the *Rumpus* count as literary magazines; these and others like them make up a welcome new class of literary publishers. Regardless of how you choose to count them, it appears that the number of online publishers having membership in CLMP may surpass that of their print magazine colleagues in the foreseeable future (though a number of our newest magazines boast a new insistence on "print culture," so time will tell).

There are some clear advantages to publishing primarily or exclusively online. Obviously, the costs of physically printing and mailing a magazine vanish, and many more people can easily access the magazine. Entire runs of a magazine can be archived and remain accessible online. Readers, through blogs and comments, can participate actively as members of a reading community, interacting with the editors, and sometimes even the writers published, to a degree never possible before. A few of my favorite online-only publishers have already established themselves as important literary curators and gathering places for those who love literature. *Words Without Borders*, founded by translator and editor Alane Salierno Mason in 1999 (though first publishing in 2003), features writing in translation from around the globe. Joel Whitney and Michael Archer started *Guernica* in 1994; it mixes literature with writing on foreign affairs and US domestic policy. *Failbetter*, founded by Thom Didato and David McLendon in 2000, acts like a traditional literary magazine featuring fiction and poetry, and has been successful in drawing a large readership and helping to legitimize the concept of an "online journal." I could easily mention many others, and new ones are literally appearing every week. One particular challenge of online publishing, however, comes from assumptions, at least for now, about what should be available for free online. Charging a subscription price for a printed literary magazine rarely covers the costs of paying a staff, but it still has that potential. Few online publications, though, can generate income. Online advertising provided an early promise of a new income stream for these magazines, but it hasn't proven successful. This means that most online magazine editors work as volunteers. While many may be happy to do this (and certainly many routinely do so in the world of printed literary magazines), online publishing presents the potential danger of devaluing the role of editors. Because few readers are likely, it is assumed, to pay to read a literary magazine on their computers, those wishing to publish online have to do so, technically, not as paid professionals.

The introduction of handheld e-readers, tablets, and smartphones, however, has been changing this scenario. *Electric Literature*, a fiction quarterly started by Andy Hunter and Scott Lindenbaum, burst onto the scene in 2009 with a digitally produced literary magazine that did the opposite of what most print magazines "going online" have done: rather than have an online version of a print magazine, or even an online-only publication, *Electric Literature* announced the availability of each new issue through every conceivable reading device, including smartphones, online, and through e-readers. Interested readers could then pay to download each new issue into their e-readers or smartphones through an app, or, if they wished, order a POD ("print-on-demand") bound copy to be shipped to them directly from the short-run printer. *Electric Literature*, existing equally as a print journal and an online journal, proved that readers will support good literature by paying for it, and that there are new models of publishing that embrace readers interested both in new technologies and in traditional print. A few years ago the magazine reinvented itself as *Recommended Reading*, an online-only magazine that uses Twitter to publish a new story every week, and does so for free, supporting its paid staff through contributions, demonstrating a highly successful new model for publishing.

The promise of digital publishing and the acceptance of e-reading suggests a bright future for literary magazines, particularly with their ability to satisfy the needs of reading communities grouped by distinct sensibilities. At the same time, literary magazines like *McSweeney's*, Ugly Duckling Presse's hand-bound with a rubber band *6X6 Magazine*, and new player *Convolution* continue to prove the unique pleasures available through printed forms. There will be a place for all of these approaches to literary magazines as long as there are readers.

Over the past nearly fifteen years, a number of other major changes have affected the community of literary magazine publishers, some technological and some philosophical. One has been a shift brought about perhaps mostly out of necessity, and perhaps equally out of practicality. Prior to 2000, few magazines accepted "simultaneous submissions." This refers to the same work being submitted to multiple magazines for consideration at the same time. Despite this hard-and-fast rule expressed by most magazines, however, few writers adhered to it. This was due in part to response times being (understandably) so very long. Few writers would have the patience for a work to be rejected before making changes (perhaps) and resubmitting it elsewhere. Accepting simultaneous submissions has become routine with most magazines, as has accepting submissions online. The question of even accepting electronic submissions was a major issue just a few years ago, when it would have meant managing countless e-mails and attachments, but with the development of online submission software and websites, the resistance to it has largely vanished. That said, the issue of ever growing, virtually insurmountable "slush piles" remains a favorite topic of conversation among editors. The ease of electronic submission, coupled with the acceptance that writers apparently submit simultaneously even if asked not to, has certainly led to what seems like an exponentially greater number of submissions. At the same time, electronic submission software and services also allows work of less interest to be rejected more quickly, and for multiple editors to examine submitted work while in any number of locations. The age of unwieldy, traveling stacks of manuscripts (and manuscripts occasionally being lost forever) seems to have ended.

Another trend I've seen develop over the past several years—a double-edged one—is the changing relationship of universities or colleges to print magazines. In recent history, a large number of literary magazines enjoyed support from educational institutions. This included, to varying degrees, paid staffs and teacher release time, office space, student interns, and having any number of things like printing and postage fully covered. Many of these affiliations still exist, and some of these magazines serve not only as exceptional publications for their readers, but also as effective calling cards for the high standards of the institutions with which they are affiliated. Increasingly, though, as these institutions have had to trim their spending significantly to match downturns in the economy, many of these literary magazines have found their budgets severely curtailed. In many cases, their very existences have been threatened. A number of magazines have been mandated to raise their own budgets or even told to take their wares and go elsewhere. This has led to a number of shake-ups in the literary magazine community, with long-beloved magazines, such as *Shenandoah*, *Antioch Review*, *New England Review*, and *TriQuarterly* (the magazine responsible for the first iteration of this history of "little magazines"), to name a few, having to fight for their survival, seek funds elsewhere, or function in an entirely new way.

While tears have been rightly shed over some of these challenges, I think the tragedy of some of these situations has produced a silver lining. I often remind people that "to publish" literally means "to make public"; and that, therefore, until a work reaches a reader's hands it has merely been printed, not published. Many university magazines, with venerable publishing histories and many "first to publish" credits to their names, because they received such a high level of support, did little to build their readerships. They may have achieved literary excellence, but very few people ever actually read what they published. Having the apron strings of academic support severed has led to many of these magazines doing more to seek out their potential readers, raising funds as they expand their subscriber bases, and becoming better magazines as a result. In some cases, these changes have had deleterious effects. Overall, though, I think that these challenges have been good for the developing history of literary magazines, at least in terms of reaching readerships beyond the walls of academia. Ironically, so many of the great literary magazine publishers of the past founded their publications in direct contrast to what could be found in the academy.

In conclusion, I will quickly mention a mere handful of outstanding magazines that started up during my first years at CLMP: Each issue of *Cabinet*, started by Sina Najafi in 2000, features a gallimaufry of literary essays on topics as varied as meditations on individual colors to home-made prosthetics or even dust. Also founded in 2000, *jubilat*, published by Rob Casper, and first edited by the poets Christian Hawkey and Michael Teig, places contemporary poetry alongside interviews and all manner of "found" pieces and rare reprints (curated by a roster of contributing editors, including myself). Hannah Tinti and Maribeth Batcha launched *One Story* in 2002 with an idea so elegantly simple it's almost astounding that nobody thought of it earlier: each issue of *One Story* consists of a single short story, and a new issue appears every three weeks (making it a magazine that publishes eighteen issues a year). They've more recently launched a sister publication featuring writing aimed at young adult readers called *One Teen Story*. Brigid Hughes, who cut her teeth working as senior editor at the *Paris Review* under George Plimpton, started *A Public Space* in 2005 and it's still one of the freshest, most vital literary magazines out there. *Alimentum*, started in 2006 by Paulette Licitra and Peter Selgin, celebrates literature inspired by food and cooking. I could easily go on and on.

This has been a pretty swell decade and a half for little magazines and I can't wait to see what lies in store in the next decades. I first came to literary magazines as a reader. It's been a privilege to be deeply involved with many of them over the years through my role at CLMP. I still love them as a reader, though, because they continue doing what little magazines do so well: publish for me what I want to read, time and time again.

Part 1:
The Editor
as Visionary

This History of BOMB

BETSY SUSSLER

BETSY SUSSLER: The story of BOMB begins about a year before the publication of its first issue in May of 1981. The visual artists, filmmakers, and
writers who were living in downtown Manhattan discussed its inception
for that long—at dinner parties, on street corners, at clubs, and over the
phone. A look at the first issue gives you an idea of who was talking: Picture Generation artist Sarah Charlesworth; avant-garde novelists Kathy
Acker and Lynne Tillman; painters Duncan Hannah and Michael McClard;
performance artist Joan Jonas; photographer Jimmy DeSana; and filmmakers Eric Mitchell and Amos Poe. I was acting and directing with a
theater group called Nightshift, founded by my then husband, Lindzee
Smith. An ensemble, Nightshift performed cutting-edge plays by Peter
Handke, Rainer Werner Fassbinder, Marguerite Duras, and the Australian
playwright Phil Motherwell. Lindzee had been part of a Melbourne collective working out of a theater called the Pram Factory where actors predom-
inated, and directors and playwrights were required to understand their
crafts through performance. They had to act. I took this as a mandate: if
you were going to tell actors what to do and say on stage, then you needed
to experience what it takes to embody that script and its directorial vision.
I acted for a few years—to better understand how to write dialogue. It
helped me enormously. In Nightshift, as with all ensembles, each partici-
pant's contributions during rehearsal were organically incorporated into
the final result. This was very much on my mind at BOMB's conception.

In 1983, two years after BOMB's first issue was published, I was still
acting and making Super 8 films. I played the character "Lurleen" in Gary
Indiana's play, *Phantoms of Louisiana*. We rehearsed at the painter David
Deutsch's studio, and the play opened at The Wooster Group's Performing

This interview was elaborated upon and adapted for *The Little Magazine in America* by
Betsy Sussler in 2013. It is based on an interview that William Corwin conducted for the
Art on Air series AirTalk and broadcast November 29, 2009. You can hear the original at
http://artonair.org/show/betsy-sussler-bomb-magazine-0.

Garage. Ross Bleckner did the sets—abstract paintings on butcher paper that had been inspired by Freud's Wolf Man character. The paintings were hung on wires that crisscrossed the stage and, between scenes, one of the actors would walk from one end of the stage to the other trailing a Bleckner painting behind them. Disciplines were not as stratified then. There were fewer commercial considerations. For instance, James Nares painted, made films, and played music. Writers acted in friends' underground films and videos; fellow filmmakers shot them. This creative fertility fed the idea that became BOMB. We talked about what we were doing; and we had a blast doing it. Or to put it another way—within any of those collaborative arrangements, you talked about a work of art's evolution: what you were thinking, what you were open to, what historical works were at play—that was a natural part of the day's conversations. And, as in any rehearsal period, the artwork evolved and transformed in a way that perhaps you'd never imagined.

It was that sort of conversation, one like the creative process itself, where you eventually come to a moment of revelation. That was the conversation we wanted to catch in BOMB. This was New York City; there was a strong sense of historical precedent. We were ambitious in the best sense of the word. We wanted to make work that was going to make a difference. Ours was the generation that followed the great minimalists and conceptualists. We were, in some ways, reared by their art and knew many of them. There was a humor and competition, a sense of play and experimentation that arose, not only from working together but from the informal conversations that occurred in each other's studios, or bars and clubs. (Downtown Manhattan had Puffy's Barnabus Rex, Chinese Chance, the Mudd Club, and Magoos.) And yes, there were fights, and struggles, and disagreements; there was envy and naivety.

WILLIAM CORWIN: Who else was at this table? I'm just curious. The historical....

BS: Well, it was many tables, at bars and restaurants, and in artists' lofts or writers' walk-up apartments. But the formal meeting table, where we finally decided what the name would be, was at a loft on lower West Broadway where I lived. The artist, Sarah Charlesworth; Liza Bear, the editor of *Avalanche*, who became an important advisor later; Glenn O'Brien, who had been the managing editor of Andy Warhol's *Interview*; Jeff Goldberg, an essayist; and the artist Michael McClard were there.

We had spent a long time discussing what to call this magazine. The actor Eric Mitchell, who had started an earlier incarnation of BOMB called *X Motion Picture* with Michael McClard and myself, had thought we should call it *Blah Blah*, because we would be talking all the time. I brought up "BOMB," because of the off-off-Broadway plays I was acting in that were opening and closing with astonishing speed, as in "plays that bomb." I thought this magazine would be a rather ephemeral, wonderful moment and would exist for three or four issues and then disappear. "BOMB?" everyone said, "No, I don't think so." Or "I hate it," or "Are you crazy?" But Glenn and I had been talking of *Blast* and he reminded them that, "*Blast* was the first artists' and writers' magazine of the twentieth century." Edited by Wyndham Lewis, Ezra Pound, and Rebecca West, its content was written by novelists, poets, and visual artists. So I said, "Great, if it lasts longer than three or four issues, we can say it was named after *Blast*." I'm not sure everyone agreed, but Michael McClard liked the idea as well, so it was vaguely decided upon and as no one else came up with a better title, it stuck.

Sarah Charlesworth and I thought we could hammer out a basic design because she had worked on the art and theory journal *The Fox* with Joseph Kosuth. Its design was spare and elegant. I wanted this avant-garde BOMB to have a classical feel. I liked the balance each gave the other, so we decided that its proportions would be based on the golden mean. But we could not remember the golden mean's formula. We were sitting at Sarah's desk, which was a tabula rasa, except for a bottle of Chanel No. 5. I looked at this bottle and said, "Coco Chanel used the golden mean; I just know it!" So we measured the bottle. BOMB's first issue was proportioned in relation to its form. As it happens, it was the golden mean.

WC: It *was* the golden mean? Well, that's lucky.

BS: Then at yet another dinner party, Mary Heilmann brought an artist named Mark Magill. I told him that we were starting this magazine but needed a designer. He said, "Funny you should bring that up, [because] I'm a graphic designer by training; why don't I do it for you?" Mark Magill designed the first ten issues of BOMB along with Michael McClard. In the early years, BOMB developed along the lines of what I call "laissez-faire anarchy." We did nothing by committee: if someone had an idea, and it was a good one, they did it. But actually editing the text—that came naturally to me. I really had learned a lot from enacting Joe Orton's or Marguerite Duras's lines. It gave me an innate understanding, an ear, if you will, for dialogue.

There really was a feeling, and I hope it still exists today, that BOMB *belonged* to its community of artists and writers, and that input is what kept it vital. That's the sort of enthusiasm that fed BOMB. That's what kept it alive. And that's how BOMB started.

WC: I want to get back to your editorial style of running the magazine. I'm curious, with a bunch of writers and poets and artists and actors, where did the money come from? Where'd you find the printer? As a tutorial for people who might want to start up a magazine: How did that happen?

BS: We were so incredibly naive. I think Arto Lindsay and the Erasers and a couple of other bands did a benefit for us and raised about $1,000—that paid what it cost to print the magazine on newsprint with thin but glossy cover. I borrowed $3,000 from someone who must remain anonymous, and actually paid a lot of it back—something they did not expect to happen. Liza had published *Avalanche*, and she was advising us. She and Michael McClard were married at the time. Michael went around with a mock-up of the inaugural issue, first to the Leo Castelli Gallery, and Leo (being such a gentleman) bought the first ad, on trust. I mean, the magazine didn't exist yet. Once Michael had the actual Leo Castelli ad in hand, he went to all the other galleries in SoHo. It was a small scene back then, and Mary Boone, Tony Shafrazi, Paula Cooper ... knew some or all of us and wanted to help out. Michael would let the Castelli ad slip out of the mock-up and lest anyone fail to notice exclaim, "Whoops, oh, Leo's ad!" Everyone adored Leo and followed his lead.

Expedi Printers, who printed the magazine for ten years, was located in SoHo then; we just really stayed in the hood. If we could walk there, we did business there. And then surprisingly enough, based on just that one issue, we got a $5,000 grant from the New York State Council on the Arts, a windfall at the time.

WC: A very interesting point that you brought up is artists talking to artists about art. What was the feeling about the more established art magazines that were all written by art critics and art historians? Was there a general feeling that they were oppressing you? It's a love-hate relationship. Obviously, if artists get rave reviews, they can change their lives. But also you never know what to do with these magazines. Did you want to create something to stand against that?

BS: It wasn't to take a stand against it. We knew perfectly well that critics have an important role in society. I mean, we had all been weaned as young artists on the great Walter Benjamin. It was much more about the desire to have our own voice as a counterpoint to being interpreted by someone else. BOMB created a real niche that needed to be filled. I didn't even fully understand it—but that the magazine is still here after 32 years certainly speaks to that need. So it was less against something but more for delivering the artists' voice. Back then I was not seeing a written form that carried that sort of oral history. The predominant art writing was being done by critics or journalists.

And when I say "we" I mean those voices that comprise the pages of BOMB. BOMB's contributors define each issue. Artists and writers have a stake in this enterprise; it belongs to them. For instance, when Joe Bradley and Dike Blair record their conversation, that transcript becomes the blueprint. They get to go back and develop their ideas. They get to say, I could have segued there, and I didn't; but let me do that now. Or a BOMB editor asks for clarification or elucidation. The editorial process follows the Socratic method. We ask a lot of questions.

Conversation brings up more conversation. That's the idea. An interview is put through several drafts but that doesn't mean that the vernacular is lost. There is a transformation from aural/oral speech to text, because in the end it's being *read*. The transformation has to be elegant, and I mean that in the sense of how the word "elegant" is used in physics; it has to be balanced between the two. Why have a conversation if you're not going to learn something, and who doesn't want to pass that on in a form that's lucid? BOMB's interviews are storytelling in one or three or five acts; there is denouement, there is catharsis.... What we have discovered is that two artists conversing—whether they be novelists, painters, or musicians—puts a whole new spin on understanding the art because in that conversation they make discoveries about their work that weren't quite cognizant beforehand. That's what I like to pull out and develop in the editorial process.

wc: So that brings us back to the point. You get a call from someone who says they're working on an interview you had no idea [about]. Or are you having dinner with someone and you agree about this guy's or woman's work? And then you call them?

bs: It used to be that spontaneous. Now it's more formal because we have so many people involved and we have a publishing schedule. We don't want to lose that enthusiasm and spontaneity, though. BOMB currently has 90 contributing editors in the fields of visual arts, literature, film and theater, architecture, and music. Contributing editors and former contributors make suggestions. People who have been interviewed get very excited about the process, and they have ideas. It's like carrying the torch, which I love. It's a great act of generosity. The only hard-and-fast rule we have is that all interviews have to be generated and conducted by practicing artists so they don't get too carried away or obsessively involved because they're busy doing their own work. And even once in a while those rules get tossed. There are some very interesting curators and then of course there are philosophers and theorists. In any case, then the editorial staff at BOMB sits down and tries to figure out how we can accommodate all the ideas—which we can't. So then we pick and choose: who are the most compelling, what's the best mix. We like to include emerging artists alongside artists who have been working for thirty or forty years, because it is about a lifetime commitment and that needs to be reflected in our pages. We just really think of the mix.

WC: I read an interview you did a couple years ago with a former employer of mine, the artist Ellen Phelan.

BS: Yes!

WC: You talked about her work, but you also talked about her life. She's a good friend of yours. How did that come about?

BS: We have become friends since the interview. Ellen is now on BOMB's Board of Trustees. I knew she had a lot to say. The interviews are an oral history of ideas. They're intellectual histories, but art doesn't get made in a vacuum but rather in the world at large, as part and parcel with life. So, yes, all those things come into it to the extent that the artist wants it to come in.

WC: You met Ellen back in the scene in the '80s?

BS: I met her when I first came to New York; Joel Shapiro brought her over to Gordon Matta-Clark's loft. Joel had made it known that this gal was the ONE, and she was; they got married.

WC: Now where were you coming from?

BS: I had gone to school in New Orleans, to Newcomb, now integrated into Tulane. I left New Orleans for San Francisco where I attended the San Francisco Art Institute for two years and studied with the Kuchar brothers, with the performance artist Howard Fried, and the painters Jerry Hatofsky, Jay DeFeo, and Sam Tchakalian. I loved them but I wanted to come back to New York. During my last year at the institute I was working for a wonderful conceptual artist, Tom Marioni, who founded the Museum of Conceptual Art. Dennis Oppenheim came to do an installation there. Dennis arrived with Christa Maiwald, who had been a star graduate student at the Art Institute of Chicago along with Diego Cortez and Coleen Fitzgibbon, who had already moved to New York and who also became friends.

I helped with the installation and Christa and Dennis said, "If you come, give us a call!" I arrived in New York with one suitcase and my Persian cat, Osmun. Christa and Dennis walked over to the subway station by Dennis's loft to meet me: they put me up, found me a summer sublet, and got me a job here at the Clocktower. I was working for Alanna [Heiss] before she founded P.S. 1 [Contemporary Art Center] or this radio station. Pretty fast work on Christa's and Dennis's part. That was my start in New York.

WC: How has BOMB changed over the years? Has it always been interviews, poetry and fiction, art—or have you seen it go up and down or change politically? How has it morphed over the years?

BS: On one level, we haven't changed—artists and writers will always edit BOMB. But we are no longer a product of one time and place; as we've matured, we've grown in vision and in formats—we now live in the digital age and our online presence has grown dramatically. But first, let's go back, to one of my favorite issues, published in 1983 and guest-edited by Mary Heilmann. It is designed so that reproductions of artwork, poems, and short stories are juxtaposed with each other on almost every page. In the early issues, this was common practice. A typical spread has a Peter Schjeldahl story about his first poem which he showed to his fifth-grade teacher ("That's nice Peter, very unpleasant. What does it mean?"), a Luc Sante gem of a short memoir ("History is the phone that rings during a fuck, not the phone, not the ringing, but the duration, the space between") and images of paintings by David Salle, Lois Lane, Robert Mangold, and Ross Bleckner. Elizabeth Murray curated a "show" of paintings—a two-page spread of reproductions of artworks by Louisa Chase, Bob Gober, Moira Dryer, and Terry Winters.... But by the '90s we were formalizing these informal juxtapositions into sections or series. The English novelist, Patrick McGrath, who lives and works in New York City and is a contributing editor to BOMB, interviewed an English author each time he went back to London—this was before anyone here was really aware of Ian McEwan, Julian Barnes, or Graham Swift. Poetry and fiction coalesced into its own journal within a journal called *First Proof*. Novelists Lynn Tillman, Francine Prose, A. M. Homes, and Gary Indiana took up the New York School tradition and conducted landmark conversations with artists Petah Coyne, Thomas Nozkowski, Eric Fischl, and Robert Mapplethorpe. We developed the latest (in the) epistolary style via e-mail interviews between Jeffrey Eugenides in Chicago and Tacita Dean in Berlin; Junot Diaz by Edwidge Danticat; and more recently, Thomas Hirschhorn by Abraham Cruz Villejas.

In 1984, we collaborated with Daniel Flores, a documentary filmmaker who was in New York working with Artist's Call in support of the freedom movements in Central America. He, along with New York writers (Kimiko Hahn and Victoria Redel, in particular) gathered a series of translations of poetry from Nicaragua, El Salvador, and Guatemala—Ernesto Cardenal, Margaret Randall, Daisy Zamora, Roque Dalton, Roberto Sosa—that BOMB published. By the new century, in the year 2000, these sections grew into BOMB's annual Americas issue: Mexican novelists Carmen Boullosa, Francisco Goldman, the poet Daniel Shapiro, and the translator Esther Allen joined Daniel Flores as its first contributing editors: Oscar Hijuelos interviewed the legendary Cuban author Guillermo Cabrera Infante; Carmen interviewed Roberto Bolaño. A photograph by Graciela Iturbide of the artist Francisco Toledo holding a Chihuahua in the air was our first Americas cover.

In the spring of 2009, 28 years after BOMB's birth, Tom Griffiths and Jessica Green of Everything Studio redesigned the magazine. We decided to go back to our past and bring it with us into our future. What was that raw and maverick quality that we had back then? We wanted to keep that core alive. So all of those things we've carried with us. And at the same time, our younger staff started an online portion of BOMB that is now BOMB Daily.

wc: But you're a quarterly.

bs: Not exactly. We have a huge online presence—and have been developing our website for some time. There's been a revolution, and we're excited to take advantage of it. We have a web editor, Clinton Krute, and two online editors, Andrew Bourne and Orit Gat, all working on daily content. So it's not simply a magazine; it's about an ongoing conversation. And because of the digital revolution that conversation can exist as talking heads in various mediums: streaming videos, podcasts, and of course there's Internet radio and Internet TV. Writing is so malleable; change is inherent to its form. I don't yet know how to find a similar quality in editing audio and video, but our younger editors mix in the new media as a matter of course.

wc: Yeah, it seems to work. Artists see things ahead anyway. BOMB began specifically as a New York manifestation. You've described how you think it's grown since 1981 when it was a bunch of people around a table. What are your plans for BOMB's future? What do you see happening?

bs: We're creating a research database for deeper searches; I think of it as constellations of influence—a Balzacean world. What began as a quarterly publication is now transforming into an innovative publishing house dedicated to the creation, dissemination, and preservation of artist-generated content. The BOMB site reaches 1.3 million online readers. And with funding from the A. W. Mellon Foundation, BOMB is digitizing, indexing, and synthesizing all of its content—over 5,000 primary cultural documents—into a searchable, relational, and free online library. When it's done, the site will provide access to the quarterly magazine, web-exclusive content, and all of BOMB's archival material from 1981 onward—BOMB's past, present, and future.

We're starting a traditional oral history series with African American visual artists that will be conducted by peers, and covering distinct groups, time periods, specifically for the web. The artists Sanford Biggers, Mickalene Thomas, Jack Whitten, Stanley Whitney, and Carrie Mae Weems, along with Thelma Golden, director of the Studio Museum, and Kellie Jones, curator, author and associate professor at Columbia, are advisors. And then we're adapting both archival and new media content, for the iPhone, iPad, and the like—why not let people create their own e-books from our archival interviews, or publish amalgamations from the past and the present? SoHo Press is coming out with an anthology of BOMB's literary interviews, *Between Authors* in 2014.... I think it's all incredibly exciting.

But this is what I would like to close with: BOMB is the sum total of its parts—that includes the voices that comprise its content, and the senior and managing editors (poet Mónica de la Torre and curator Sabine Russ, respectively), contributing editors, and interns who work with me to make them manifest. As one of our past senior editors, Nell McClister, so aptly wrote for the Association of Art Historians on the occasion of our twenty-fifth anniversary, "BOMB foregrounds the work of art as always in dialogue, with the artist engaged in the world, and the reader as instrumental in the construction of the work's meaning."

And finally, I think we've just gotten better at revealing the truth. Storytelling is my beat, and as an amalgamation of so many of its forms, the Bible is exemplary. At one point I came across this: "Seek the truth." In that context, the Torah is speaking of God. But another interpretation of truth, mine for instance, might say that while the truth can be ephemeral—a paradigm, complex, or many-sided—it does exist. It can be found out. Although it doesn't always match with the views of one group in relation to another, and as a result you might think that the truth is negotiable. But perhaps it's that we have to negotiate among ourselves for its release. Because even if the truth is ineffable, we are obliged to at least circle its essence. That's what we try to reveal.

The Life of *Ontario Review* (1974–2008)

GREG JOHNSON

Ontario Review, for thirty-four years one of North America's most prestigious literary magazines, began as an image.

One day in 1973, Joyce Carol Oates was simply looking out a window, daydreaming, and saw a white bird in flight. She immediately thought that the image would be an ideal logo for a literary journal. She sketched the flying bird, discussed the idea with her husband, Raymond J. Smith, and the couple decided to inaugurate a magazine as soon as possible. In fact, Ray and Joyce had long harbored such a notion. Joyce once wrote,

I was simply intrigued by the idea of a little magazine. Not a glossy magazine — never — but a *little magazine*. (Not too little: the original *Kenyon Review*, say. Remember those gorgeous covers?) I was fascinated from about the age of eighteen onward by the notion, the abstract, almost Platonic notion, of a physical thing that was at the same time a communal phenomenon. That is, one picks up a magazine, weighs it in the hand, it appears to be a *thing*, but in fact it isn't a *thing* at all. It's a symposium. A gathering. A party.[1]

Since both Oates and Smith were then teaching at the University of Windsor in Ontario, Canada, *Ontario Review* seemed the appropriate name. The journal's subheading, "A North American Journal of the Arts," suggested its ambition to seek out the best work available from both Canadian and American writers. As Ray once remarked, in an interview he gave me for *Invisible Writer: A Biography of Joyce Carol Oates* (Dutton, 1998), "It was intended to bridge what Joyce and I ... felt to be a widening gap between the two literary/artistic cultures. We tried to do this by publishing writers and artists from both countries, as well as essays and reviews of an intercultural nature."[2] Ray once wrote that a distinct feature of the maga-

1. Joyce Carol Oates and Raymond J. Smith, "On Editing *The Ontario Review*," in *The Art of Literary Publishing: Editors on Their Craft*, ed. Bill Henderson (New York: Pushcart Book Press, 1980), 145.
2. "About *Ontario Review*" on *Celestial Timepiece: The Joyce Carol Oates homepage*, https://www.usfca.edu/jco/aboutontarioreview/; accessed March 29, 2014.

zine was "its character as a North American journal of the arts—'North American,' I say, though for purely practical reasons it focuses mainly on the English-speaking cultures of the continent. As Americans teaching in Canada, in the border city of Windsor, knowledgeable about the literary traditions and in contact with writers of both countries, Joyce and I felt that we were in a fine position to start such a journal."[3] By 1978, when Ray and Joyce moved to Princeton, the magazine already had a distinguished reputation and so the name of the journal remained unchanged.

Ontario Review, whose first issue had appeared in fall 1974, grew in size and scope over the years, so that in 1984 Ray and Joyce decided to start publishing books as well, under the "Ontario Review Press" imprint. More than once they have been compared to Leonard and Virginia Woolf, who similarly began a home-centered publishing concern, the Hogarth Press, with the purpose of publishing friends whose work was too experimental for the rather staid literary tastes of 1916, the year their press began. Leonard and Virginia published such luminaries as T. S. Eliot, Katherine Mansfield, and E. M. Forster, in addition to their own work, and like Ray and Joyce they were "hands on," even setting type themselves, and wrapping books in parcels to send off to book buyers.

In 1974, it's doubtful that Ray and Joyce were thinking of any comparisons to the Woolfs, and their reasons for inaugurating *Ontario Review* were unique to them. Ray, despite having earned his PhD in eighteenth-century literature at the University of Wisconsin, had, as a young man, his own literary ambitions, producing a couple of novels and some short stories that, he later said, "didn't pan out"; and he'd always maintained a lively interest in contemporary literature. Unlike Virginia Woolf, who saw her Hogarth Press work as a form of psychological therapy, Joyce simply had a desire to contribute to the literary establishment, especially to the world of small presses and magazines that had been so instrumental in launching her career. Perhaps her most famous story, for example, "Where Are You Going, Where Have You Been?," had originally appeared in a little magazine published at Cornell University, *Epoch*, and other journals such as *Southern Review*, *Kenyon Review*, and *Shenandoah* published her work early in her career, and often.

Once *Ontario Review* was underway, Ray took the helm as editor, with Joyce listed as associate editor. Though the magazine was always a joint endeavor, Ray did most of the work of reading submissions, dealing with printers, handling subscriptions and the myriad other details involved in putting out a magazine. Joyce, for her part, read many of the submissions as well, and conferred with Ray on what work should be accepted for pub-

3. Oates and Smith, "On Editing *The Ontario Review*," 146.

lication. She often sent personal notes (as did Ray) to writers, commenting on the submission at hand and/or encouraging them to submit further work. As with the Woolfs, all this work was done out of their home, where Ray and Joyce had adjoining offices.

Many years later, in her 2011 memoir, *A Widow's Story*, Joyce recalled that publishing a journal did have its frustrating moments: "Starting a literary magazine is an adventure not for the faint-hearted or the easily discouraged. Neither Ray nor I knew what to expect. Ray's first experience with a printer was a near disaster—the printer had never printed anything more ambitious than a menu for a local Chinese restaurant—the page proofs were riddled with errors that required hours of Ray's time and patience to correct, and when the copies were finally printed, for some reason we never understood, a number were smeared with bloody fingerprints." Joyce adds that "I wish I could recall Ray's exact words, when he eagerly opened the box from the printer, and saw the mysterious stains on the covers. I want to think that he'd said something appropriately witty but probably what emerged from his throat more resembled a sob."[4] He may have sobbed more over the fact that most of the roughly 1,000 copies he'd ordered did not sell. As Joyce observed in her memoir, many years would pass before circulation reached 1,000.

Yet Ray's efforts as the editor of the journal won him praise and gratitude from the writers with whom he worked. One of Joyce's colleagues in the Princeton creative writing program, the distinguished novelist, memoirist, and biographer Edmund White, noted in an interview for *Invisible Writer* that "I've known several writers (I'm one of them) who'd been manhandled by New York editors and who turned with relief to Ray's thoughtfulness and politeness and genuine perspicacity. He was a superb line-editor. His taste was flawless."[5] Similarly grateful was the well-known poet Albert Goldbarth, a particular favorite of Ray's and a poet who contributed to *Ontario Review* for more than a quarter of a century. Goldbarth has saved every note that Ray sent him over the years, and said in his *Invisible Writer* interview that "in every jot of Ray Smith's side of the vast accumulation of paper implied in this, the wit and generosity, the liberal humanity, the abundant love of getting every editorial detail hammered down just right, is evident. He was a warm, gently intelligent and civilized presence at the other end of that quarter-century of mailed envelopes, singular as a person and, sadly, increasingly rare as a type."[6]

4. "I am Sorry to Inform You," *Atlantic* (May 2010): 78–83, at 81.
5. Personal correspondence with the author.
6. Greg Johnson, "Remembering Ray Smith," *Celestial Timepiece: The Joyce Carol Oates homepage*, http://www.usfca.edu/jco/rememberingray/, accessed March 28, 2014.

As Joyce noted in *A Widow's Story*, Ray was a natural at editing the journal. "As he was revealed to be a born gardener with a gardener's zest for
working in the soil with his hands," she wrote, "so he was revealed to be
a born editor with a zest for working with writers, nurturing their work
and publishing it. Many of his closest friendships were editor/writer relationships forged in the intimacy of letters, phone calls, faxes. With his
Jesuit-trained scrupulosity for 'perfection' Ray was an ideal line-editor
and made it a principle to read, reread, and reread material—in manuscript, in galleys, and in page proofs."[7]

Thanks to the strong reputation of *Ontario Review* in the literary world,
Ray was able to attract a roster of distinguished contributors: fiction writers in the magazine included Nobel laureates such as Saul Bellow and Nadine Gordimer in addition to such luminaries as John Updike, Margaret Atwood, Raymond Carver, Donald Barthelme, and Philip Roth. Well-known
poets whose work appeared in the magazine included Joseph Brodsky, Rita
Dove, Maxine Kumin, W. S. Merwin, and C. K. Williams. Ray sought out his
own "gorgeous covers," too, by featuring the work of such artists as Matt
Phillips and Gloria Vanderbilt. Such a variety of talent helped produce a
singular tenor for *Ontario Review* that was described in *Library Journal*, in a
1976 review by Bill Katz: "The style is as relaxed as it is meaningful, and the
review is not burdened with dense scholarly prose whose primary appeal is
to the expert. No, this is for the average intelligent reader who seeks a professional, honest approach to the arts … and for once there is a solid balance between 'names' and lesser-known figures of equally high standards."[8]

Indeed, Ray prided himself on finding and publishing writers at the
beginning of their careers. One of these was Joyce's former Princeton student Pinckney Benedict, who published stories in the magazine as well
as a 1987 collection, *Town Smokes*, with the press when Benedict was only
twenty-three. At that time, Benedict recalls, he "had no idea—because
I'd published very little and had never had another editor outside the
classroom—what good care he was taking of me." Later professional experiences, Benedict notes, made him realize that he was "blessed by Ray from
the very beginning and far above any merits I might have possessed." Like
Goldbarth, Benedict greatly valued the personal notes Ray would send
about his young author's work. "The notes were doubtless second nature
to Ray," Benedict observes in his *Invisible Writer* interview, "and I never
communicated to him how precious they became to me."[9]

---

7. *A Widow's Story* (New York: Ecco, 2011), 387.

8. "*The Ontario Review*" (review), *Library Journal*, May 15, 1976.

9. Greg Johnson, "Remembering Ray Smith," *Celestial Timepiece: The Joyce Carol Oates
homepage*, http://www.usfca.edu/jco/rememberingray/, accessed March 28, 2014.

Another grateful author published by the magazine and the press was Sheila Kohler, who recalls that Ray once rejected something of hers, "but with the kind of letter that is rarely sent with a rejection—a helpful one." Eventually editor and writer came to terms over her work, and she vividly recalls first meeting Ray and Joyce in person one rainy evening in 2002. "The couple immediately put me at ease. Ray looked at me with his signature benevolent gaze and spoke very kindly of my stories. I realized to my surprise that he had read them very carefully—always the ultimate compliment to a writer." As a line editor, Ray was "diligent and patient," Kohler remembers, "willing to sit on the telephone and make small corrections of punctuation and style. He made larger suggestions, too, pointing out contradictions and confusions in the text, but never forcing an opinion or insisting on anything if I felt it was not right.... Here, I thought, was someone who was interested in the product rather than in himself. I felt that it was possible to grow as a writer, to blossom, in the sun of such interest and appreciation."[10]

Yet another fiction writer who appreciated Ray's qualities as an editor was Richard Burgin; he was in a unique position to value Ray's work because Burgin himself edits an excellent literary magazine, *Boulevard*. Burgin recalls Ray's editorial sensibility: "While generally not effusive, he was always sensitive and gentle, insightful and fair. You never felt he was being anything less than honest." Burgin had been drawn to the magazine because of the "excellent overall quality of the publication. The fact that a writer of Joyce Carol Oates's stature was involved with it was also a definite plus. I especially admired the openness to different types of writing in [the magazine]. It published first-rate 'mainstream' (for want of a better term) fiction and poetry, but also edgy, 'experimental' work as well. I always felt Ray Smith had impeccable taste."

Beginning in the late 1970s, when I was a graduate student at Emory University, I worked with Ray often, being fortunate enough to have a number of stories and other work published in the magazine, and to publish three books with the press; my experience was similar to that of the other writers quoted above. With Joyce's welcome input, Ray attended carefully to every detail regarding my work and its appearance in *Ontario Review*. It might be said that he, Joyce, and I were "workshopping" my fiction long before I started teaching my own workshops. Knowing that I was only one of dozens of writers he was helping, I found the amount of work he did, and the care with which he did it, to be nothing less than astonishing.

Despite the manifold problems involved with publishing a magazine—

10. Ibid.

such as dealing with dilatory printers, or with well-known authors (and friends) who might submit an inferior piece of work—Ray stressed the many rewards of his endeavor. In "On Editing *Ontario Review*," he wrote:

> I see editing a magazine not as *compiling* but *creating*, and the finished product as a work of art in its own right.... The rewards of the job are many—discovering a well-shaped and compelling story or poem by a previously unpublished writer, watching hitherto disconnected material gradually assume a focus, getting some positive reactions from people you admire. Finally, the editor, for better or worse, contributes (no matter how little) to the shaping of a culture. He need not, and perhaps should not, be doctrinaire; nevertheless, he will have values—aesthetic, cultural, even moral, that will be reflected in what he chooses to publish. I have never thought of it this way before, but I suppose that the *Ontario Review*, whether quixotically or not, is tilting with the dragon of anti-art—resisting the deadening commercialism of modern Western civilization.[11]

Such thoughtfulness and purpose underlay all of Ray's work with the magazine over a publishing career of more than thirty years.

For those who knew Ray, however, his personal qualities are what will most be missed. On a couple of occasions I "house-sat" for Ray and Joyce when they went on extended trips, and what most stays in my memory is Ray showing me how to care for their cats, their canary, and their plants. No detail was too small for him to discuss, and it struck me that he was an inherently nurturing person, whether dealing with animals, his garden, his authors, his friends, or his wife.

He, along with Joyce, was nurturing likewise in the largest sense, creating a sense of community for the writers he published. Again the authors who published in *Ontario Review* have been eloquent in enumerating both Ray and Joyce's special qualities. For instance, Edmund White recalls in his *Invisible Writer* interview: "I can picture them sitting on opposite ends of the couch under the twin floor lamps and listening to recordings of Chopin, reading and working, writing and correcting proof. They thought of themselves as 'lazy,' but never was there a more disciplined and productive couple, yet the discipline never felt harsh. They were doing what they wanted to do and with the ideal companion." White adds of Ray that he "was so kind, so twinkly, so quick to catch the joke, so gently satirical about the foibles of our friends—he didn't have to say anything, it was all there, sparkling in his regard. He led an exemplary life."[12] Richard Burgin notes:

11. Oates and Smith, "On Editing *The Ontario Review*," 149–50.
12. Greg Johnson, "Remembering Ray Smith," *Celestial Timepiece: The Joyce Carol Oates homepage*, http://www.usfca.edu/jco/rememberingray/, accessed March 28, 2014.

He was a true gentleman, one of the kindest, most considerate people I ever dealt with in a publishing world that needs many more Ray Smiths—people of integrity, true dignity and simple human kindness.... What I think I admired most about Ray as an editor, superb though his literary sensibility was, was the way he treated me. He was not a man of many words, but he used the right words. He respected your intelligence and your feelings and he thought about what was best for you as a writer.... I never met anyone like him and doubt I will again. I miss him dearly.[13]

No one has been more eloquent in enumerating his special qualities than Joyce, who often has written in her journal about her husband. Noting that her marriage has "made my life stable," she listed her husband's virtues: "Kindly, loving, sweet, at times critically intelligent, sensitive, funny, unambitious, with a love for idleness that matches my own. Ray is an extraordinary person whose depths are not immediately obvious." Two years later, she noted similarly: "He is an extraordinary person, in a number of respects: his kindness, his good nature, his sense of humor, his wit (which is so rarely shown in public), his reserve, shyness, intelligence ... sweetness.... That he should be so *sweet*, and that I should have guessed so ... what a miracle."[14]

13. Personal correspondence with the author.
14. *The Journal of Joyce Carol Oates: 1973–1982* (New York: Ecco, 2007), 203, 291.

The Word *Sacred* Is Not Misplaced

DAVE EGGERS

Publishing other people's work is a hell of a lot more enjoyable than publishing your own. Publishing your own work is fraught with complicated, even tortured, feelings. Invariably you believe that you've failed. That you could have done better. That if you were given another month or another year, you would have achieved what you set out to do.

Actually, it's not always that bad. But usually it is.

Publishing someone else's work, though, is uncomplicated. You can be an unabashed champion of that work. You can finish reading it, or finish editing it, and know that it's done, that people will love it, and that you want to send it into the world. That feeling is strong, and it's simple, and it's pure.

That's what's driven *McSweeney's* for fifteen years now—far beyond the four or eight issues we originally thought this journal would run. We thought the fun of it would end after a year or so, but that feeling, of finding a new voice, or a new piece by an established voice, and setting it into type and printing it and mailing it and connecting writers to readers, is still just as good as it was back when we started in 1998.

Back then it was me opening submission envelopes in my kitchen, and being astonished that anyone would trust this new quarterly with their work. When I was the only one reading the submissions, I was an easy audience. I was so overwhelmed with the whole thing that I pretty much accepted every other story. And then I couldn't wait to get them into type. Actually, I would usually accept a piece and lay it out the same day. If I couldn't get a digital version of it soon enough, I would just retype the whole story and lay it out that night. This is what I'm talking about: this simple and good feeling of knowing you'll be able to introduce a new writer to new readers.

This is adapted from Eggers's introduction to *The Best of McSweeney's*, edited by Dave Eggers and Jordan Bass (San Francisco: McSweeney's, 2013).

Early on, most of the writers in *McSweeney's* were lesser known, or were starting out in their careers. After a few issues, we began getting work from some established authors—even without asking, which was startling—and since then, our goal has been to balance these known quantities with the newcomers, and balance both of them with an eye toward occasional experimentation, some of these efforts improbably successful. Sometimes these experiments were simple acts of matching a great writer to unusual subject matter. Thus we sent Andrew Sean Greer to a weekend NASCAR rally in Michigan. Sometimes these commissions were based on iffy notions that yielded great results—for example, when we asked dozens of writers to each write a short story in twenty minutes. In one issue we asked our writers to write stories based on the notebook jottings of F. Scott Fitzgerald. In another, we asked them to help resurrect dead forms like the pantoum and *biji*.

But most of what we've published over the years has simply come through the mail. We still open every submission envelope, and each time we do, we want to be surprised, we want to be reawakened. I'm rarely the person opening these envelopes anymore, but the other day, while talking to the volunteer readers about the responsibility entrusted to them, I found myself using the word *sacred*. It was hyperbole, I'm sure, but here's what I meant: it takes a particular mix of madness and courage to write short stories—they do not pay the rent, they are not widely read—and it takes even greater courage to put them in the mail, submitting them for judgment by strangers. So thinking about these senders, batshit crazy and full of hope and dread, and the fact that they would entrust our readers to judge their work, and for us to print their work, I said the word *sacred*. It still seems right in some way.

Art is made by anarchists and sorted by bureaucrats. Thus, over the years, there have been a few bureaucrats who, feeling the need to categorize and label, have posited that *McSweeney's* has some house style. But this is not the case. Even the earliest issues, which even I assumed did lean toward the experimental, always balanced these formal forays with more traditional storytelling. Issue 3, for example, included a story by David Foster Wallace that we ran on the journal's spine, but it also featured a 25,000-word essay about Gary Greenberg's correspondence with Ted Kaczynski. This balance has held true ever since. We've sought to publish the best work we can, no matter its genre or approach or author. We've published everything from oral histories from Zimbabwe to experimental prose-poems from Norway. The only thing common to all the work in every one of our forty-five issues so far is that the work was good and told us something new.

Some years ago, I was in Galway, Ireland, and happened to meet a man named Timothy McSweeney. I got to know him and his wife, Maura, who also had the last name McSweeney. We talked about a writer she liked, and she said, "He writes like he's seeing the world for the first time." And that about summed it up. That's what we look for—writers who make us feel like they're seeing their world, whatever world that is, with fresh eyes, and who, through their words, allow us to do the same. Is this easy to do? No, it is goddamned hard to do. But a lot of writers manage to pull it off, and a lot of these writers then send their work to small, or tiny, literary magazines—there are no big ones—and it's our honor and pleasure (could it even be our duty?) to try to get them read.

On *n+1*

KEITH GESSEN

In 2003, at the age of 28, I escaped from grad school and moved to New York. A friend offered to sublet me his rent-controlled apartment on the Upper West Side. The sublet was not technically allowed by the building, but it was unlikely anyone would notice. My friend had just one request: I was not to receive any mail. No problem. For a nominal fee, I opened a PO box at the post office around the corner.

All of *n+1*'s early mail came to that little box, at Columbus Avenue and 95th Street. But I'm getting ahead of myself. First there were many meetings. We met at my subleased apartment, on West 93rd, and we met at Ben Kunkel's apartment, on West 16th Street. Mark Greif and Marco Roth were both doing PhDs at Yale, and they would come into the city and stay with relatives: Mark with his grandmother on the Lower East Side, Marco with his mom on the Upper West Side. Ben and Mark had been good friends in college; I'd met them after graduation, when we were all reviewing books for *Dissent*, the *Nation* (where Ben had been an intern), and the *American Prospect* (where Mark had been an editorial fellow). Mark met Marco in grad school, where both were active in the movement to organize a graduate student union. Throughout that year, 2003, we'd meet up and talk about our "magazine." We were all literature majors of one kind or another, but we were all also interested in left-wing politics and history. We felt like there was no space for those things to come together—the political magazines we wrote for didn't ultimately care that much about literature, whereas the literary magazines that were coming out seemed intent on keeping themselves at a distance from the world. Why couldn't you have both things? Literature used to; magazines used to. We sat around and talked about all this, and about how our magazine was going to change things. We talked about it so much, and had so much fun doing so, that it didn't feel like we'd ever actually have to do anything about it.

I think we never would have, in truth, except that we were in New York, where things can take on a momentum of their own, just from talking about them. At some point we decided that we needed a place to meet that wasn't our apartment; as it happened, my childhood friend Matvei Yankelevich had started a poetry press in Brooklyn called Ugly Duckling Presse, which had a rent-free office space in DUMBO, an abandoned industrial neighborhood squeezed in between the Brooklyn and Manhattan Bridges. I asked Matvei if we could hold our meetings at his office, and he said yes. It was a large basement space, with twenty-foot-high ceilings and a tiny bit of light through the tall windows. UDP had one computer, an eMac, a letter press printer, and a huge industrial table on which they folded booklets, placed tea mugs, and hand-rolled cigarettes in breaks between folding.

We started meeting there. Having an office space gave our project a reality that it didn't previously have. And suddenly we began to argue. We argued about everything: the title, the subtitle, the distribution of articles, the question of whether we'd have contributor bios. (For the record, we all thought "n+1" was a terrible title—Chad Harbach, another of the early editors, who at this point was in Wisconsin, had come up with it as a kind of joke when we'd first imagined starting a magazine, years earlier. "There are already so many magazines," I had said. "Well," said Chad, "n+1"—meaning, why not another? It was a placeholder, but every other title we came up with during our endless arguments at the UDP office—the only one I remember now is *The Reverberator*, after a Henry James novel, also sometimes *The American Reverberator*—was even worse. And we kept calling it *n+1* despite ourselves.) So we argued. Now the Ducks, as we called them, were very chill people. They drank their tea, rolled their cigarettes, talked about poetry. Meanwhile, in another corner of the room, we'd be yelling our heads off at one another. Marco would storm out; I'd throw my hands up in despair; Mark, out of anger, would simply stop talking. It was embarrassing. But having that office, showing, to other people, that we were lunatics—this was incredibly important. After all that, it would have been very embarrassing not to start our magazine.

What's more, the Ducks were incredibly helpful. One of their founders, Ryan Haley, agreed to design the first issue. The design process led to more fights—we had to decide on a logo, a cover, the layout, the font. And once we had a layout and a font, we had to finalize the texts. Now things got ugly. All our files were on Ryan's laptop, which he would leave at the office if we needed to work on something. Whoever was at the office latest got to change things. I changed something in one of Mark's texts; Marco and Ryan changed something in one of mine. There was a period of time when we stopped talking to one another. Even mild-mannered Ryan, who was basically held hostage by our inability to finalize the texts—we kept having to use his computer, and he kept having to reflow the text in the design program—eventually slammed a file drawer shut with great violence when we admitted to him, sheepishly, that we'd need a few more days to finish up a few more things. Said the mild-mannered Ryan: "Fuck!!"Our first publication was a stapled "prototype," a kind of try out. It consisted of our very first "Intellectual Situation"—attacks on the *New Republic*, the *Weekly Standard*, and *McSweeney's/The Believer*; part of Mark's essay "Against Exercise"; part of Ben's short story "Failure"; and something I wrote specifically for the prototype, about the Martha Stewart trial for insider trading, which I'd attended because a friend of mine from high school was the star witness. The attacks on the other magazines staked out our position: For us, the *New Republic* was smart, well informed, and serious, but fundamentally conservative: for years it had used its intelligence to denounce anything new, difficult, or interesting in literature or art. (We connected this, fairly or unfairly, to the magazine's support for the Iraq War.) *McSweeney's* and the *Believer*, meanwhile, could not be accused of aesthetic conservativism: *McSweeney's*, a literary quarterly, published all sorts of literary experiments, while the *Believer*, a book review, had as its explicit policy that it would only celebrate new work, rather than criticize it (the *Believer*, too, had pushed off the *New Republic's* literary criticism in its initial statement of intent). Yet it seemed to us like an explicit policy of niceness and editorial strategy of "anything goes" vitiated the whole purpose of literature, which was to put forward one's most intimate and passionately held thoughts and ideas. What if one's ideas were bad or wrong? For us the *New Republic* and the *Believer* were two sides of the same coin. They deserved each other. We wanted to go beyond them.

In March 2004 we printed and stapled the prototype at the Ugly Duckling office, then threw a party where we asked people to subscribe. We e-mailed all our friends. Somehow or other, by the time we printed our first issue four months later, we had around 250 subscribers. We figured we could think of another 250 people to send the issue to for free. And the rest we could put into bookstores.

By this point we'd been joined by Allison Lorentzen, who was just out of college and interested in getting into publishing and who agreed to be our managing editor. We began taking our disputes to her, and she would adjudicate. For a while, the arguments died down.

It came time to print the issue, and those of us who could—Marco, Ben, Mark, and I—chipped in $2,000, for a total of $8,000. We printed 1,000 copies at the printer recommended by Ugly Duckling, McNaughton and Gunn in Michigan. But here we ran into another problem. That spring, Ugly Duckling (and by extension *n+1*) had been kicked out of the free arts space to make room for paying customers. Where were we going to send the issue? Mark's grandmother's apartment was not a good option; Marco's mother's apartment would have worked, but this seemed too juvenile.

Ben was out of town. We decided to get it delivered to my sublet, despite the fact that I wasn't allowed to receive mail. This wasn't, after all, technically mail.

The issue was finished in early July and shipped from Michigan in a truck. Chad was just then visiting from Wisconsin, and every few hours we checked the tracking information on my computer. The truck was in Ohio. The truck was in Pennsylvania. The truck was in New Jersey! It was expected to arrive the next morning. Chad and I went out to get a bagel. When we came back, two very frazzled Pakistani guys, one of them holding a bill of lading, were arguing with two equally frazzled security guards about whether a Keith Gessen lived in my building. The Pakistani guys were sure that he did; the security guards were equally sure that he didn't. This was 2004, not 2002, but there was still a lot of tension around terrorism in New York, and you could see the guards were uncomfortable about whatever it was the Pakistani guys were trying to deliver. But they were only trying to deliver 1,000 issues of *n+1*. I admitted that I was Keith Gessen, and the delivery guys unloaded our boxes onto the sidewalk, and Chad and I took them up to the apartment. I then had to explain to the doormen that I was staying in my friend's apartment. I then had to confess to my friend that this had happened. He was understanding but asked me to get out of the apartment for a little while, in case the building management freaked out. That summer, for the first few months of *n+1*'s existence, as we launched our website and tried to drum up publicity, I lived in Massachusetts, in my father's basement, and checked my e-mail as often as I could.

The first issue, while imperfect, did pretty much what we'd set out to do. Every piece in it was both literary and political. Marco wrote an essay about the success of the memoir *Reading Lolita in Tehran*, wondering why it was that Americans could take literature seriously when it was in other countries, but not when it was in our own; the excellent literary critic Patrick Giles, whom I'd met a few years earlier, wrote a piece on the gay novelist James McCourt which doubled as a memoir of the AIDS epidemic and its effects on gay culture. Chad wrote an essay on his favorite writer, David Foster Wallace. I translated part of the classic anti-Soviet conceptualist novel *The Norm*, by Vladimir Sorokin, about citizens of a country who are forced daily to eat shit.

The first issue also included a piece by Mark, "Mogadishu, Baghdad, Troy," about contemporary American warfare. It is still, to me, the prototypical *n+1* piece, because it took a political phenomenon—the shape and feel, the murderousness, and ultimately the ineffectuality at actually solving conflicts of the way the US now fights its wars—and explained it, with great brio, through a reading of the *Iliad*, Simone Weil, Elaine Scarry, and Mark Bowden's *Black Hawk Down*. This was politics seen by literature and literature seen by politics. It was awesome. So we had created an issue that we liked. Now what? As the process advanced, practical complications piled onto one another, and we split the business side of things into five areas:

Accounting
Ads
Distribution (to bookstores)
Publicity
Subscriptions
Website

At first Mark was in charge of accounting and subscriptions; I was in charge of distribution, publicity, and the website. I was also, once I got back to New York, responsible for checking our post office box, which meant that I received the checks that came in from new subscribers. My record keeping left something to be desired. Under Mark's supervision, I bought a proper ledger at Staples, but that was the end of the good news. I had a jacket that I always wore at this time, and in order not to lose track of the checks I simply stuffed all of them into the same pocket of the jacket until I got around to laying them out, entering them into the ledger, and depositing them all at once at our bank. I would then mail the ledgers to Mark, who would enter them into a database and fill any outstanding orders from the post office near where he lived. My jacket technique filled the methodical, well-organized Mark with both apprehension and glee. "Sometimes people write me to claim that they have a subscription," he would say. "And I tell them, 'Look, Keith checked his jacket pocket. He checked it very carefully. Your check was not in Keith's jacket pocket! Sorry, you are not a subscriber to *n+1*.'"

Distribution was my most fervent interest. There were thousands of bookstores in the US—but how many of them would actually be interested in us? Before we even printed the first issue, we had our first intern, a Columbia student. For two months, she and I would meet once a week at a coffee shop near my house and talk about bookstores. I had a list of potentially sympathetic bookstores that I'd gotten from a friend at Dalkey Archive Press, and our intern would call them on the phone, using a phone card I'd bought so she wouldn't run up her parents' long distance bill, and tell them to be on the lookout for *n+1*. It's hard to know whether this was effective. In New York, we visited the stores in person: some of them said that they didn't sell magazines and others that didn't want yet another one. Those stores are now out of business. Others, like St. Mark's and Labyrinth (now Book Culture) and the Community Bookstore and BookCourt in Brooklyn, were much more receptive. And in any case we soon learned about the existence of distributors: places that already knew all the bookstores and would send our magazine to all the good ones in exchange for a small percentage of our sales.

Unfortunately it was not so simple. For one thing, the distributors were overwhelmed by requests. We were initially rejected by the biggest distributor, Ingram, after I sent them a long explanatory letter, a printed-out pdf of our first issue, and our stapled prototype. Mistaking the prototype for an actual issue, they responded that it would be difficult to get people to pay $9 for the thing. A friendlier place was Deboer, based in New Jersey, which had once distributed the *Partisan Review*. They took two hundred copies of the first issue. But they had fallen on hard times. They immediately fell behind on their payments. We, in turn, refused to send the next issue. They pleaded poverty—these were difficult days in a low-margin business. Did we want them to disappear? We played hardball: what good were they to us if they distributed our product, then failed to pay us? They made a partial payment. We sent them the second issue, and celebrated. We were business geniuses! Not long after, Deboer announced that it was going out of business.

Deboer's main competitor was Ubiquity, based in Brooklyn. I visited them, in a small, nondescript warehouse on Degraw Street, near the body shops and gas stations of Fourth Avenue. The first level was staffed entirely by a small crew of Caribbean men who placed various literary and culture magazines—I saw *Open City*, BOMB, *Raritan*—into boxes and shipped them off to bookstores, though for New York, to save on postage, Ubiquity sent a van out once a week to make deliveries. Upstairs was the business office, staffed by a family that had been in the business for several decades, but I didn't get to go upstairs until year later, when we published our book about hipsters and the owner of Ubiquity, Joe Massey, got excited and, in the stuffy business office upstairs on Degraw, said an amazing thing. "In the '80s there used to be a thing called Semiotext(e)," Joe said, referring to the legendary American publisher of Baudrillard, Paul Virilio, and Deleuze and Guattari. "Do you know them? We distributed their books. You could be like them!" It was truly one of the most incredible moments in the history of our magazine, but Joe's dream was not to be. Even if our books had been the same caliber as Semiotext(e)'s, Joe, increasingly squeezed by the giant distribution companies, would not have been able to move very many of them. We gave him two hundred copies of *What Was the Hipster?* A couple of years later, most of them came back.

So that was distribution. What about publicity? Anyone who's been around the literary world has seen small publishers put out excellent, worthy work which they then do nothing to promote. Which is understandable. Self-promotion is different from literature; great writers are seldom great self-promoters. And still: as a group we had decided that, within certain limits, we would do what we could to promote our magazine. As someone who has since had to promote his own work, I can say that it was much easier, and more enjoyable, to promote a group project. We decided to throw big parties and invite everyone we humanly could. In New York, this turned out to be very easy. Three hundred people came to our first issue party; five hundred people came to our third. The parties were effective, especially in the pre–social media era, in getting our terrible name out into the ether. At the same time I think it was these parties that gave us a reputation for being a "hip" or even "hipster" magazine, which was irritating.

Six months after our first issue came out, we looked at our bank account and saw that it was back to where it'd been when we started—around $8,000. Clearly we were business geniuses. Then it occurred to us that we'd all spent six months working full-time, or close to full-time, for free. If you do that, you really can break even, in any business.

But it *was* a business, and when I think about the past ten years, a lot of what I think about are business decisions, or turning points. For years we spent all our time in post offices, mailing issues, books, tote bags. We'd take a backpack to the post office for regular mailings, and for the big issue mailing at the start of the cycle we'd borrow a car. Then someone—it must have been Ali Heifetz, our first full-time managing editor—discovered that the post office will actually come and pick up your mail at your office if you ask them to. Nothing was ever the same after that. Other turning points revolved around our office spaces. After we got kicked out of the Ugly Duckling space, we made the second issue in Allison Lorentzen's apartment in Park Slope; not long after that, Chad and I rented a place on Eastern Parkway, in Prospect Heights, in Brooklyn, and that was where we made our third issue. Ben's novel, *Indecision*, came out at the same time as the third issue, and Ben felt flush enough to make a donation to the magazine: he'd pay for an office for a year, a significant investment. We rented a small office on Chrystie Street, just below Houston, in a liminal neighborhood between SoHo and the Lower East Side. It was tiny, poorly lit, and the ceiling seemed to be dripping asbestos, but on the other hand the location was unbeatable. If we needed help unloading issues from a truck (after issue 3, we switched our printer to Sheridan, in Pennsylvania, partly because it was cheaper, and partly because a certain number of the third issue had come back from McNaughton with the reviews section upside down, and partly because we wanted to save money on shipping and thought, correctly as it turned out, that we could do so by driving a truck to Pennsylvania and picking up the issues ourselves), or we needed some advice, or we just wanted to throw a party, we could send out an e-mail and there'd be twenty people there within the hour.

That first real office was a great advance for us; so was our first office manager, Isaac Scarborough, who worked for free in exchange for getting to sit in the office and do his other (paid) work there. In 2006, Isaac went off to the Peace Corps in Turkmenistan, but we were able to hire our best intern, Alexandra (Ali) Heifetz, to a barely livable wage as our business manager. Ali heroically remained on the job for as long as she could, doing everything—subscription fulfillment, accounting, distribution, layout—in that dark office, until she could take it no more and went off to law school. It wasn't until 2010 that we were able to hire a second full-time employee, so that we had both a business manager and a managing editor. As of this writing, we're at three and a half full-time employees, which seems about right. Aside from a few months over the past decade when a few of us were too impoverished to carry out our magazine duties (running production, in one case; overseeing the office, in another) and asked for a stipend, none of the founding editors has been paid.

The first issue of the magazine we pretty much wrote ourselves. I wrote three pieces, Mark wrote four pieces, Marco and Chad each wrote two pieces. The only non-editors in it were my sister, Masha; Patrick Giles; and Joshua Glenn, the founder of the 1990s Boston intellectual magazine *Hermenaut*. How would we find new writers? We discussed it. I remembered reading an incredibly funny piece in our college literary magazine by a woman named Elif Batuman about a summer she'd spent in Moscow interning for a Russian publisher. "Let's find her!" said the other editors. I looked her up and learned that she was ensconced in a PhD program in literature at Stanford. I was prejudiced against PhD students, because of their terrible prose. "It's not going to work out with Elif," I reported back, "she's in grad school in California." "You don't know what she's doing out there!" Mark, himself a grad student, shot back. "What if she's like Foucault, hanging out in the desert and practicing S/M?" Reluctantly I agreed to give it a shot. I got in touch with Elif and sent her the first issue of the magazine, saying that I'd thought of her because we were looking for a new kind of essay, one that mixed narrative, polemic, and memoir, much in the way her essays in the college literary magazine had done. After reading the magazine, Elif wrote to say that she'd been thinking about writing something about an Issac Babel conference that she'd recently helped organize at Stanford, which, among other things, featured the appearance, in Palo Alto, both of Babel's daughter, from his first marriage, and his widow, from his second, both of whom were over ninety. A few months later she sent a 20,000-word essay called "Babel in California," which we published in our second issue. It was a masterpiece, a mixture of academic satire, literary criticism, and a memoir of the loneliness of graduate school. Looking at it now, you think, any magazine in the world would publish this. But none had. For us it was a breakthrough on two fronts: on its own, and because it meant that we could get people outside our immediate circle to produce remarkable work. It meant the magazine would survive.

From then on, just about every issue brought someone new into the magazine, an unpublished or under-published writer whose work we felt strongly about. We never wanted to publish established writers—or "famous people," as we half-facetiously called mid-career writers who weren't, of course, famous at all. We wanted people who were just beginning the long climb and could use our help. (Mark, who was writing his dissertation partly on the *Partisan Review*, kept recalling how they'd rejected some poems from William Carlos Williams, despite their admiration for the poet. Eventually we too would have our chance to reject second-tier work from first-rate writers.) In issue 3, our discovery was J. D. Daniels, who'd written us a furious denunciatory letter from Boston about the first issue, then produced a taut, angry piece about rich white kids affecting the fashions of poor white people in the form of "wifebeaters" and trucker hats. "When you wear the Fordson tractor belt buckle my father gave me, you're a hipster," the piece began. "When I wear it, I'm a redneck." Now we had opened a front in a game we couldn't win: a class war against ourselves.

What mistakes did we make? I think there were three main ones.

One was that we didn't take criticism very well. It was one of the primary goals of the magazine to bring back a combative, argumentative, engaged ethos to literary life. But of course you can't do that just by talking about your "ethos"; you can only do it by attacking people. Over the years we published polemics against literary readings, author photos, the publishing process, cell phones, the *Wall Street Journal*, the *New York Times*, Gawker.com, Pitchfork.com, Jewish magazines, right-wing magazines, lit bloggers, video games, the university, AOL chat, the iPod, book reviews, cultural sociology, *Harper's*, the *Atlantic*, the South Asian diaspora, and "world literature," to name just a few. Some of these institutions didn't mind being attacked (the publisher of *Heeb* wrote politely to correct our spelling of the Israeli porn site "Assraelis.com"); others did. The trouble was that we ourselves didn't much like being attacked, for a magazine that so enjoyed attacking. We were too touchy.

A more serious mistake was in the makeup of our editorial staff at the very start. There's a sense in which we didn't take ourselves seriously enough. This is an odd thing to say, since one of the criticisms leveled against us has been that we've taken ourselves too seriously. And we did take our writing, and our editing, very seriously. What we never really believed until it happened was that anyone would care, that people would pay as much attention to our magazine as they did. I think if we'd known that, we would have looked around and seen that we were almost all men. There were five men, and Allison Lorentzen, our managing editor. Could we not have found women to edit the magazine? It wasn't like we didn't know brilliant women. Yet it was easier to keep our group as it was, and because we didn't think it would matter very much, in the end, what we did, we didn't do anything about it. That ultimately limited how good a magazine we could be, and it's a mistake that, as of this writing, we're still recovering from. (Issue 15 was the first issue with an equal number of male and female contributors.)

A final mistake was that we never really created a working system for the distribution of labor. In a group of three, or six, or, as it eventually became, eleven or twelve, this meant that someone was always doing more work than someone else. For a long time, I thought, and believed, and still in a way believe, that the more you put into the magazine, the more you got out. The more publicity I did, the more control I had of the kind of events we put on, and the more I enjoyed them. Mark, as subscription czar, literally knew the name of every single one of our subscribers. When we threw one of our early parties, he would walk up and down the line that formed at the front door and say hi to everyone. "Frank!" he'd say, to a surprised recent subscriber who'd quietly given Mark his name. "How are you?? It's great to meet you at last! I just mailed out your issue last week!"

But inevitably the inequality of labor bled into the editorial process. Why should person X tell me this piece I edited is no good, when he's not editing any pieces himself? When was the last time he went to the post office? Does he even know how much a media mail package costs these days? Etc. The conflicts tended to happen toward the end of the issue cycle, when we had to make real decisions about what went into the magazine, in what order, and in what form. It was not uncommon, when production was finished and we sent the issue off to the printer, for several of the editors to no longer be speaking to one another, a situation that would last a few weeks or a month, until we all had a talk about it and resolved to move forward. It had been this way from the very start: one of the few early photos of us (we started the magazine before everyone's phone became a camera) is of Mark, Marco, and me in front of City Hall in early 2004. We'd just finished the prototype. Ever-organized Mark had gotten us to go to City Hall to register ourselves as a limited liability company; at the Registry of Deeds, they gave us all blowpops, to congratulate us on our new corporation, and so in the photo, Mark and I are sucking on blowpops and laughing. In fact, I remember very well that we'd had a huge blowup the day before about the preamble to the prototype. We hardly said hello to one another when we got to City Hall.

We always made up after these fights, but the fights kept happening. In Russian there is a term for what happened next—*vyyasneniya otnosheniy*—"sorting out of relations." The editors were always fighting, then sorting out our relations. At times it felt like that's all *n+1* did. Eventually, we were going to have a fight and not make up afterward.

Working on *n+1* I lost years of my life; lost my temper; lost money; and lost one of my two best friends in the world. Without the magazine to push us into a place where our relatively minor differences about how to do things would force a crisis, we would have remained friends for a long time. But without the magazine, too, we would have not spent years talking nearly every day on the phone, plotting business strategies, figuring out how we were going to outsmart, outwrite, outmaneuver all the forces intent on ignoring us. I suppose the thing to say here is that I would not have traded one thing for the other, would not have done things differently. I don't know if that's true. But it's too late now.

By the time you read this, we'll have published our twenty-first issue. There are some very good things in it. I hope everyone subscribes.

Part 2:
Politics, Culture,
and the Little Magazine

Callaloo: A Journal of Necessity

CHARLES HENRY ROWELL

"... his dream of the beautiful, needful thing."
ROBERT HAYDEN, "Frederick Douglass"

To recall the founding or origins of *Callaloo* is, first and foremost, to speak of necessity, as it was then and remains so today: the necessity of inventing and providing a site from which a marginalized group of people as literary poets, fiction writers, creative nonfiction writers, and countless other artists and intellectuals may freely speak. As I have written and spoken many times, *Callaloo* is "a journal of necessity." In a democracy, a people's right to develop their artistic talents, and their right to be allowed access to forums for their literary voices are as necessary as their right to vote or assemble peacefully and speak freely. In the American South, we, African Americans, were being denied—through state-sanctioned laws and through pernicious forms of economic deprivations—those as well as countless other necessary rights. We were, in fact, denied access to the very institutions and other venues that we as a people, since the seventeenth century, had helped to create, develop, and maintain. Such was the norm in the Deep South until I published the first issue of *Callaloo* in 1976. In fact, *Callaloo* was—and remains—a response to those desperate arresting circumstances throughout the African Diaspora, especially those in the American South. The conception, founding, and development of *Callaloo* are my response to violations of human and civil rights—this necessity, this right to voice, public and private: "This freedom, this liberty, this beautiful / and terrible thing, needful to man as air, / usable as earth," as Robert Hayden concluded in his poem "Frederick Douglass."

In 1976 and before, there were no nationally recognized literary and cultural journals or magazines focusing on or available to the Black South. During the 1970s, the South was still in the throes of the Civil Rights Movement, whose focus was addressing basic rights of all people in the United States, especially of those who lived in the American South, where black writers were not only ignored but were also forced to look beyond their region for publication outlets. That is, African American writers in the South did not find regionally located journals, such as the *Southern Review, Georgia Review, Mississippi Quarterly, Virginia Quarterly Review*, or *Sewanee Review—white only* periodicals—either interested in or supportive of work black writers created. These white-only journals operated exclusively and obviously for European American writers. Although a number of White South literary journals were supported by public funds, they, like other public institutions of the region, were in fact closed to Black South creativity, and their white editors, themselves defenders and perpetuators of the system of white racism and domination, were hostile to black creative writers as well as to balanced nonfiction work by or about African Americans. Neither written nor publicly announced, one of the racial tenets of the white-only literary journals of the region was to act as a White South vanguard to protect, defend, and perpetuate white racism and privilege, by using their power of exclusion and other nefarious means to arrest the creative development and the intellectual advancement of people of African descent, thereby helping to dominate and ultimately silence the Black South. What could help counter those inherited intentions and actions of White Power? A literary and cultural forum, what became *Callaloo*—I had hoped then, and I now declare.

During this same period, African American writers in other regions of the United States did not suffer the absence of periodical publication outlets that continued to arrest the development of creative writers and intellectuals in the Black South. In fact, during late 1960s and 1970s, a sizeable number of black literary journals and magazines suddenly appeared in regions beyond the South, but most of those periodical forums focused on the current phenomenon of the Black Arts Movement, the arts and culture branch of the Black Power Movement, both of which originated in the "urban North." *Black Theatre, The Black Scholar, Black World, Journal of Black Poetry, Black Dialogue, Black Creation*—these are but a few of the various periodical publications that served African American writers outside the South. It is important to remember that the Black Arts Movement, as an urban Northern phenomenon, did not subscribe to the integrationist ideology of the Civil Rights Movement, whose urgent focus was the festering racial segregation of the South. The continuing racial integrationist concerns of the Black South were not a part of the ideology of the Black Power Movement or of its arts and culture branch. The magazines that supported the dicta of the Black Aesthetic, which the architects of the Black Arts Movement formulated, became their mouthpieces, some of the forums through which they spoke. In the Black South, we, as artists and intellectuals, were more inclined to use as our aesthetic models the best work of Zora Neale Hurston, Sterling Brown, Melvin Tolson, Robert Hayden, Ralph Ellison, Albert Murray, Al Young, Ernest Gaines, and Alice Walker—writers whose poetics and cultural affirmations that the architects of the Black Arts Movement sometimes spoke against. No wonder then that the different periodicals available to advocates and practitioners of the Black Aesthetic were not interested in our Black South voices or what we would speak. Not until the fall of 1976 would our need be fulfilled in the publication of the first issue of *Callaloo* from my office in the Department of English at Southern University in Baton Rouge.

ii

Celle qu'on a fabriquer ensemble pour suivre.

It was not in my new hometown, Baton Rouge, Louisiana, but in Auburn, Alabama, the site of my birth and early youth, that I conceived *Callaloo*. One April morning in 1974—the year I had taken a five- or six-month refuge to write in my father's home on his farm, just outside the city limits of Auburn—I began to realize that we ourselves in the Black South needed to create and provide a publication outlet for our writers and intellectuals. Fortunately, during the 1973–1974 academic year, I was awarded a research fellowship from the National Endowment for the Humanities for a proposed project on African American writers' use of vernacular traditions in their work. For the first time in my academic career I was afforded days and evenings of uninterrupted reading, thinking, research, and writing.

I had recently returned to Auburn from my visit with the poet, literary critic, and long-term Howard University professor of English Sterling Brown in Washington, DC, where, in his home, I recorded a lengthy interview about his life and extraordinary work as an artist, academic, and intellectual. I recalled some of the engaging narratives Sterling Brown had recounted to me about his invaluable administrative and editorial work as head of the Office of Negro Affairs of the Works Progress Administration (WPA), and I began to think about how he had helped a number of black writers who worked on this important federal government project. Sterling Brown's example as administrator and editor led me to wonder what I could do in support of black writers in my native region, especially for those potential poets and fiction writers I had advised in the creative writing workshop I offered at Southern University and in the city of Baton Rouge.

Two years after I returned to my teaching duties at Southern University, I published the first issue of *Callaloo*. But first I had to create a coherent mission statement, find a name for the journal, locate funds for the first issue, identify a local printer, call for manuscripts, and take care of a number of other responsibilities. I knew that I could get assistance from a number of friends and colleagues from New Orleans and Baton Rouge, and did—as consultants, advisors, copy editors, proofreaders, fundraisers, promoters, advertisers, and marketers. I also knew that some of my colleagues and friends would contribute financially to this project, whose mission was simply to support and nurture new and emerging, along with established, Black South writers by providing a forum from which they could speak to the world. I had watched how and why Melvin A. Butler's *Black Experience*, a general periodical covering various Africana concerns, had folded shortly after its first issue in 1969: the Southern University administration did not see a need to continue to fund it. The funds to defray the costs of printing, advertising, and distributing the first issue of *Callaloo* came from a variety of sources: contributions from colleagues and their spouses, from a few black Southern writers and scholars, from funds begged on the streets of Baton Rouge by members of our nonuniversity workshop, and from my own impecunious pockets. How we would support the next issues of the newborn Black South literary journal was a luxury we could not contemplate or plan for. I had to focus on the immediate need of creating an attractive and seminal first issue of the journal—a number that would convince potential financial supporters to help us fund the journal into a long future.

How I arrived at the name of "callaloo" for the journal is a narrative I have recollected a number of times. In an interview with my colleague Shona Jackson for one of the thirtieth-anniversary issues of *Callaloo* (vol. 30, no. 1, Winter 2007), I told her that

I came upon the name for the journal as I was engaged in a telephone conversation with my Southern University colleague Lelia Taylor. We were both talking ... about cooking, and I told her that what we called gumbo at my home in central east Alabama (a mixture of vegetables, including okra, and maybe pork sausage or beef stew meat, all stirred together like a succotash) was different from Louisiana gumbo. Lelia told me that what I described as our gumbo sounded more like callaloo, a dish her family also made at home there in Baton Rouge. Before that telephone conversation I had never heard the word "callaloo," so I asked her to repeat it and spell it for me. She repeated it, and its musical sound again rang in my ears. Lelia and I held this conversation during the period when I was trying to find a name for the journal that I was planning. I knew I wanted a name for the journal that would, like blues or jazz, evoke blackness; I wanted a word or some words that would express the focus of the journal without having to name the race.... Look at the people of the African Diaspora: racially and culturally, we are a callaloo, a mixture. Look at the journal: it is a literary mixture [a cultural mixture]. Only the ancestors knew that, when they gave me the word "callaloo" through Lelia Taylor.

This narrative is a testament to the communal roots of the journal, which place Louisiana people and other black Southerners at the center of the origin, development, and continuation of *Callaloo*. This narrative about naming not only underscores *Callaloo* as an idea originating from a collective need of a specific locale; as a recording of a moment of the past, this narrative also signifies what the journal has become as an ever-evolving collective project of necessity that is now both national and international.

That same collective spirit reveals itself in the generosity of the twenty-seven contributors to the inaugural issue of *Callaloo*. Because Tom Dent—like Mercedes Broussard, Verda Talton, Oneada Spurlock Madison, and Johnnie Mae Arrington—had advised and worked closely with me in assembling the first issue of the journal, I asked him to write the introduction. After all, his name as poet, essayist, playwright, and political activist, which was known in many literary quarters across the country, would help promote the journal beyond the South. So would Alice Walker, Alvin Aubert, Pinkie Gordon Lane, Arthenia Bates Millican, Lance Jeffers, Kalamu ya Salaam, Amos Zu-Bolton, Lorenzo Thomas, and some of the other creative writers who contributed poems, fiction, and nonfiction prose to the first issue of *Callaloo*. Roy Lewis's front cover photograph, along with those in "River Road," the photo essay he and Tom Dent created and contributed, anticipates *Callaloo*'s continuing commitment to publishing images of visual art, a practice that culminates in *Callaloo Art*, an annual focusing on selective creative facets of visual culture in the African Diaspora. Sometime shortly after the publication of the first issue of *Callaloo*, the journal became a national and international journal, and yet we have remained especially vigilant in our goal to identify, nurture, encourage, and publish new and emerging Southern writers, for our first commitment is to our own community, the Black South.

iii

Because I had not identified a sponsor or a group of benefactors for *Callaloo* before I published the first issue of the journal in December 1976, I began to drift toward a state of anxiety: I did not know what the future would portend for the needful regional project we in Louisiana had together created. I did know, however, that capital, like imagination and intellect, is essential to the operation and development of a literary journal. Shortly after the publication of the first issue of *Callaloo*, I, by chance, met Chester Grundy at a region-wide Black South cultural meeting in New Orleans. As director of African American Affairs at the University of Kentucky, Chester Grundy invited me to apply for a teaching position at the university. In fact, he told me that, when he returned home to Kentucky, he would strongly urge the Department of English to invite me up for an interview. He too knew the importance of financial support to nonprofit cultural projects, and he, working to support the needs of the Black South, also knew that the University of Kentucky could afford to defray the cost of the basics for the continued publication of *Callaloo*. By the fall of 1977, I had joined the English faculty at the University of Kentucky, where the journal began to transform itself from a regional to a national journal.

When I moved the journal to the University of Kentucky in the fall of 1977, *Callaloo* continued for more than a year as a forum exclusively for the Black South. *Callaloo* no. 2, the first issue we published from Lexington, consisted largely of contributions by such Black South writers and critics as Tom Dent, Sharon Stockard Martin, E. Ethelbert Miller, William Wiggins, Jr., Electa Wiley, and Harryette Mullen. But the voices of three non-Southern writers also appeared in the same issue—Melvin Dixon and Gaoan-Ugandan Peter Nazareth with fiction, and Keorapetse Kgositsile in an interview, entitled "'With Bloodstains to Testify.'" The publication of this South African poet's interview, as well as the practice of publishing visual art as cover images and as portfolios by individual artists, helped to establish the tradition of publishing interviews with creative writers and art by visual artists in literary magazines across the United States. One of the central features of *Callaloo* no. 3 is not only its exclusive focus on the Southern novelist Ernest Gaines but especially the attention to his interview and the photographs he himself made of the plantation complex and its environs, where he spent his early childhood in southern Louisiana. The next two issues, however, contained work by a number of writers who were not Southerners. By the publication of the next two issues, no. 4 (1978) and no. 5 (1979), our readers could discern that *Callaloo* had become a national African American literary and cultural journal. John Edgar Wideman, Jayne Cortez, Clarence Major, Charles Johnson, Naomi Long Madgett, Robert Chrisman, Ron Welburn, and Ntozake Shange—these are only a few of the non-Black South writers I selected for the fourth and fifth issues of the journal. By 1980, African American writers were certain that *Callaloo* was their publication outlet also, thanks to the late Melvin Dixon, a New York poet, fiction writer, translator, and literary critic.

I had already noticed the disappearance of the different magazines that were popular and visible during the height of the Black Arts Movement. So when Melvin Dixon warned more than once of the consequences of the folding of the different periodicals that supported writers in the North during the Black Arts Movement, I felt a need all the more to open *Callaloo* to African American writers nationwide. This opening up to writers across the United States increased our readership and provided for us a wide range of writers from whom we could invite as potential contributors to different issues of the journal. This change in editorial policy also accelerated the development of *Callaloo*, while enhancing its reputation as a national journal. Our new policy, moreover, helped us in judiciously selecting and carefully organizing a dedicated corps of referees—creative writers and literary and cultural critics—whose thorough evaluations of manuscripts helped us to raise the quality of work we published to a level that suddenly established *Callaloo* as the premier literary and cultural journal in the African Diaspora.

I have no doubt that the very positive reputation *Callaloo* garnered while I was employed as an associate professor of English at the University of Kentucky motivated the faculty of the Department of English at the University of Virginia to recruit me there, provided I move the journal with me. In light of the offer, especially with my new rank as professor with tenure, the solid financial support offered to *Callaloo*, the bucolic setting of the University of Virginia, my acceptance of the appointment was swift and immediate. No longer would I have to work without an office assistant; no longer would I have to mix the work of my academic teaching with that of the journal; no longer would the journal suffer from inadequate operation funds; no longer would I have to publish, advertise, promote, and distribute the journal and its series from my academic office.

The move to Virginia was indeed a relief, and it was also a very good site from which I could raise the national and international visibility of *Callaloo*. Again, thanks to Melvin Dixon, who became very supportive as an advisory and contributing editor, for advising me to transform *Callaloo* into an international publication. Melvin Dixon himself was an international traveler; he was in constant movement from New York to Dakar to Paris to Johannesburg to Rio de Janeiro. And the poems in his first volume, *Change of Territory*, tell us as much. When I traveled with him to Dakar and observed his exchanges with Francophone African writers, I knew that internationalizing *Callaloo* could only improve the journal. However, Africa itself seemed too vast and complex to attempt to cover in the journal. In fact, my working knowledge of that vast and beloved continent and its cultures, languages, etc., was narrow. As a result, I decided to limit the scope of *Callaloo* to a quarterly journal of black literature produced in the Americas. But what of those descendants of Africans creating poems, fiction, nonfiction, etc., in France, England, the Netherlands, for example? Where are they publishing? Where in the African Diaspora could people of African descent hold, however directly or indirectly, a conversation about art on their own terms? Why can't we speak with them through one literary organ? Once I answered these and other related questions, I set out to transform *Callaloo* into an international organ, which would focus on the African Diaspora. And to do so, I needed first to begin traveling in parts of the African Diaspora to introduce the writers and literary critics, along with their readers, to the journal and its mission. Shortly after I moved to the University of Virginia, *Callaloo* became an African Diaspora journal in name, words, and practice.

A few semesters after I became an active citizen of "Mister Jefferson's 'Academical village'," the dean of the College of the University of Virginia gave me a leave to travel throughout the Caribbean and Western Europe to promote *Callaloo* and to meet and speak with writers who would later become contributors to *Callaloo*. In late January of that year, my promotional trip began in Jamaica—in Mona, to be exact, about two or so hours after our nonstop Jamaica Air flight from Baltimore put down in Kingston. In Mona I made "my campground" the Senior Common Room at the University of the West Indies. From there I ventured out, always with a guide, to meet and visit with faculty in literature, language and culture, and with Jamaican writers. Carolyn Cooper, the literary and cultural critic, and the venerable Edward Baugh introduced me to a number of individuals whom I needed to know. They also introduced me to Mervyn Morris, Velma Pollard, Lorna Goodison, Pamela Mordecai, and Olive Senior. The very first stop on my promotional tour of the Caribbean was, in countless ways, an education for me. It was an education about culture and literary writing in Jamaica, and it was also an education about me and my responsibilities as an editor if I wanted to make *Callaloo* a comprehensive forum for the multicultural voices across the African Diaspora.

My Caribbean tour took me next to Curaçao, where I met the celebrated author Frank Martinus Arion, whose novel *Double Play*, originally published in Dutch as *Dubbelspel* in 1973, has brought him much critical attention. Meeting him made it possible for me to set appointments and engage other writers of African descent who wrote in Dutch—for example, Astrid Roemer and the now late Edgar Cairo, both of whom I met and with whom I recorded interviews in Amsterdam on the European wing of my promotional tour. These encounters occasioned the special Dutch Antillean issue of *Callaloo*, a veritable anthology, the first of its kind in the English-speaking world. From Curaçao, that Dutch Antillean island, I flew to Trinidad. While there, I got a chance to speak with the distinguished literary critic Kenneth Ramchand, who, not long after, contributed an article to *Callaloo* on the history of Anglophone Caribbean literature.

From the festive Trinidad, I made my way to Barbados, where I had hoped to meet the internationally read George Lamming, who, to my misfortune, seems never on the island when I travel there. At Cave Hill's University of the West Indies, I did, however, have a number of conversations with faculty members in the Department of English, some of whom have subsequently contributed critical work to *Callaloo*. From Bridgetown, Barbados, my 1980s Caribbean promotional tour moved from "Little England," as Barbados is called, to two of France's most important *départements*, Martinique and Guadeloupe.

My visits in Guadeloupe and Martinique were the beginning of a major encounter for the transformation of *Callaloo* into an African Diaspora journal, for the exchanges I had with creative writers and intellectuals on those two islands awakened me to the need to begin the practice of publishing non-English language texts in translation in *Callaloo*, which is obviously oriented toward English-speaking readers. The first of such English-language translations published in *Callaloo* was "Eloge de la créolité" ["In Praise of Creoleness"], a controversial essay that Raphaël Confiant, Jean Bernabé, and Patrick Chamoiseau authored together. Not only did the publication of that essay expand the readership of *Callaloo*; Mahamed Taleb Khyar's translation of "Eloge de la créolité" for the journal, the first version to be published in English, signaled to other writers of African descent whose work does not originally appear in English that *Callaloo* is also their forum. No wonder then that Aimé Césaire was willing to record an interview with me; that Maryse Condé agreed to be featured in an issue devoted exclusively to her work; that numerous Haitian writers—Jean Méttelus and René Deprestre in France, Stanley Péan and Joël Des Rosiers in Canada, and Jan J. Dominique, Frankétienne, Lyonel Trouillot, and Yanick Lahens in Haiti, for example—freely and gladly contributed work to the two-part special Haitian issue of *Callaloo* (Spring and Summer 1992). Like those of African descent in the United States, Brazil, the United Kingdom, and the Anglophone Caribbean, these French-speaking writers knew, for the first time, that *Callaloo* had become the first literary journal to serve specifically writers throughout the African Diaspora—their primary language not withstanding.

As I was leaving Maryse Condé's home in Guadeloupe, I informed her that my last stop in the Caribbean would be the Spanish-speaking Dominican Republic, to which she responded with a question. "Charles," which only Maryse can pronounce with regal authority, "are you not going to visit with writers in Haiti," to which I answered, "Our government has warned us about travel to Haiti, while it is politically unstable. I am afraid to go there." "Charles," she pronounced again, "you Americans are always afraid to travel anywhere." Underneath her unapologetic declaration, I could hear a subtext, a command, and about a year later I followed it: I flew to Port-au-Prince to begin work on a special two-part issue of *Callaloo* (vol. 15, nos. 2 and 3), "Haitian Literature and Culture," for which we won our first national prize in 1992, an honor from the Awards Competition of the Council of Editors of Learned Journals (Modern Language Association of America) for the best special issue of a literary journal.

The academic leave and travel funding I received from the University of Virginia laid the foundation for the international quarterly journal *Callaloo* has become. Without funds beyond our regular operating budget, how could we have mounted the special African Brazilian issue honoring the seventeenth-century black freedom fighter Zumbi, the last known leader of the *quilombo* known as Palmares, a maroon society created by enslaved Africans as a free and self supporting nation-state inside Brazil, from 1605 to 1694, before the white government of Brazil destroyed it? Without support from the University of Virginia, how could I have otherwise traveled to Brazil to meet writers and academics to prepare the special African Brazilian *Callaloo*, which contained visual art and essays as well as creative literature? How could I have met and, more than once, published the words of the engaging poet and intellectual Edimilson de Almeida Pereira of the state of Minas Gerais? Or print images of the sculpture of Emanuel Araújo, director of the Afro-Brazilian Museum in São Paulo, or the fiction of Conceição Evaristo of Belo Horizonte, for example? Dean Hugh Kelley of the University of Virginia did more than he knew. When he supported the practice of travel as research and afforded me the privilege of visiting African Diaspora writers in the Caribbean, the United Kingdom, and those other European countries that enslaved African peoples and later colonized them in the Americas and elsewhere, Dean Kelley helped to transform *Callaloo* into the premier journal of the African Diaspora.

In addition to developing the quarterly journal, grants from the Virginia Humanities Council, Virginia Arts Council, Lannan Foundation, and National Endowment for the Arts also assisted in the funding and developing of two *Callaloo*-supporting projects: readings/lectures/symposia as audience development and the annual creative writing workshops developmental service to black writers. Beginning at the University of Virginia, these two projects have now become international also. Offering local readings by creative writers, and lectures and symposia involving intellectuals and artists of various kinds as vehicles for audience development for the general public and the "academical village," was a relatively easy task. By far the more expensive and work-driven project was the workshops, which were originally mounted at selective predominately black colleges and universities. After staging them with such poets and fiction writers as John Edgar Wideman, Lucille Clifton, Percival Everett, Toi Derricotte, Harryette Mullen, and Yusef Komunyakaa as workshop leaders in their respective genres, we concluded that it would be less costly, more broadly serving, and more manageable to mount the workshops on *Callaloo*'s home grounds, the University of Virginia. This shift in site occasioned other changes in the writing project and constructed the *Callaloo*

Creative Writing Workshop, with selective admission, as a two-week nationwide engagement, serving new and emerging black writers across the United States and from other countries, especially those where English is the primary and official language of discourse.

With these changes in the workshops came others. When I was recruited to join the faculty of the Department of English at Texas A&M University in 2001 and moved *Callaloo* with me to College Station, we started to employ workshop leaders who were closer in age to the participants—Natasha Trethewey, Tracy K. Smith, Mat Johnson, Tayari Jones, Terrance Hayes, Vievee Francis, Maaza Mengiste, Ravi Howard, and Gregory Pardlo, for example; and I also began again to stage the workshops at different academic campuses, as well as at Texas A&M University. And, recently, we have begun to offer weeklong workshops for black fiction and poetry writers in the United Kingdom and for Anglophone Caribbean writers in Barbados—to the excitement of writing communities in those and nearby English-speaking countries. It should be remembered, however, that, since their beginnings in the mid-1990s, our two audience and writer-oriented projects have maintained and followed their original missions: to encourage and develop engaging critical readers for contemporary poetry and fiction, and to encourage, nurture, develop, promote, and, when possible, publish excellent new poets and fiction writers.

Sponsored by Texas A&M University in College Station, *Callaloo* continues as a nonprofit literary and cultural journal published quarterly by the Johns Hopkins University Press in Baltimore, Maryland. Since I moved the journal from Virginia to Texas in 2001, it has remained dedicated to promoting and publishing the best of the diverse literatures of the African Diaspora, and provocative and engaging critiques of them. For example, we have featured such authors as Derek Walcott, Rita Dove, Yusef Komunyakaa, Édouard Glissant, Olympia Vernon, Lawrence Hill, Jamaica Kincaid, Austin Clarke, and Audre Lorde, and we have devoted numbers of the journal to blacks in Mexico, Peru, Cuba, and other sites in Latin America, and to such subjects as politics, postcolonial studies, race and racial politics, and issues of gender and sexual practices. The journal will soon begin publishing features that document and illuminate continuously living settlements that people of African descent in the Americas founded as sites of resistance against enslavement or as communities formed as havens of freedom, self-development, and independence, such as San Basilio de Palenque in Colombia and Mound Bayou in Mississippi. In other words, most of our practices of providing a forum for the diverse literary and cultural voices of the African Diaspora have remained the same. So, too, have our efforts to inform and educate our readers about marginalized people and their will to prevail—and when and wherever possible—triumph through their own aesthetic productions and their different cultural and social practices.

At Texas A&M University, *Callaloo* and its allied projects have multiplied and expanded as publishing and service entities. In addition to publishing the journal each quarter, we have created an annual called *Callaloo Art*, the purpose of which is to promote art criticism as well as print images of the visual art that various artists across the diaspora are creating. Readers familiar with the aesthetic practices of the journal and its thirty-six-year history will not think it odd that *Callaloo* would produce a visual art annual. That I have made and continue to make space for our visual artists can be well documented by the images of and comments on work by such artists as Lorna Simpson, José Maria Capricorne, Chester Higgins, Martin Puryear, Wilson Bigaud, Wangechi Mutu, Lois Mailou Jones, Roy DeCarava, Manoel Araújo, Frank Bowling, Yeda Maria Correa de Oliveira, Romare Bearden, Kerry James Marshall, Alison Saar, and Julie Mehretu. And the list goes on and on, which further signals the need for at least an annual publication featuring full-color reproductions of African Diaspora visual artists' works, along with critical readings of them. Therefore the founding and publication of *Callaloo Art*.

Edwin C. Hill, Jr.'s *Black Soundscapes White Stages: The Meaning of Francophone Sound in the Black Atlantic* (October 2013) is the inaugural volume of the *Callaloo* African Diaspora Series, whose purpose is to duplicate in book form what the journal does in critical articles devoted to diasporic discourses in literary studies and cultural studies—that is, to provide another forum for academics whose working interests are African Diaspora literatures and cultures. We will also hope to identify a publisher that might be interested in restoring life to the two creative writing series we founded and published from my faculty office at the University of Kentucky. Like our literary and cultural critics, our creative writers, especially our poets, are in much need of book publication outlets.

The new service efforts of *Callaloo* are not unrelated to the mission of the *Callaloo* African Diaspora Series. I am speaking of the services that the annual *Callaloo* Conference offers creative writers and academics, as well as the general public. Around the early 1980s, I began to notice how the worlds of contemporary writers, especially that of the poets, had drifted far from those of the literary and cultural critic, a reality which occasioned in me a desire to experiment: to begin to publish side-by-side critical articles and poems, and to publish short fiction next to literary and cultural criticism—all with the hope of nudging the one kind of author to read the work of the other. Apparently, that approach was not working as effectively or as rapidly as I had intended, or so one poet implied when he complained to me in 2007 at the end of the Thirtieth Anniversary Celebration of *Callaloo* in Baltimore. "I didn't understand a thing those critics talked about. I wish they would speak English," he said without concealing his impatience, apparently not only referring to their ideas and arguments, but also to the theoretical nature of the English in which they were couched. "A group of us [*of us poets*, I assumed he meant] got together last night and talked about that problem."

Over the past ten years, not less than four to six of my friends in literary studies have confessed to me that they don't try to read contemporary poetry. "I don't have the patience or the time. It's too difficult," one told me. Another said, "They're nothing like those poets who wrote back during the high point of the Black Arts Movement. Now those were real poets! I could understand all of the righteousness that they laid down. Those were poets then." Today (or ever) immediate accessibility is neither an aesthetic virtue nor a reliable yardstick one uses to judge poetry, but I could not be so rude as to make that kind of direct response to her. My response to her and to the poet who complained is this: start reading widely in those contemporary literary genres and academic fields outside your immediate interests and practices and you will begin to experience a new world of useful language and ways of being that will enhance or prove quite useful to what you do in your own critical and creative productions. Such is the general and foremost important mission of the *Callaloo* Conference.

Where we have been meeting is as important as what we have accomplished during our short visits at these institutions. First of all, the locations where we have strategically staged our annual conferences have contributed immensely to our efforts to expand the reaches of *Callaloo*'s readership. Second, we have continuously brought critical minds and creative imaginations together in public and private exchanges on critical and creative matters of production and reading. We have begun to understand each other's modes of translations of the world, and the media and forms through which we represent them. As a result, poets and fiction writers, for example, have begun to work together with literary and cultural critics in the selection of ideas or themes on which to plan, build, and coordinate conferences, with panels and readings we all attend in support of each other and for our own common good. Because we invite the general public, as well as academic communities, to our conferences free of charge, we are continuing to develop audiences for literature and the critical studies about them. Like the quarterly journal *Callaloo*, the *Callaloo* Conference not only serves those who produce texts published in the journal; our annual gatherings also help to inform the world of the creative and critical productions of a long-exploited, denigrated, and marginalized people. *Callaloo* and its allied projects, then, are a necessary education for twenty-first century people, the world over.

It has become quite clear to me that, since its move from the University of Virginia to Texas A&M University in 2001, *Callaloo* has become a veritable African Diaspora literary center, serving some of the aesthetic, intellectual, and cultural needs of a great number of people in a vast territory, however scattered in regions where almost half of the world's population resides. Wherever *Callaloo* moves or with whom I elect to work, the journal and its allied projects will remain a center of learning, practice, and production for future memory. That is, while extending and expanding the scope of African American literary and cultural studies, *Callaloo* is a recorder, arbiter, and enabler of the literary culture of the African Diaspora.

iv

The distance between my father's kitchen table in Auburn, Alabama, to the Throne Room of Haile Selassie's first palace in Addis Ababa, Ethiopia, is far, but so is the distance between Southern University in Baton Rouge, Louisiana, to Princeton University in New Jersey, and so too is the distance between Texas A&M University, College Station, to Oxford University in the United Kingdom. But with the ancestors as my guiding companions, I have no fear of or concern for the distance. With the ancestors beside me for safe passage, I think only of the charge to keep I have: the collection and conservation and deliverance of the words of the people, as Sterling Brown did so almost a hundred years ago.

Critical Thinking from Women

AMY HOFFMAN

During the 1970s and 1980s, as befits a city with its distinguished literary heritage, Boston was a center of alternative publishing. The first thing any group of likeminded people did when they got together was to put out a publication. Community organizers, feminists, New Left politicos, hippies, rock and rollers, LGBT liberationists, racial and ethnic groups, current and former students, poets and drifters created newsletters, newspapers, monthly magazines, literary quarterlies, books, calendars, leaflets, and unclassifiable ventures such as the gay anarchist *Fag Rag*. And you could buy them in the big Harvard Square bookstores as well as in one of the country's first feminist bookstores, New Words; in the LGBT-oriented Glad Day Books; or in the leftist Redbook.

This proliferation of publications and book culture meant that in the late 1970s and early 1980s, feminists could choose among three monthlies: *Sister Courage* (socialist); *Sojourner* (capitalist); and *Equal Times* (liberal). Hipsters had the *Real Paper* or the *Phoenix*. There were two competing LGBT weeklies, *Gay Community News* (radical) and *Bay Windows* (liberal—tagged "Gay Bimbos" by the *GCN* crowd). I volunteered for *Sister Courage*; worked at *GCN* from 1978 to 1982; and was an editor at South End Press, a collectively run, left-wing book publisher, for a couple of years after that.

All this is to place the founding of *Women's Review of Books*, in 1983, in context. Like most of the people involved in such ventures, *WRB*'s founder, Linda Gardiner, had no publishing experience (and it probably didn't occur to her or anyone else that she needed any): she was a philosophy professor at Wellesley College. Denied tenure, she persuaded the college to set her up in an office at the Center for Research on Women (CRW), raised about $20,000 in seed money from her sister academics—and it was let's-put-out-a-journal time.

WRB was different from other alternative publications in a couple of ways. For one, it had the support of a prestigious institution behind it—although that support has always been mostly moral. Wellesley College and the Wellesley Centers for Women (the now-merged CRW and Stone Center) generously provided WRB with space and other infrastructure, but never with any money. And Linda never had any pretense of striving for a democratically run organization: *Women's Review of Books* was her creation and hers only.

From Cambridge, where I hung out, *WRB* looked a little stodgy, with its college backing and professor-editor. Of course, that may also have been because an ex-girlfriend of mine was its first poetry editor (as the old joke had it, there are only ten lesbians in the world, and the rest is done with mirrors), and when she accepted a poem of mine, Linda vetoed it—probably because the poem was a paean to said ex and contained words that you still can't say on the radio. Linda was worried that the college would literally pull the rug out from under her if it found objectionable content in the magazine—although then as now, the college barely knows that *WRB* exists. I wrote a letter to the editor, which Linda also refused to publish, and the censorship of my poem became a brief and satisfying cause célèbre among my friends and acquaintances—although, as with Virginia Woolf's famous defense of the publication of Radclyffe Hall's *The Well of Loneliness*, more because of the principle of the thing than because of the merit of my poem. (Writing to Lady Ottoline Morrell, Woolf said of *The Well*, "The dullness of the book is such that any indecency may lurk there—one simply can't keep one's eyes on the page.")[1]

The early issues of *WRB* are what now seems an odd amalgam of radical political rhetoric and academese. It seemed less odd at the time. The gulf between feminist scholars and activists had not yet opened wide, and indeed it was taken for granted that they were all participating in the same project. The discipline of women's studies was young, and it was just about possible to thoroughly cover even its more specialized and obscure productions as well as women's fiction, poetry, and memoir in twelve issues per year.

Which was a good thing, because the exciting research, criticism, analysis, and creative work with which *WRB* was concerned was getting no attention in the mainstream media, and even on the alternative and literary scenes there were few publications devoted solely to books—or women. During its first decade, *WRB* grew to about 10,000 subscribers, a huge number for an "alternative" journal, since it published ideas and information that readers could find nowhere else. Even the back-page "books received" list was valued, especially by librarians—although it was basically a random jumble of everything from review copies the editors had

1. Virginia Woolf, *The Letters of Virginia Woolf*, vol. 3: *1923–1928*, ed. Nigel Nicolson and Joanne Trautmann (New York: Harcourt, 1975–77), 556.

requested to self-published poetry that had appeared spontaneously in the mailbox. It was a time when writers such as Kate Chopin, Zora Neale Hurston, and Charlotte Perkins Gilman, now canonical, were just being rediscovered and reinterpreted; and finding the new work and ideas coming out of the global women's movement took a fair amount of digging.

As *WRB* entered its second decade, though, the situation began to change. Women's studies became more established as a discipline, with its own peer-reviewed journals and university press books. Dissertations abounded. Queer studies was emerging. Creative writers associated with the feminist movement such as Adrienne Rich, Audre Lorde, Margaret Atwood, Toni Morrison, and numerous others won prestigious prizes and stellar reviews on the front pages of newspaper book sections. Not only independents but also chain bookstores gave shelf space to feminist and LGBT works. Any self-respecting college curriculum included *Their Eyes Were Watching God, The Woman Warrior*, and even *Our Bodies, Ourselves*. By the end of the 1990s, the Internet was facilitating communication and the spread of information.

Ironically, in large part because of these positive developments, *WRB* lost ground. You no longer had to be a member of the club to find out who was publishing and thinking what; you could Google it. *WRB*'s funky design and academic associations looked increasingly old school, carrying little appeal or relevance to younger readers; while the review's original subscribers, now on fixed incomes, canceled or died. At conferences, women's studies graduate students commented to the *WRB* editors staffing the exhibit table, "*Women's Review of Books* ... oh, yeah, my mom used to read that."

After a heroic twenty years of service, Linda Gardiner retired in 2003, and I joined the *WRB* staff as editor in chief. Books and feminism: my two favorite things. I felt the job was made for me. But, it came with several problems: the subscriber base had by that time dropped to less than 5,000; the review had been operating at a loss for several years, subsidized by Wellesley Center for Women (WCW), which could not afford to continue doing so; the staff was demoralized and quarrelsome.

Finally, in 2005, the review suspended publication. During the next year, we reorganized, returning in January 2006 as a joint venture between WCW, where our editorial offices are located, and Old City Publishing, a scholarly publisher in Philadelphia, Pennsylvania, that handles our subscriptions, advertising, and production. In addition to the print edition, *WRB*'s archives are available in libraries through the JSTOR database. We publish a blog with additional insights from *WRB* writers on our website, www.wcwonline.org/womensreview, and the future of *WRB* may involve even more of a presence on the Internet—although we're very fond of print, and it's the money we bring in from ads and subscriptions that continues to sustain us.

But a question continues to nag. If things had reached such a low point in 2005, wasn't it about time to pack it in? Times had changed, and surely so had the need for a publication featuring current work in women's and gender studies, reviewed by women writers. In the twenty years since *WRB*'s founding, it had become easier to find women's bylines in mainstream glossies, and feminist thinkers in their pages. Right?

Well, actually, no. VIDA, a group founded several years ago by a group of women who were outraged that the *Publisher's Weekly* best books of 2010 list included zero women—in a year with notable publications by Margaret Atwood, A. S. Byatt, Rita Dove, Lorrie Moore, Alice Munro, and Alicia Ostriker, among many others—has been monitoring the percentage of books by women and women reviewers in major publications and posting the results on www.vidaweb.org. The annual tally has produced some useful, though depressing information. A pattern emerges. In some publications the gap between women and men is wider than in others (*WRB*'s namesake, the *New York Review of Books*, is particularly egregious), but in no case do the numbers even approach equality—nor have they changed much from year to year.

Summer reading lists, holiday book lists, and just about any other lists you can think of (except perhaps chick-lit and romance novel lists) tend to tilt heavily toward the straight white male—even though women, people of color, LGBT folks, and others write and read at a great rate. You'd think the publishing industry would see us as an important market, if nothing else. (Of course, expecting rational capitalist behavior from an industry that regularly produces products—"midlist books"—that it makes no effort to market may be unrealistic.)

Several years ago, I had the opportunity to attend a lecture by an editor of the *New York Times Book Review*. He probably got off on the wrong foot by saying, "Now I am going to have my Larry Summers moment" by way of introducing his discussion of the dearth of women reviewers in his publication. The problem was not, he said, that he and his colleagues were consciously sexist, although he speculated that they might be unconsciously so, but rather that qualified women reviewers were simply rare. For example, he said, he knew of no women who could review works of military history. He explained that he and his colleagues were always on the lookout for good new writers, and that they regularly perused the *New York Review of Books*, *Harper's*, the *New Yorker*, etc.—basically, the publications VIDA monitors—in search of them.

For once I had a comment to contribute during the question-and-answer session! You don't have to psychoanalyze yourself to find the unconscious sexist or racist remnants, I reassured him. But you're looking in the wrong places. You and all those other editors are passing the same old names back and forth. I offered to refer him to excellent, expert reviewers from *WRB*'s list—which even includes a few military historians (although I've never noticed that this is a major topic of concern for the *NYTBR*)—but for some reason he never took advantage of the opportunity. (To its credit, since then, the *NYTBR* has improved its ratio of male to female reviewers: in 2013, VIDA reported, it was almost equal. In April 2013, the *Book Review* appointed a woman editor, Pamela Paul.)

This experience, the statistics, and the fact that the books we cover in *WRB* have remarkably little overlap with those covered in mainstream publications all convince me that even after all this time, *WRB* still has a role to play in promoting writing by women and in bridging the gaps among scholars in various disciplines, activists, and interested, thoughtful readers.

The *Bitch* Interview

LISA JERVIS AND ANDI ZEISLER

As interviewed by Joanne Diaz

JOANNE DIAZ: The *Bitch* website features a brief history in which you recall the impetus for the first issues of the magazine. You say that you "looked around at a landscape of self-published zines" and decided that you wanted to start a zine of your own that provided an analysis—and critique—of women's images and issues in popular culture.[1] What zines were you reading in the early '90s, and how did they influence the mission and aesthetic of *Bitch*?

ANDI ZEISLER: Our decision to start *Bitch* as a zine was in a lot of ways a practical decision: We knew that starting small and growing incrementally was a better strategy for longevity than trying to have a full-fledged magazine launch with a business plan and ads and investors and all that. But we also liked the ethos of zines, and were also very zinelike in tone— our first few issues were all pretty much written by the two of us, and consisted of rants and opinion pieces and reviews. We didn't start hewing to journalistic conventions—like fact-checking, for instance—until later.

The zines I was personally reading in the early '90s were personal zines and Riot Grrrl zines that I ordered from *Factsheet Five* when I was in college, and then bigger zines like *Ben Is Dead*, which thoroughly confused me because I wasn't sure what it was supposed to be about, but it covered pop culture in a funny, off-kilter way I could relate to. Another one that Lisa and I both liked a lot was called *Hermenaut,* and it sort of synthesized philosophy and pop culture in an irreverent, smart way that we emulated a little bit.

I think one big difference between a zine and a magazine is that a zine is often an expression of one or two people's thoughts, whereas a magazine is more of a forum. In the early issues, we had a pretty firm idea of what we wanted to print in the magazine—namely, our own personal ideas

Interview conducted via e-mail correspondence, fall 2010.

1. "About *Bitch*: History," http://bitchmagazine.org/about/history, accessed June 22, 2010.

and peeves about feminism and pop culture. Over time, as we established our identity, we started opening it up—printing points of view that we didn't necessarily agree with, printing letters to the editor that were negative, and refusing to toe specific party lines, and I think that's where we started to become more of a magazine. And though we always hoped to transform the zine into a magazine, we never doubted that starting as a zine was right for us.

LISA JERVIS: I wasn't actually much of a zine reader—it was more that they were out there, and that showed us what was possible. We always had magazine ambitions, design- and production-value-wise. So we never considered doing something messy and handwritten, which really is the "true" zine style, if such a thing can be said to exist.

The reason we chose the zine format was its accessibility. The web was in its infancy, so print was the only thing we knew. And we didn't have a lot of money, so there was no way we were going to print in color. But a black-and-white photocopy (which was our intent even though the first issue ended up getting printed, via miscommunication at one of those copy shops that also does low-quality offset printing) was totally within our reach. And the existence of all those other zines made clear that that was a total possibility.

I don't remember having any doubts about the format—it seemed like the natural way, and the only way.

JD: The earliest issues of *Bitch* have a refreshingly witty, colloquial, often sardonic rhetorical style that you've maintained throughout the magazine's history. How did you adopt and manage to maintain this rhetorical stance?

AZ: That was really just the voice that came out of us when we started. We were definitely influenced by the voice of *Sassy* magazine—Lisa and I had both been interns there before starting *Bitch*, and were inspired by *Sassy*'s way of speaking to its readers. Rather than talking at its audience in a voice of older authority, as most teen magazines did, *Sassy* spoke to their readers as peers, and the effect was really different and refreshing. It felt honest and empathetic without being disingenuous.

So because we wanted *Bitch* to be similar to *Sassy* in making feminism accessible and attractive to women our age and younger, it seemed natural to aim at striking a relatable tone, where we were essentially writing exactly like we talked in daily life. It also reflected the fact that we weren't professionals at what we were doing, and were open to growing and evolving. And I think people responded to it.

I'd say that, over time, we've tried to keep the tone while also professionalizing it a bit. There's less gratuitous cursing, for one thing. And while we do try to emphasize to contributors that they can feel free to sort of let loose and snark up their writing voice, not all of them necessarily want to or feel comfortable doing so. If it was still two or three people generating all the content, I think the tone would be much the same as it was, even nineteen years later. But we're showcasing a wider range of voices now, and that means that the overall voice and stance have changed.

LJ: It started because that's just the style that came naturally to us. We just wanted to say our piece and that's what it sounded like. Of course, as time went on we definitely were conscious of cultivating a certain voice, because it had become clear that our tone and style was really hitting a nerve with readers.

And as far as maintenance of the style, well, especially in the early years we were very, very heavy editors. We had hit on a voice for the magazine and we wanted to establish it as ours. So we worked hard to maintain a consistent voice. Later, we loosened up on that, especially as the number of contributors expanded—but I think writers were also attracted by the tone they could take, 'cause it's a fun style to write in. And it just made sense for the material, as well.

JD: Since the first issue was published back in 1996, *Bitch* has been committed to the analysis and critique of women in the media. In the early years of publication, you had plenty of material to critique: not only glossy women's magazines like *Glamour* and *Redbook*, but more allegedly progressive magazines like *Sassy* and *Jane*. When you look at magazines that are committed to women's issues today, what do you admire and what concerns you most?

AZ: Women's magazines haven't changed much since 1996; in fact, one could argue that everything we complained about then—the commercialism, the lack of diversity, the beauty and fashion imperatives—has gotten more pronounced. Part of this has to do with the way that celebrity culture has really taken hold of the popular imagination, and as a result the aspirational nature of women's magazines has increased exponentially as celebrity culture has grown. Just one example of this: Models no longer appear on magazine covers, only celebrities. And, increasingly, the cover subjects of "mature" women's fashion magazines like *Elle* and *Vogue* are the same teen starlets that are on the cover of magazines for teens and tweens. That's really different—you never would have seen, say, an '80s teen star like Debbie Gibson or Alyssa Milano on the cover of *Vogue* in those days.

Also, with magazine sales on a decline across the board, and ad-page sales down industry-wide, and so many magazines folding, the ones that remain seem increasingly interchangeable. For instance, *Glamour*, at the time we started *Bitch*, was actually pretty progressive when it came to women's issues; now, it's almost indistinguishable from all the others. And the more supposedly edgy and progressive titles that launched between the late 1980s and mid-1990s (*Sassy, Jane, Fierce, Suede,* and others) folded, many after short runs.

With magazines geared toward a specifically female audience today, I'll say that although I wish there were more unapologetically feminist magazines out there, the ones that exist, including *Ms.* and *Bust,* do an excellent job with their specific focus. *Ms.*, as always, has institutional heft and great reporting, and *Bust* makes feminism seem hip and accessible and fun. Oddly, the women's magazine I like the most at this point is *Elle.* It takes for granted a readership that's intelligent and thoughtful, and always devotes lots of pages to reviews of books by women, particularly nonfiction books.

LJ: I don't actually look at a lot of women's magazines anymore; I'm just not interested. But I don't think things have changed much — print media aimed at women is still driven by advertisers' ideas of what women think about and by their demands to have their products featured. Online media has opened things up a little — you have *Jezebel* covering celebrity gossip and who wore what to which awards show, and at the same time running posts on stoning in Iran, electoral politics, the pay gap, etc. But to be honest, I don't read that much on blogs, either — it's information overload for me.

JD: In 1996, your print run for the first issue of *Bitch* was 300 copies. By 1998, you had a circulation of 5,000, and your current circulation is approximately 47,000. How has this increase in distribution necessarily affected *Bitch*? Most zines assiduously avoid wide readership. In the early years, did you want for *Bitch* to be widely read or was circulation not something you were thinking about?

AZ: I think the pipe dream we had when we started out was that the zine would quickly become a "real" magazine, with an attendant circulation. We didn't have the mindset of, "Oh, we can't get a bar code because that'll mean we've sold out." We weren't wedded to the sort of stereotypical zine ideals of anticapitalist purity — we wanted all the readers we could get, as long as it didn't mean compromising the kind of content we wanted to publish. But none of us really knew anything about zine distribution, or magazine distribution, or the way the business of growing a magazine quickly becomes both incredibly expensive and potentially incredibly wasteful. That certainly counts as a disadvantage of growing so quickly.

The advantage was that at some point the rapid growth of the magazine forced us to make a decision that it would be our full-time job. Lisa and Ben[2] and I all had "regular" day jobs and would work on the magazine in our spare time, but after several years that really took a toll. We were all exhausted, interpersonal tensions were pretty high, and our personal lives were really compromised by having no free time. Reaching a certain level of growth made us realize that either we either had to really do it—as in, quit our other jobs and make the magazine really happen—or we were going to have to fold. Continuing as we were just wasn't an option.

LJ: We definitely wanted it to be widely read! We used to joke about the goal being world domination. Being so passionate about our message, we wanted to reach every last person we possibly could. But when we started we had no idea how many people would be interested. It was incredibly gratifying to see that a lot of people were.

So the advantages of growing fast were that we were really succeeding in our mission to reach a lot of people, and also the newsstand income gave us the resources to print more pages, to print color on the cover, etc. We were able to move aesthetically toward what we had wanted all along. Which I think then helped us grow even more. And having a larger circulation meant more reader feedback, which was one of the great things about doing the magazine: people would write to say how much the magazine meant to them, how it made them feel less isolated as the only feminist in their class, their school, their town, their whatever, and that was tremendously gratifying. And we'd also get critiques of articles, arguments about them, which was also great. We'd have these long letters sections and people would write in with responses to the letters, and it would go back and forth. Of course with blog comments all that is instantaneous now. But regardless I saw it as a real measure of how engaged people were.

The disadvantages were that we had to learn a tremendous amount about the magazine business really fast. And it took a big toll on me personally. I never set out to be running a business and there I was having to do it—all while learning how, really from the ground up. I worked a lot of seven-day weeks, between *Bitch* and my day job. It was my whole life, which ended up not being the best thing for me and it took a long time to realize how damaging that was. There was also a lot of pressure from distributors to make a production schedule and stick to it, which is hard

2. Benjamin Shaykin, cofounder and original designer for *Bitch* from 1996 to 2002.

enough when it's your full-time job but harder when you have to go to work also.

JD: How were you able to stay in business when other zines fell by the wayside?

AZ: As a nonprofit, we did a fair amount of donor cultivation, and the few major donors we had, including family members, were a huge, huge part of how we managed to survive really tough times. And being able to call on a very loyal and very dedicated readership with fundraising pleas is also a huge factor. We've tried to make our readers see that we really can't exist without them, and that we're accountable to them, and the result is a pretty symbiotic relationship. It definitely hasn't always been easy or fun to admit publicly when we're in dire financial straits, and we've taken steps to ensure that it doesn't happen as often as it has in the past, but we all feel that transparency is a really important part of being a mission-driven organization.

LJ: The way we went about growing was really organic and demand-driven: basically, distributors started coming to us and asking to carry it—they'd started hearing about it from bookstores. And once the distributors had it they kept increasing their orders, because it did well and sell-through was always really high. Until our circulation was about 30,000 (maybe 25,000?), our sell-through was never under 80 percent. So we were able to be (barely) financially sustainable to get us to the point of being able to pay ourselves a little, and then to develop a donor base among readers to keep us going. And we've been able to call on that base when we need to. And we have needed to. The economics of small magazine publishing have always been incredibly difficult, and over the magazine's first ten years, paper and postage costs both increased a lot. There's no way the magazine would be in print today without the financial support of the readers. It's community-supported and community-driven.

JD: A brief survey of *Bitch's* cover art shows a progression from black-and-white illustrations to elaborate four-color covers that feature photography and art by contemporary artists. Can you tell us more about the aesthetic and editorial decisions that went into the early covers, and how (if at all) that differs from your current aesthetic?

AZ: I drew the early covers, and really there wasn't a lot of discussion that went into them—Lisa and Ben and I talked about them, but ultimately they trusted me, I guess, to do something that was reflective of the content inside. At that point, we were very much a zine, and we weren't necessarily grappling with a lot of the concerns that later went into deciding on cover imagery, like: How will this look on the newsstand? Will there be room for cover lines? Where's the bar code going to go?

Our current covers take newsstand visibility very much into account, and are much more of a collaborative decision. We still have the same challenge, which is that we have to try and be eye-catching without using celebrities or huge, neon cover lines. We try to portray something of the theme of each issue on their covers without being really literal, we try to make covers both aesthetically interesting and visually witty, and we try to make the covers as a whole seem coherent, so that when they're all grouped together they read as having a somewhat consistent aesthetic.

LJ: We also had access to the donated skills of an excellent professional photographer, Jeff Walls, Andi's now-husband. That was a big part of it—we couldn't have afforded to pay anyone. So we started doing photographs of illustrated items. I still love that mix. One of my favorite covers ever is for issue 12, the one where Andi painted these nesting dolls and Jeff photographed them. Later, with different art directors, we moved into other styles.

JD: Katherine Marino has observed that editing a little magazine takes "a balance of nonconformity and of tradition, resisting the mainstream and seeking out new and inventive works."[3] How did you balance this tension between nonconformity and tradition in the early years, and how is it different now?

AZ: Lisa and Ben and I were very much magazine geeks, and really interested in adapting conventional formal elements of a magazine in a zine format, which is why even the earliest issues kind of aped the format of "real" magazines—cover lines, table of contents, short front-of-book content, features well, reviews at the back of the issue, and a short last-page feature. It was fun to play with conventions and make them specific to the work we were doing.

It's maybe a bit different now, in terms of editing, because we have an existing audience that has expectations for consistent features and content in each issue, but at the same time we're always trying to grow our readership as well and draw in new readers and people who've never heard of the magazine, so we need to keep accessibility in mind. The interplay between the cover imagery (which really doesn't read explicitly "feminist,"

3. "The Man in the Back Row Has a Question," *Paris Review* (Fall 2003): 374–413, at 381.

or political at all) and the content is one way we kind of balance the non-conformity and tradition, though to be honest I've really never thought of it that way!

LJ: In the early years it was all about nonconformity in the writing and the topics, with the tradition coming from the design and from very intentionally using the conventions of magazines, though tweaked. We've always had a front-of-the-book section, reviews were always at the end, and we always had a one-page piece, often funny, on the last page. We made our folios very traditional, with the season and page numbers exactly where you'd expect them, but we'd write wacky text to describe the season. (Well, we also kind of had to since we weren't on a normal magazine schedule most of the time.) We always stressed readability and generous white space with the design, classic magazine attributes.

JD: *Bitch* has featured articles and interviews with important feminist voices, including scholars Judith Halberstam and Susan Bordo, the activist group Guerrilla Girls, NPR personality Terri Gross, comedian Margaret Cho, cartoonist Lynda Barry, writers bell hooks and Barbara Ehrenreich, and graphic memoirist Marjane Satrapi. Why were you drawn to these feminists and what have they contributed to current discussions of feminism?

AZ: Almost all of the women (and men) *Bitch* has interviewed are people we genuinely admire, love, and want to talk to. It's not that every one of them self-applies the term "feminist," but most of them create work, or art, or criticism that has shaped a cultural dialogue in a way that inherently foregrounds experiences that are relevant to feminism and social justice.

The "feminist" in the subtitle refers to the fact that we view everything—in particular, the mainstream media and popular culture—through the lens of feminism. But "feminism" is still a really misunderstood word, and still assumed in many ways to be a monolithic ideology. Our conception of feminism is that it's not about man hating or female superiority, and it's not about just women—it's about understanding that our culture really is set up as an antagonism between both men and women as well as between women and "feminism," and between "moral" and "immoral," and dozens of other harmful binary distinctions, and that it's important to look at cultural products with that in mind. So that has absolutely informed the people we've profiled and interviewed.

In general, the starting mission of the magazine has stayed much the same as it's become the mission of the organization as a whole (which doesn't just produce a magazine these days, but has expanded into non-profit programming including symposia, lecture series, a lending library, and more). We want to be a critical forum for people who love pop culture, see it as a locus of activism, and work to both highlight existing pop culture that foregrounds and elevates women and carve out more female-friendly places in the mass media. And we want to point out the ways in which there is still a lot of work to do with respect to making feminism, and women's voices in general, more visible and tangible in the media and in popular culture.

JD: How would you characterize your relationship with contributors? What is the editing process like?

AZ: I've always felt like we have been incredibly lucky to have the contributors we have—many of whom have been contributors almost since the beginning. We don't pay anything approaching industry standard, and in the early years we couldn't afford to pay contributors at all. And we also have always had really high standards with regard to the quality of writing. So some writers, over the years, have (quite rightly) said, "Wait, you want me to go through two rounds of developmental editing on a piece that I'm barely getting paid for?" But so many others are willing to do that because they believe in the work, they love the magazine, and in many cases they're writing a piece that wouldn't work in any other magazine because of the angle or the feminist standpoint. And that's all really great. It's also been gratifying to work with contributors at the very beginning of their writing careers and see them go on to make a name for themselves as writers.

The editing process has changed over the last few years because of personnel changes. Historically, *Bitch* had two people who worked together on all the written content, the editorial director and the managing editor. Once features and columns were accepted, a lead editor was assigned. That person was the first point of communication for the writer, and (for consistency) usually the only person to communicate with the writer during the bulk of the editing process. The editorial director and managing editor split the work more or less evenly, with each acting as lead editor on about half of the features and columns. Whoever wasn't the lead editor was given drafts to comment on, so that the burden of editing entire pieces wasn't on one person.

Budget issues for the past two years have made the managing editor position obsolete, which means that the editorial director (that's me) is the sole editor on staff. This has been really difficult, and is something I hope can change in the future. What this has meant for the editing process is that I'm the sole point of contact for contributors, and that our editorial interns have become involved in the editing process at a higher level than they were when there were two editors on staff.

LJ: I always saw the writers I was working with as partners in producing a great magazine. Of course I had a vision for how I wanted things to go, but in the end it was their writing, their names going on it—and I always made that totally clear, which interestingly made writers more likely to take my advice.

My style as an editor was to read and ask a lot of questions: "What about X?" "As a reader, I'm wondering why you're not mentioning Z here." Or just, "I'm confused, can you unpack this a little more?" Sometimes I had a specific direction I wanted them to go in, but sometimes it was just about feeling a loose thread in the argument and wanting to see what would happen if I pulled on it.

Also sometimes I think it's an editor's role to play devil's advocate. Even if you agree with the writer's analysis, you have to present an alternate view and see how to respond. It just makes the original analysis stronger. So I would definitely push like that. And sometimes (especially early on when I had less experience) things could go a lot of rounds. But even though it was a lot of work, I know the writers really appreciated the careful reading and commenting, and the pushing. We got a lot of feedback about that from a lot of grateful authors. Though sometimes I wondered how many of them were tearing their hair out and cursing my name during the editing process.

JD: What has been your most difficult moment?

LJ: Um, I have to pick just one?

Choosing to leave was hard—not that that was one isolated moment, it was a multiyear process of me figuring out what I wanted/needed to do and also finding and training someone to take over for me as publisher.

We also had a time in summer 2000 or early 2001 when we actually decided to fold; the burnout was too much. After some outside convincing and some concrete budget advice from some colleagues, we decided instead to increase our frequency and start to pay ourselves. That was a big, scary leap and definitely a hard moment, both the deciding to fold and the deciding not to.

The ominous letter from the US Postal Service telling us that a back-cover vibrator ad was obscene and thus in violation of some postal codes was no fun, either. Many of our readers weren't particularly happy about that one—one person wrote and said (I'm paraphrasing), "I'd like to choose when my four-year-old learns about vibrators, and at the mailbox this morning was not the best time." That made total sense, and I did feel bad about not thinking it through more carefully. Then again, another letter we got from a mother said that she was upset about the ad because of her teenage daughter. And we were all like, Lady, if there's anyone in the world who needs to know about vibrators most, it's a fourteen-year-old girl! Don't you want your kids to have information about the safest sex there is?

And when I did the bell hooks interview, I had an equipment malfunction. I'd plugged in the recorder wrong and I had my voice but not hers (it was on the phone). I had to call up one of my most long-standing intellectual idols and tell her I'd made a dumb mistake and ask her to do the interview again! She was incredibly gracious about it and so generous with her time, but I was terrified and mortified. It was really awful.

I could talk about the late nights and trying to proofread at 2 a.m. and all that, but I actually found the production process and its crazy hours really fun much of the time. It's the times in the middle of the day when I'd be staring at a cash-flow statement wondering how the hell we were going to close the gaps that were way worse.

JD: While *Bitch* provides a consistent engagement with and critique of mass media and advertising, you do use advertising as well. What is your guiding principle?

AZ: Advertising has never accounted for more than about 7 or 8 percent of *Bitch*'s operating budget, and since it isn't necessarily crucial to the magazine's survival we've been able to be choosy about what kind of advertising we accept. I don't think we've ever had an official list of guiding criteria, but our sniff test has been this: If the advertisement is something that *Bitch* would criticize if we saw if in another publication, we probably shouldn't run it.

Recently, we rejected the ad art from Voodoo Donuts, a Portland institution known for its edgy donuts. The ad was using a sexualized image of a woman—actually, it was basically a disembodied crotch shot—to sell donuts, which we just couldn't see a way to justify to ourselves or readers. The funny thing is that the guy who made the ad made it specifically for *Bitch*, and thought we'd love it: He was like, "It's edgy! And you're edgy! I don't get why you don't like it!" And we were like, "How do you figure that using a woman's body to sell a product is edgy?" It's pretty much the biggest advertising cliché ever. Why not give us an ad with a woman actually chowing down on a pile of donuts? That might actually be edgy. (Interestingly, after we scrapped the ad, it ran in *Bust*.)

LJ: For individual ads, our metric for rejecting an ad was to ask ourselves whether, if we saw the image in a mainstream magazine, we would write about it. That was our basic metric, supplemented by putting ourselves in our readers' shoes, seeing if we thought they'd be bugged by something. For the bigger picture, we were very clear from the beginning that advertising as a category was never going to be a big source of income for us — like, never more than 10 percent of our revenue. That meant that if an advertiser walked away (or threatened to) because they didn't like something we wrote, the damage would be relatively small and there would never be any temptation to change the content.

Debbie Rasmussen, who succeeded me as publisher, oversaw a complete overhaul and redesign of the website, and from the start she was really committed to it being ad-free, in response to the density of advertising messages on the web and just the way that advertisers are encroaching on public space and our mental environment to an unprecedented degree. And also because being ad-free just allows so much more design flexibility on the web, things can look so much better when there doesn't have to be space reserved for banners. There was talk internally of whether we were cutting ourselves off from an important income stream, but when the website went ad-free I think it was the right call.[4]

JD: The *Bitch* website uses web technology to raise money. "The B-Hive" page allows users to quickly set up a monthly contribution to *Bitch*, and the "BitchMart" page sells *Bitch* merchandise, including books, T-shirts, and aprons. Tell us more about your approach to web technology and merchandising.

AZ: We're still figuring it out, honestly, but what we realized several years ago was that we weren't using the web as much as we could be, given that a huge part of our readership is college students for whom the Internet is the default technology.

As for merchandise, we've gone through a few different phases of having merchandise and not having it. A lot of it hinged on finding sourcing and manufacturing that the organization could stand behind, from an environmental and ethical perspective, and that hasn't always been easy to find, so rather than compromise we just held out until we found a company that could provide that. We eventually found one, last year, and so we've been kind of ramping up efforts to offer merchandise.

---

4. That decision to remain ad-free only lasted through Debbie's tenure, and *Bitch* soon went ahead with a model for the web that is technically sponsorship-based, but whose "visibility spaces" for sponsoring organizations look indistinguishable from ads.

JD: How does social media affect your relationship with your readers and contributors?

AZ: I think mainly it's just made them much less of an abstract mass. Facebook and especially Twitter enable readers to interact with us, and have made readers' responses to articles, blog posts, or the organization in general seem, for better or worse, much more instantaneous and insistent. If someone doesn't like something we've posted on Facebook, or disagrees with the author of a blog post, it can easily blow up and turn into that person demanding to hear back from a staff member right now. And because the Internet never sleeps—but the staff has to—it can be challenging, to put it charitably, to accommodate demands like that.

We really love the way Twitter and Facebook are great for responding to pop cultural events or circulating timely activist alerts. But we haven't changed things like our submissions policy or our internship- or job-application process to accommodate the easy familiarity of Facebook and Twitter. I'm surprised sometimes when we get a direct message on Twitter that's like, "I want to write about X. Can I?" Or when someone contacts me via my personal Facebook account to say, "I'm graduating from college and I want to work for you guys!" Not to sound like an old fart, but really? Is that how we're doing things now? We try not to encourage that, since we have equally simple channels by which people can pitch stories or apply for internships. Just because the technology exists doesn't mean we necessarily want to use it for everything.

JD: The Bitch Media website features links to selected features from the *Bitch* archive, important feminist websites, blogs, and podcasts. How do you approach online content?

AZ: I think what we've realized is that the audience for the magazine is not necessarily the same audience for the website. Some magazine readers never read the blogs; many blog readers don't read the magazine. Many people who subscribe to our Facebook page don't read either one—or, at least, not regularly. They come to the Facebook page specifically to interact with the community there. It's something that we talk about as a staff a lot: If the readers of the magazine and the website are different, should the mission and goals of those two things be different as well? Again, it's something that we're still figuring out, and that will probably evolve as we continue to exist and technology becomes more and more entwined with the way people read and experience media.

The World Doesn't Stop for Derek Walcott, or: An Exchange between Coeditors

GERALD MAA AND LAWRENCE-MINH BÙI DAVIS

GERALD MAA: When I think of race, I use the census form as my hieroglyph. I am constantly astonished at how baldly and succinctly the census form displays the way race is fundamentally figured in contemporary American politics and culture.[1] There is no obfuscation from the top. Here is the race question:

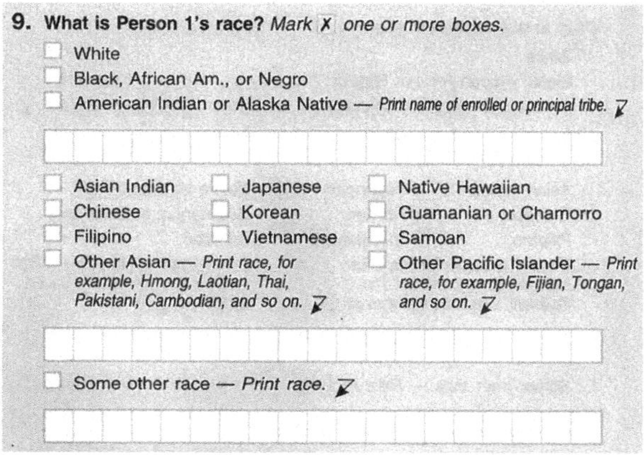
9. What is Person 1's race? *Mark X one or more boxes.*

☐ White
☐ Black, African Am., or Negro
☐ American Indian or Alaska Native — *Print name of enrolled or principal tribe.*

☐ Asian Indian ☐ Japanese ☐ Native Hawaiian
☐ Chinese ☐ Korean ☐ Guamanian or Chamorro
☐ Filipino ☐ Vietnamese ☐ Samoan
☐ Other Asian — *Print race, for example, Hmong, Laotian, Thai, Pakistani, Cambodian, and so on.*
☐ Other Pacific Islander — *Print race, for example, Fijian, Tongan, and so on.*

☐ Some other race — *Print race.*

FIGURE 3. 2010 Census Form. Source: US Census Bureau.

Whereas there is one box for White Americans and one for Black, Asian Americans have eleven boxes to choose from, and two of them are "others." Those of Spanish, Hispanic, or Latin origins—the face of our immigration

1. LAWRENCE-MINH BÙI DAVIS: Since Gerald opens with the census, here is poet Srikanth Reddy, from *AALR* vol. 2, issue 1 (Spring 2011), on precisely this subject:

The last famous census-taker in American poetry came up with a surprising finding indeed. Walt Whitman discovered that the United States was populated by precisely one person—himself—though, of course, that solitary singer contained multitudes within the imaginative precincts of his literary persona. Counting himself as a Hoosier, a Badger, and a Buckeye—and even crossing the border to assume "Kanadian" citizenship in "problem"—have been quarantined to a preceding question about "ethnicity," not "race." These are the racial terms set for us.

Half a century ago, the race question looked like this:

P5. Color or race

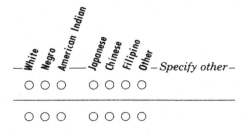

—*Specify other*—

FIGURE 4. 1960 Census Form.
Source: US Census Bureau.

Decades of the accomplishments and pitfalls from the civil rights era, the Reagan years, the years of multiculturalism, and the subsequent ones in which we live have proliferated the boxes for Asian Americans, but not for Black or White Americans. According to the census form, the difference for Black Americans between pre–Civil Rights America and our supposedly post-racial one is a few names tacked on to their still singular box. The variegated field for Asian Americans is the one James Baldwin nostalgically yearns for in "Color." In his essay, written for *Esquire* in 1962, Baldwin mourns usurpation of *colored* by *negro* as the prominent colloquial term for Black Americans. He prefers the "vivid, many-hued" connotations of *colored* to the singular blankness of *negro*. Although I sympathize with Baldwin in assessing the place of *negro* more onerous than that of *colored*, I want to emphasize that neither is void of its own turmoil. As Baldwin notes in "The Price of the Ticket," everyone, even White Americans, who ostensibly and really profit most from the racial structuring of American culture, pays a price for living in this racialized country.[2] In

---

this passage—Whitman shows how great art can interrogate our most basic assumptions about census and consensus, polity and identity, pluralism and union (8).

Art doesn't somehow imbue race with contradictory energies; those tensions were always already there. No, as Whitman shows us, Reddy reminds us: art undoes the normalizing work of the census, finding complexity where that project gives us blessed, and accursed, simplicity. And of course the census is just a symptom. Not the disease itself.

2. LAWRENCE-MINH BÙI DAVIS: I have always been particularly enamored of this essay. To paraphrase, Baldwin outlines the price of the black ticket as having to want to be white when one can never, in fact, be white. Meanwhile the price of the white ticket:

"Color" Baldwin notes that, whether called *colored* or *negro*, the racialized American is caught in "some utterly unbelievable cosmic joke" in which one's skin color can be used to elicit mutually exclusive assumptions of that person[3]—for example, that an Asian must be a terrible driver; that an Asian must be a street racer.

I say this as an act of diagnosis rather than prescription. The census form clearly conceptualized at the borders of the White box the diametrically opposed Black, Negro, African American box and the set of Asian American boxes. With this multidimensional racial structure, each group has its own prominent capacities and concerns. As an editor of the only literary print journal that foregrounds issues about and work by Asian Americans, I deal with the capacities and concerns of our several boxes. The day Lawrence and I got a green light from the University of Maryland for our journal, we celebrated with dinner. Over dinner at Paul Kee and on the ride back we celebrated with dreams of what we could do. We had to find a name. I for one insisted on a one-word name, something catchy and memorable. Fifteen minutes into shouting out and then shutting down a list of candidates reminded me of the primary pitfall those who work in Asian American culture must consider, always. One must work with the awareness that the most common public cry, the most damned heresy, the most cardinal sin of all within the Asian American community, is exclusivity,[4] for good reason. Each of the names that I blurted out seemed

---

having to want to be white when one can never, in fact, be white. In other words whiteness is constructed, aspirational, an unreachable horizon. It's helpful to think of what we're up to at *AALR*, in running an Asian American literary journal, along these lines. What it means to publish under the banner we publish under must be understood in the context of cost, economies of representation, yearning, white supremacy. What it means to be Asian American, to make Asian American art, to create space for Asian American art, must be understood in relation to—within and beyond—the structures imposed upon us: the Census, the whims of the publishing industry, popular racial representation.

Here is something Gerald may disagree with: literature not simply as the product or reworking of this system but the price. This is a recurring question of Asian American lit (and writing by people of color and/or other marginalized communities more generally): what price do writers feel, take upon their shoulders, agree to pay?

3. *The Price of the Ticket: Collected Nonfiction, 1948–1985* (New York: St. Martin's, 1985), ix–xx.

4. LAWRENCE-MINH BÙI DAVIS: Set this fact alongside what has come to count for "Asian American" in mainstream publishing history: a narrowing to a handful of recyclable tropes.... Think just of the remarkable number of women of Asian descent who grace Asian/Asian diasporic/Asian American book covers, always seeming to want to face away from us, backs bared.... This must be culture. Pan-cultural practice to hang around topless facing away waiting to be photographed/painted.

to be too egregiously exclusionary. These Asian Americans don't eat that. We can't use that name with what those Asian Americans went through sixty years ago. These Asian Americans would find the title ludicrous. That word would only pertain to those Asian Americans. Although there are obviously titles and names for Asian American institutions that toe this line quite well, we happily conceded to the most rudimentary title of all: *The Asian American Literary Review*. And in this spirit we saw the importance of carefully crafting a mission statement that would be a sure lodestone for our future travels.

LAWRENCE-MINH BÙI DAVIS: AALR's mission statement is as follows:

The Asian American Literary Review is a space for all those who consider the designation "Asian American" a fruitful starting point for artistic vision and community. In showcasing the work of established and emerging writers, the journal aims to incubate dialogues and, just as importantly, open those dialogues to regional, national, and international audiences of all constituencies. We select work that is, as Marianne Moore once put it, "an expression of our needs ... [and] feeling, modified by the writer's moral and technical insights." *AALR* features fiction, poetry, creative nonfiction, translations, comic art, interviews, and book reviews.

We formulated this mission against mainstream publishing's rendering of "Asian American." "Asian American" as *starting point*—as opposed to the more common understanding, as endpoint: "Asian American" as marketing strategy, library/bookstore shelving category, and discrete, confirmable idea of culture and community. *AALR*'s goal is to unsettle any ending points, to avoid confirmation in favor of complication. To open rather than foreclose conversation. Endpoint: it's impossible for *AALR* to cover every camp and community the designation "Asian American" encompasses—in terms of ethnicity, region, gender, sexual orientation, generation, class, and so on. We cannot even hope to offer more than gestures toward fairness or evenness—but you'd better believe we're held accountable for doing so; those left out remind us they've been left out. But in process of selection, radical openness is a matter not simply of representation for the sake of pleasing everyone (or no one, as in any good compromise!) but of ethics. Openness, in other words, not simply for the sake of a census-taking sort of inclusion but—and I'm realizing this sounds awfully precious and somewhat sanctimonious, but I'll say it nonetheless—for the sake of enriching dialogue, giving voice to what's beneath the grain, some brand of literary and cultural empathy.[5] As Asian America changes

5. GERALD MAA: Audre Lorde comes to mind here. "The Transformation of Silence into Language and Action," a paper first presented in 1977 at the MLA's "Lesbian and Literature Panel," starts off by observing how silence isolates a person from those around

in response to internal and external pressures, there must be some space for imaginatively and critically engaging those changes.

GERALD: When it comes to our fundamental wish to cultivate dialogue and empathy, another strong interest of ours is classroom adoption. We have invested a lot of effort into finding ways to carve out hospitable space for *AALR* in university classrooms. In the fall of 2011, a number of university courses used our issue that commemorated the tenth anniversary of September 11th.[6] In Fall 2013 we piloted a synchronous teaching program. Some eighty classes from around the world used our mixed race issue as a core text. For the month of October 2013 the classes interacted with each other virtually by way of digital labs. With the help of CUNY Binghamton,

---

her, especially when that silence enshrouds a matter of difference. Poetry, language at its most powerful, should transform silence into language and action so that differences can be bridged. One of the trailblazing voices for intersectionality, Lorde understands that the best way to validate and valorize one's own community is to bridge the differences with communities outside of one's own. "The Transformation of Silence into Language and Action," in *Sister Outsider: Essays and Speeches* (Berkeley, CA: Crossing Press, 2007), 40–44.

6. LAWRENCE-MINH BÙI DAVIS: Afterward we gathered a group of teachers to discuss the experience of teaching Sept. 11th on the ten-year anniversary, and one of the fascinating points of conversation had to do with regional difference—how responses to Sept. 11th and its legacies by students in the Midwest and West Coast were radically unlike those of students living in NYC.

Which importantly informed our upcoming teaching program on mixed race. For years I'd been having conversations about mixedness with *AALR* assistant editor Alicia Upano; I was born and raised on the East Coast, whereas Alicia, also mixed-identifying, was born and raised in Hawai'i, and comparing experiences has been an eye-opening enterprise. Regional difference seems so obvious, and so obviously generative, but it's rarely capitalized upon in classrooms, or only in limited fashion.

The basic idea of our teaching program is to stage a cross-classroom conversation writ large, connecting, as Gerald says, eighty or more classrooms across the world, with regional difference front and center—teaching and learning together about race and how and why we understand race in the ways we do.

When it comes to the publication at the center of this project, our special issue on mixed race, we've taken something of an unusual approach, a sort of "inverse" approach, working with teachers who've agreed in advance to take part in the teaching program to help conceptualize the issue together. We've opened up the editing circle, more or less, inviting a range of folks into our tiny little dark room with us!

So for this project at least we've moved to a kind of boutique, hyper-curated, nearly crowd-sourced model of publishing—something in keeping with new trends in publishing but also consonant, importantly, with our fundamental investments in dialogue and community building. But damn hard work!

we offer these digital hubs as meeting grounds for instructors to share curriculum and find ways for classes miles apart to collaborate.

At the root of this interest is the question, "What does it mean to have a literary journal in the classroom?" Like its sibling, the old standard-bearing anthology, the journal collects work from various authors. Both are defined as such. The journal, however, aspires to timeliness, whereas the anthology aims for timelessness. In essence the former's work is ephemeral, the latter immortal. Or so they both would wish. At least for me, our classroom push is not meant to exalt the journal above the anthology, have the bastard son usurp the long-standing monarch. The push is meant to trumpet a need for both. (My thoughts on what I see as a presentist streak in contemporary American literature will have to wait for another day.) In perhaps my favorite passage from all of English literature, Samuel Taylor Coleridge describes the difference between the types of awe an aspiring writer feels for a piece of contemporary literature and one from ages past:

> The great works of past ages seem to a young man things of another race, in respect to which his faculties must remain passive and submissive, even as to the stars and mountains. But the writings of a contemporary, perhaps not many years older than himself, surrounded by the same circumstances, and disciplined by the same manners, possess a reality for him, and inspire an actual friendship as of a man for a man. His very admiration is the wind which fans and feeds his hope. The poems themselves assume the properties of flesh and blood. To recite, to extol, to contend for them is but the payment of a debt due to one, who exists to receive it (*Biographia*, chap. 1).[7]

An aspiring writer needs both the fervor stoked by contemporary literature and the sublime awe brought on by literature from deep in the past. (I guess the implication is that *AALR* (1) views its readers as young aspiring writers, (2) sees students in academic classrooms likewise, and (3) understands the classroom's initial task as inspiring the students—talk about precious and sanctimonious!) There is a particular sort of indebtedness that can only arise from contemporary literature because of a perceived shared milieu.

It is important for students, especially young ones, to acquaint themselves with editors invested in the project of timeliness to foreground aspirations literature can take other than Parnassus.

LAWRENCE:
Then mother grabbed my little brother and forced it into his mouth, the breast looked much bigger and fiercer than my little brother's head, and mother looked still bigger and fiercer

---

7. *Biographia Literaria, or Biographical Sketches of My Literary Life and Opinions*, ed. James Engell and W. Jackson Bate (Princeton, NJ: Princeton University Press, 1983), 12.

than that, the bubbling milk came squirting from its smiling, split tip, with resignation
my brother took it in his mouth, mother squeezed and stroked it two or three times, I heard
the sound of him swallowing one gulp after another, gurooosu, he said, his mouth dripping
with her white milk.

From *Wild Grass on the Riverbank*, by Hiromi Itō, trans. Jeffrey Angles, *AALR* vol. 3,
issue 1 (Spring 2012)

Hace días que estoy hipnótico en el centro
del Atlántico. La única referencia para saber que avanzo
es mi propio pasado: está ahora delante
como un tigre que me dio una tregua.

For days I've been mesmerized at the center
of the Atlantic. My only point of reference
is my own past: there it lies ahead
like a tiger that has lent me a hand.

From "Regresando al Perú en barco" ("Back to Peru by Boat"), by José Watanabe,
AALR vol. 2, issue 1 (Spring 2011)

little fish   packed in vats   limed with salt
                                pressed
Pressed until your bones are worn into the salt water
                    pressed until you no longer exist between the layers
From "Love Poem to Nuoc Mam," by Mong-Lan, *AALR* vol. 1, issue 1 (Spring 2010)

There's that age-old literary maxim: an era without significant translation
is necessarily weak, the strongest era, strongest by virtue of, by force of,
exchange.[8] I'll let Gerald the translator say more here.[9] But if as he writes
we need to attend to history, to rich-contextualize not only in a given time
zone but in what scholar Wai Chee Dimock has called "deep time," then
we also need to contextualize by way of geography—and movement. Or,
rather, as editors our work is to invest in projects of both timeliness and . . .
space-liness?[10] To foster exchange across regional/cultural/linguistic borders, especially because those borders are so often porous and mobile.

8. GERALD MAA: Ezra Pound: "A great age of literature is perhaps always a great age of
translations; or follow it," *Literary Essays of Ezra Pound*, edited and with an introduction
by T. S. Eliot (New York: New Directions, 1968), 232.

9. GERALD MAA: Cf. the Audre Lorde quote above.

10. GERALD MAA: Yes—a country is as much a boundary marking off time as a border
marking off space.

Hiromi Itō comes to the US late in her career, almost entirely unknown to American readers, still writing in Japanese but now about Japanese immigrants or Japanese American realities, writing about motherhood and what it means to be a woman in ways as perhaps startling to American sensibilities as to Japanese.[11] José Watanabe, Peruvian of Japanese descent, becomes a national treasure in Peru before passing away in 2007, his corpus of work almost entirely untranslated from Spanish into English—or Japanese. Mong-Lan, born in Saigon, comes to the US at the end of the Vietnam/American war, later remigrates from the US to Argentina, where she teaches tango and lives and writes in both English and Spanish. What it means to be Asian American, already impossibly multifarious, becomes even more so when we think diasporas, when we think remigrations and transnational traffic, spatial and linguistic complexity, cross-cultural intersections and America as just one part of the Americas.[12] These are the kinds of exchanges and hybridities we need to at once track and stage.

GERALD: I capped off the 2013 Labor Day weekend with a barbeque at the home of Michelle Har Kim, José Watanabe's translator. She, the poet Brandon Som, and I spent much, but not most, of the night talking about her work-in-progress, a translation of Watanabe's *Historia Natural*.[13] Our

11. GERALD MAA: Her first volume of poetry in English, *Killing Kanoko*, is a hidden gem in contemporary English literature. The title poem is as famous in Japan as "Howl" is here, both in literature and in the courts. And if you have the chance to catch her read, it's perhaps one of the best readings you'll ever experience.

12. GERALD MAA: If the task is Herculean, think the Hydra: for every head lopped off three more grow. I'm no Hercules, however; I don't care to slay the unwieldy beast.

13. LAWRENCE-MINH BÙI DAVIS: More from *AALR*'s excerpt of this project—a portion of the poem "El nieto" ("The Grandson"):

Una rana	A frog
emergió del pecho desnudo y recién muerto	emerged from the bare and newly-dead chest
de mi abuelo, Don Calixto Varas.	of my grandfather, Don Calixto Varas.
Libre de ataduras de venas y arterias, huyó	Freed from a mesh of veins and arteries, it fled
roja y húmeda de sangre	slick and red with blood
hasta desaparecer en un estanque de regadío.	until it disappeared in an irrigation ditch.
La vieron	They saw it
con los ojos, con la boca, con las orejas	with their eyes, mouths, and ears
y así quedó para siempre	and remained this way always
en la palabra convencida, y junto	in the cogent word, beside
a otra palabra, de igual poder	other words of equal power
para conjurarla.	to conjure it.
Así la noche transcurría eternamente en equilibrio	That night continued in eternal balance
porque en Laredo	for in Laredo

talk branched off into discussion about the merits of her unconventional choice to introduce this renowned poet to the English-speaking world with a single volume rather than a book of selected works. At times devil's advocates, at times out of principle, Brandon and I defended the conventional stance. Starting with a selected work, a translator has to convince the reader only of the author's abilities. With a single volume as the inaugural translated work, she has to convince the reader first of the author's power and then the single volume's relevance. Michelle understood the rationale behind the protocol, but took issue with the value behind the rationale. Why limit readers only to a greatest hits paradigm? When so much of Anglo-American poetry is invested more in writing books and series than discrete poems, why present the poetry of the rest of the world merely as poems? As a concession to Michelle, I mentioned the odd double standard with selected works: whereas selected works generally introduce non-English poets to the English reading public, they are a prestigious landmark for English poets. Brandon looked at me with a longish pause and a look inscrutable because purely contemplative. "No," he quietly retorted, "it's really not that different because the fact of being translated *itself* is a mark of distinction."

I could go on and recap the entire conversation, but I want to stop here: what is this mark of distinction? Obviously Brandon is right: to be translated is an honor, de facto, just as it is a sign of respect to learn at least a smattering of someone else's language. We have thankfully progressed to the point where one does not assume an Asian American can speak Chinese, Korean, or Japanese. We, however, also have to remember that Asian American literature can also be written in languages other than English. For starters: the US is not the only American country.[14] Canada and Latin American countries each have a robust Asian American tradition and scene with writers of its own. The scarcity of these authors even

---

el mundo se organizaba como es debido: the world was organized like it should be:
en la honda boca de los mayores.   by the profound lips of elders.

14. LAWRENCE-MINH BÙI DAVIS: Love this idea of literary work annotating the critical, so again! From "On the History of the Marvelous Afternoon (a recycle)," by Canadian poet Ray Hsu:

Which map (and dome cage) does humanity not sail out from?
Even time, at recreation, is its table: humanity is one which has been set
especially from country, as wire.
Landing there, way inside: a world with compartments. Always birds'
small-scale sleeping. The barbarian, seeing better passageways, seemed ice
set for display.

within Asian American studies is a crime. We too fall prey to an American myopia.

Translation is where two cultures linguistically meet. "Directive," Robert Frost's comic anti-pastoral, sarcastically describes a phenomenon that happens all too often: "The height of the adventure is the height / Of country where two village cultures faded / Into each other. Both of them are lost."[15] Having two cultures meet is not necessarily a productive instance; it, Frost reminds us, can be devastatingly destructive. Frost, the good old American poet (and I personally underscore the "good") is an odd source because Frost famously proclaimed that "poetry" is what gets lost in translation. I agree, but I find Percy Shelley's note in "A Defense of Poetry" more thorough: "Hence the vanity of translation; it were as wise to cast a violet into a crucible that you might discover the formal principle of its color and odor, as seek to transfuse from one language into another the creations of a poet. The plant must spring again from its seed, or it will bear no flower—and this is the burden of the curse of Babel."[16]

LAWRENCE: Gerald once told me this story, passed along to him by a friend, perhaps passed along to that friend by a series of other tellers, but no matter: it's true even if it isn't true. Derek Walcott sets up shop at a conference, unfolds his own card table, drags over a folding chair, hauls over a heavy suitcase of books, unpacks and stacks the books one by one. No one notices. The world doesn't stop for Derek Walcott, and Derek Walcott doesn't stop for the world.[17]

---

15. Frost, Robert. "Directive," in *The Poetry of Robert Frost*. (New York: Henry Holt, 1969), 377–78 (citation is ll. 33–35).

16. *Shelley's Poetry and Prose*, edited by Donald Reiman and Neil Fraistat (New York: Norton, 2002) 514.

17. GERALD MAA: I remember James Longenbach saying, either in a workshop or at a reading, that one shouldn't go into the business of literature for individual fame. If you go to any street corner and take a straw poll on how many people know who someone like Wallace Stevens is, one would be easily convinced, I think, that name recognition is a foolish reason to dedicate your life to this mug's game. I'm not saying this to proclaim literature dead, the public illiterate, yada, yada, yada—all of which I don't necessarily believe. Longenbach continued by saying that writers shouldn't go in for name recognition, but rather to help feed the great river that is a collective literary tradition. Even Milton, whose work Hazlitt described as "a perpetual hymn to fame," understood that the muse is, ultimately, "thankless." I offset the pessimism, or invert it into optimism, by thinking about the deep *individual* impression one gets when one finds a deep connection with a literary figure. I tell every one of my classes that reading is the most antisocial act ever—exhibit A: the easiest way to not make friends at a party is to crack

American letters are shot through and through with humbling. Humbling, not humility, mind you. Literature breeds the inner peacock in all of us. We are not humble, and this isn't only self-inf(l)ected. We want and need literature to occupy a more central place in our collective life—and in pockets, and in moments, it does. All of us who do literary work can tick off a handful of instances instantly; we hold these in mind as totems. And then are reminded, constantly, of literature's lack of everyday purchase.[18] The little magazine is particularly far down the food chain, and ours, a new-ish one, an "ethnic" one, without institutional home, is in the ooze of the swamp. We could take an ironic or perhaps politicized joy in marginalization, in our role as marginalia-provider, as ostensible decenterer, or attempted decenterer, anyway. Another story: a few years ago Gerald and I attended a banquet dinner for the Asian Pacific American Librarians Association. This was not long after the publication of our inaugural issue, and hoping to secure some institutional subscription interest, we had plenty of copies on hand to distribute, gratis, to banquet attendees. At one point a gentleman walked past us without taking his complimentary copy, so we chased after him, offering—

"No!" he said.

"No, not for sale," we assured him—*"for free."*

"No!"

"It's complimentary."

"No, I don't want it, please no!"

---

open a book. But, the flip side is that, then, a connection with a literary person can be purely Edenic.

18. GERALD MAA: There has been a "notes" section at the bottom of this document ever since I started the process. I'm the only one that has used it, I guess because I marked it off "Notes / Gerald," and there have been only a handful of thoughts throughout. The longest-standing one is "I am convinced that one of literature's primary tasks is to make the reader's every day bearable." I couldn't find an appropriate time to bring this in, although I was tempted more than once to shoehorn this note into the essay. I suppose it's best that this ends up as marginalia because this statement is, at the moment, one of faith, not conviction. (What's the deal with "convinced," then?) Gleaning from my experiences as a reader, I believe these words true. But I can't articulate even to myself the reasons for its truth. The humbling that Lawrence talks about is certainly at the root of the matter. John Keats is certainly one of English literature's most prominent models for a writer. I like to telescope his "negative capability" out into the writer's life. Keats is the one who can say, within one abbreviated lifetime, both "I think I shall be among the English Poets after my death" as well as "Here lies One whose Name was writ in Water" with equal amounts of sincerity and conviction.

Come back to me later, and I might have an answer that would have turned this faith into a conviction.

And then he was gone, and we were perhaps less dignified than we had been a few moments earlier. An Asian American librarian of Asian American collections at an Asian American librarians banquet saying no to a free Asian American literary text? Humbling, but no humility—we kept pushing copies all night.

Most of us at little magazines must be accustomed to humbling, and what lies after it, and after it, we antiquarians, we anachronisms, we upstarts, we dreamers. But blessedly there is support, too—not to offset or counter the struggling; trying to draw an equivalence is foolish. But there is support, heartening support. There is need reflected back. In our literary journal readers at once see heritage, see public forum, see crowd-sourced architecture for the future, and for that, we can be both thankful and hopeful. The world doesn't stop for literature. But I had it wrong earlier. In his labors, Derek Walcott—in all of our labors, we poets and writers and editors, we readers and students and teachers, we communities, we upstarts, we anachronisms, we humbled: this is literature stopping for the world. In laboring, stopping for the world.

Part 3:
Innovation and
Experimentation:
The Literary
Avant-Garde

Exquisite Corpse

ANDREI CODRESCU

From the beginning we meant to do harm. Not mean harm, the kind writers do to each other when they exact revenge for gossip intended or imagined, but the kind of harm that promotes health. American literature, poetry in particular, is sick from lack of public debate. Where I come from, Romania, it was possible for writers to fight in the morning papers and continue to do so in person at the café in the evening. The issues were not personal: culture was at stake. In the process, feathers were ruffled and persons became indignant. But it was clear to all that literature was bigger than us because it could not exist without passionate ferment. In the late 1960s when I came to America ferment was the order of the day. The New York poets of the Lower East Side among whom I found myself were making literature against the status quo. On street corners people handed out pamphlets against the war, calls to spiritual enlightenment, poetry written on LSD and mimeographed on speed, esoteric manifestos and sexual proclamations. That was as complete a world of expressive assault as anyone would have wished. And yet, at the age of twenty, even all that seemed somehow insufficient.

To my natural Surrealist sympathies, the Lower East Side in the 1960s was a vast *cadavre exquis*, or "exquisite corpse," a form of collaboration much practiced by Andre Breton's circle in Paris several decades earlier. To make a *Corpse*, one wrote or drew something and then folded the paper in such a way that the next person who wrote or drew something didn't see what came before. The end result, when the paper was unfolded, was not the work of individuals but the creation of an *esprit*.

In San Francisco, where I next went, there was intense collaboration among writers, many of them refugees from New York, but the accent here

Portions of this essay originally appeared in *The Stiffest of the Corpse: An Exquisite Corpse Reader, 1983–1988* (San Francisco: City Lights Books, 1989) and *Thus Spake the Corpse: An Exquisite Corpse Reader 1988–1998*, Vol. 1: *Poetry and Essays* (Santa Rosa, CA: Black Sparrow Press, 1989).

was not on the printed word. Instead of street literature there were poetry readings and experimental theater.

In the mid-1970s, however, collaboration suddenly ceased. The corpse of the 1960s was suddenly unfolded and the huge wings of a terrifying bird descended on it and snatched it away. The age of the "moral majority" cultism, microchips, conservatism, Reaganism, computers, structuralism, and curricula was suddenly upon us. The esprit was silenced and its practitioners went back inside, back to school, back to work, back to silence. The Outside disappeared. The metaphorical *Corpse* of rebellion gave way to the literal Corpse of conformism.

At the University of Baltimore, where I went to teach in the 1980s, they had something called a "Publications Design Department," a graphics lab where students were always working on "magazine concepts"; I proposed that we make something people might actually want to read. I had in mind a long and skinny newspaper, patterned after Tudor Arghezi's pre-war Romanian sheet, *Bilete de Papagal*, whose mixture of muckraking and high tone bohemianism had brought down two governments. I wanted to publish polemics and travelogues, capsule reviews, poetry, and drawings. The name suggested itself spontaneously. It referred both to the Surrealist game and to the current state of the culture. Even longer and skinnier than Arghezi's sheet, it was designed for reading with one hand in the subway or the bus. It also folded perfectly for mailing, and had the added advantage of being the occasion of instant curiosity when people first beheld its seventeen erect and six wide inches. Arghezi's journal was literary, political, and polemical, and it earned its editor a few months' imprisonment by the fascist government in the 1940s, and a glorious reputation for showcasing the most brilliant modern-minded writers of post WWI Romania. I didn't share Arghezi's fate, but neither did I expect the *Corpse* to be around long enough to see a great many of our contributors die before the publication did.[1] At some point, we dreamt of becoming financially solvent by selling "lifetime subscriptions," an advertisement that didn't specify whose lifetime your $100 would get: the subscriber's or the magazine's. I knew that all the contributors to *Exquisite Corpse: A Monthly of Books and Ideas*, would eventually be corpses, but only some of them exquisite.

How *Exquisite Corpse: A Monthly of Books and Ideas* (1983–1984) became *Exquisite Corpse: A Journal of Books and Ideas* (a quarterly, 1984–1986), then

[1]. In the U.S. we don't jail writers for political opinions, though it might have a salutary effect on public discourse. At the very least, we should jail writers for being boring. In 1983 American literature, especially poetry, was a sluggish and tired beast (after its burst of energy from 1965 until 1977) feeding off the meager teats of government grants and badly paid college sinecures.

A MONTHLY OF BOOKS AND IDEAS   VOL. 1 / NO. 1 / JANUARY 1983

AUTO-DA-FE CLAIMS RICHARD HOWARD'S HEIR APPARENT
by David Hilton

Seasonal Rights, Daniel Halpern, Viking.

The only time I ever burned a book came during the last minutes of the 1970s. A few friends had gathered hearthside for the purpose of ridding America of the horrors and curses that had accumulated throughout the previous ten years. Into the fire went things like a plastic Pill compact, Nixon campaign literature, a Kiss album, Weight Watcher's guides, a divorce decree, etc. My contribution to the pyre was *The American Poetry Anthology*, editor Daniel Halpern (1975). This was a casebook of all that had gone wrong and gotten worse for poetry during that dreadful decade: precious, monotonous solipsism (feebly disguised as isolato melancholy); obsessive technique (all lines broken with surgical precision; the establishment of "you" as the major character in contemporary poetry; "stones and bones" diction and a fondness for self-cancelling lines ("you return to the place you never were"); a great fear of music. In short, poems that crumbled at the whisper of the question, "So what?"

In Halpern's new book, *Seasonal Rights*, the abuses are committed so slickly that they might be called rarefied. Absolutely nothing is at stake in these poems, not even language. Instead, these poems reside in that scoundrel's first and last refuge called "voice". How is it that all the blurb reviewers praise Halpern and his like for their "distinctive voice" when their voices all sound the same? Any of Halpern's poems could as well be a collaboration among a random dozen poets in the *American Poetry Review*. His lines sound as if they've been passed around every important Poetry Conference in the land until purified of all the blemishes: "The old neighbors have passed quietly into the earth"; "Come back, the fields are gone and your friends are gone"; "that sleep is pressed from me"; "In the darkness the black pennies of death"; "They beg for the bodies of light"; "Outside the weather gets colder, then warmer."

Clearly it is time again for The Strangler! If this journal decide to start a "Poems We Never Finished Reading" section, let me offer this Halpern opening: "In one of Watteau's pencil sketches. . ."

Halpern's book serves to remind us of the basic flaw in Establishment poetry today. Call it the Flat Fallacy: the assumption that any banal, grammatical, toneless utterance is "charged" with understated tension and "taut" rhythms.

The Flat Fallacy has nothing to do with the masters of the Plain Style from George Herbert to Charles Reznikoff. It is instead the 70s and now 80s corruption of Image/Persona/Vernacular breakthroughs of our great-grandfathers. Halpern has reached bottom; his directness is evasion, his honesty platitude. Consider the ending of "Late":

I say what comes to mind.
What comes to mind is unsaid—
inflection your sweet device—your profile
at the window the day you turned to me to say
that those who never lie are never wholly alone.
It is late and the night air is fat with water.
I sit with you here, waiting for you to turn
again from that window and talk to me.

Matthew Arnold was much hipper, wittier, more crafted than this. Halpern has a peculiar deftness for the instant cliche ("night air. . .fat with water"). If only, like a Hemingway, he had ever written truly, we could be kind enough to call this stuff self-parody. Unfortunately, with *American Poetry Review* poetry what you get is what you see—the "voice" moving its passionless punctuations across the page, where even an exclamation point is self-mocking: "How much the same it is!" ("Return, Starting Out").

I won't try burning this book. Why not? It's from Viking/Penguin and costs $12.95, and anyway bookburning is a bad habit. This is a horrible book, the State-of-the-Art in America right now.

THE AVANT-GARDE AS ARRIERE-GARDE: RICHARD KOSTELANETZ'S CEMENT SHOES
by Nadia Marin

The Avant-Garde Tradition in Literature, edited by Richard Kostelanetz, Prometheus Books.

I used to think Mr. Kostelanetz was a kind of professional literary paranoid who railed against the publishing industry and the academic establishment for all the right reasons, with all the right facts but with totally the wrong tone. I still think that, after glancing through *The End of Intelligent Writing* again, a book full of ominous indictments of the tiny cliques that make up America's intellectual taste-octocry. But while the tone is still totally off, I now know why and have a little sympathy for the man. The reason why he sounds so irritated is because no one paid any attention to Mr. Kostelanetz's pet "literary revolution," namely "concrete poetry," a

thing which sank long ago under its own weight.

Now, in an anthology which orders a number of contributions in a sequence which is meant to prove that art is progress and that the pinnacle of progress is "concrete poetry," Mr. Kostelanetz finds his true vocation: that of anthologist. An anthologist, to be sure, is a taste maker, an authority figure and the very prototype of the conspirator reviled in *The End of Intelligent Writing*.

With the exception of two extraordinary essays, classics in their own right for quite some time, this Anthology is ineluctable proof, if any was needed, why the term "avant-garde" should be put in mothballs once and forever. The attic smell of some of these tedious treatises is lethal. The central piece of the book, something called "Literature" by L. Moholy-Nagy, has the same freshness as Nagy's art, which has long been incorporated by advertising. Moholy-Nagy used to sadly think, until the day he died actually, that his squares and circles were going to revolutionize the world. They only brightened up fashion. The problem again is that the seriousness of this presentation is unbearably academic. What was once fresh is now downright torture, and the reason why the avant-gardists revolted in the first place should be the same reason we won't put up with their own dated pompousness. Italian Futurism, and especially Russian Formalism which is having a great revival recently, has been trashed I don't know how many times by history. After Mussolini, Bauhaus, and Stalinist architecture, I see little of interest there, no matter what the wounded cries of being misunderstood.

The two essays worth the book are "The New Spirit and the Poets" by Guillaume Apollinaire, written at the beginning of the 20th Century, in which Apollinaire is totally wrong about technology but totally right about poetry, and "Modernism and Post-Modernism: Approaching the Present in American Poetry" by David Antin, an essay which, despite its title, is invaluable to anyone who wants to know why the boring academic poets of the 1950's (and by extension their present-day epigones) were blown right out of the water by the live Beat Generation.

NOWHERE BUT HERE
by Minna Doskow

Utopian Thought in the Western World, Frank E. Manuel and Fritzie P. Manuel, Belknap Press, Harvard University Press.

To speculate on the intended audience or purpose of this history of western utopian thought is unnecessary. Its mere bulk provides an incontrovertible answer; for it precludes comfortable reading in bed, makes armchair reading a doubtful venture, and virtually demands a solid desk, adequate lighting, and an active pencil. It provides a comprehensive history for the thoughtful reader and a useful reference work. Yet the prodigious learning of its co-authors is not burdensome, but is rendered with grace, style, and wit that keeps the reader absorbed for hundreds of pages at a time. Taking a multi-disciplinary approach, they provide insights from diverse fields but free of the particular jargon of each and couched instead in literate prose with just the hint of an occasional academic sneer.

Authors of numerous articles and books on various aspects of utopian thought, Frank and Fritzie Manuel present their present readers with a distillation of over a quarter of a century of scholarship and thought. Their knowledge and scope is impressive. They seem to have read everything and although they do not claim to be exhaustive, but only to cite exemplars and suggest several lines of development, the book presents a vast panorama of utopian thought from its beginnings in Judeo-Christian Edenic or millenial literature and Greek golden age literature through five other major utopian "constellations" of common elements from the renaissance through the nineteenth century to what the Manuels call its contemporary post-Darwinian and post-Freudian "twilight."

Although the term "utopia," taken from a Latin adverb meaning "nowhere," was first used by Thomas More in the title of his sixteenth century classic, the Manuels trace the "utopian propensity," that human desire for an ideal society and a reformed human nature, back to ancient Greece and Israel. They avoid a rigid definition of utopia and relate the changing meaning and expressions of this propensity for social transformation through time, analyzing it both as a reflection of the social and economic problems of the times and as creations of individual imagination.

The Manuels end on a rather bleak note since they see an impoverishment of contemporary utopian expression in the outworn conceptions, dreamlike musings, consumer paradises, new fangled cults, scientific utopias of space colonies or psychologically and pharmacologically controlled societies, and statistics-laden futurologists which make up the contemporary utopian outpourings. Yet, they add a call for new efforts: "To cultivate wisely the ancient art of wishing as an antidote to the present saturation with the pseudoscience of prediction and the busyness of the masters of applied utopistics may be a paramount moral need of the age." (page 814).

FIGURE 5. Cover page of the first issue of *Exquisite Corpse* 1, no. 1 (January 1983). Source: Special Collections, Wyndham Robertson Library, Hollins University.

Exquisite Corpse: A Journal of Letters and Life (1986–1996), then *Exquisite-Corpse* or Corpse.org (1996–2012), and then the *Secret Corpse* (corpse.org, 2012–present) is a book (or several). Moreover, this is not a book the editor could write, if only because editing and life were so closely woven that I'd have to write a fifth autobiography. The first four just skim the surface of my own life and writing: I cannot imagine what kind of oceanic epic would hold the stories of the *Corpse*. But if I didn't write something, the *Corpse* might miss being "historical" within the very history that it helped create. There is probably little more awful than being kicked out of the history you made. Add to that the fact that, among little magazines, we have lasted at least as long as the Habsburg Empire (proportionally), and that we published most of the writers I care for, and hundreds that came to us unbidden and have (sadly) thrown their lives into the leech-infested pool of letters (or just thrown them away), and an awful kind of regret descends. It doesn't make things easier that for the past four years I have moved to a secret woods to practice "the art of forgetting," which, unlike Alzheimer's, allows one to forget what one needs to forget, in order to make room on the hard drive for the things one might wish to remember. Like, where did I put my glasses? Is that iPhone mine or yours?

In midst of these strictly personal conundrums I did remember the obvious: *Exquisite Corpse*, for the entire three decades of its existence, made sure to recapitulate and memorialize itself, not just from issue to issue, but in three remarkable anthologies: *The Stiffest of the Corpse: An Exquisite Corpse Reader, 1983–1988* (City Lights, 1989, editor Andrei Codrescu), and *Thus Spake the Corpse: An Exquisite Corpse Reader 1988–1998*, Vol. 1: *Poetry and Essays* (Black Sparrow, 1999) and *Thus Spake the Corpse, an Exquisite Corpse Reader, 1988–1998, Fictions, Travels and Translations* (Black Sparrow, 2000), editors Andrei Codrescu and Laura Rosenthal. We closed the twentieth century by collecting ourselves, but kept going into the twenty-first full speed ahead on the Internet, one of the first publications to do so. We almost invented Facebook, when we opened a "chat room" to accommodate real-time conversations on the material in the cyber *Corpse* (as we briefly called it). The chat room turned into an unmanageable din of conversation about everything in the world, a process that we tried to manage by first hiring a "moderator," then giving our most-often present voices their own section or "channel." If we hadn't been so hungup on "content," so-o-o twentieth century a habit, we'd have let everyone make their own affinity circle in their own room where they could post whatever they wanted to. The curse of being in the avant-garde, even by five seconds, is not getting the money, plus missing the very future you inhabited for those five seconds. Vindicated prophets end both poor *and* condescended to by the mobs for whom they opened the doors. Serves them right. "There is no such thing as an avantgarde body," to quote the poet.

Given these insurmountable alps of memory, prose, and denial, I thought that it would be best to reproduce the cover and the editorial of *Exquisite Corpse: A Monthly of Books and Ideas No. 1* (January 1983), offer the simple and touching story of our first stab at financing, the hallucinatory moment when we captured our first backer, and provide some insight into what made our magazine so extraordinary. This story is written now, as if never told before (and in truth, never in such luxuriating detail). I hope it "works," as we used to say in that high age of poesy when labor was admired and literature was composed of "works" we produced through high-minded labor.

The Birth of Funding, or The War of Zero

The financing of the first issue was borne by the University of Baltimore, thanks to the English Department chair, Lawrence Markert, who earned himself a title on the mast for his good work. (And publication of two of his poems which, having been rejected by the academic quarterlies, belonged by default to the Rebels.) Continuing to publish was another matter, but fate intervened. (As did "faith," later.)

I had been writing op-ed essays for the *Baltimore Sun* to earn extra cash; a reader wrote to me at the paper, asking for the honor of my *acquaintance* at a special dinner to be held before his impending demise from cancer. Even if I hadn't been the editor of the *Corpse*, I'd have responded positively, but dinner with an imminent corpse looked promising. The soon-to-be deceased was the wealthy owner of six bowling alleys in the Baltimore area.

I taxied up on time to what looked to me like a ritzy suburb, with a stack of *Corpses* no. 1 under my arm. The host was a roundish pale man planted in a deep armchair, being tended by a chain-smoking middle-age woman with red toenails in open-toe sandals. A morose young man dressed in a business suit was planted in another deep chair opposite the host, tended in his turn by his anxious young wife, who turned out to be the host's daughter. I took a seat and a double scotch, after placing the *Corpses* ostentatiously on a tiled table holding a flower vase with plastic tulips. An ashtray joined the stack of *Corpses* and the tulips, and I lit up. My smoking visibly cheered up the hostess, and visibly depressed the young couple. The host looked sedated and unreadable. We exchanged pleasantries, as I looked for an opportune moment to make my case for a *Corpse* subsidy to the dying bowling alley king. I couldn't quite find it. So I drank. And smoked. The red-toes hostess started to have quite a good time, and I was soon racing her chain-smoking with my own, as the other couple sank into deeper gloom. I couldn't smell anything coming from either the dining room or the kitchen, so I started to doubt that dinner would ever come. I drank more. And then we ran out of cigarettes.

The smoker jumped to her feet and announced that she was going out for cigarettes and did I care to join her? Yes, I did, and we were soon racing in her new Mercedes convertible to a convenience store in the ghetto that started just outside the ritzy burb. On the way I found out that the driver was the bowling alleys mogul's mistress, and that she had been chosen to entertain the B-list of people the mogul wanted to meet before he died. The wife, who lived in a much bigger house, tended to the A-list. This information cheered me up considerably, since I felt that the *Corpse* was very much in the same position versus the mainstream as the mistress was to the wife. Come to think of it, Literature, for which both the mainstream and Bohemia worked, was also on the verge of dying. I was definitely going to get some money out of the old Bowling Macher. When we returned, in an even better frame of mind, with a carton of Marlboro Lights and another bottle of scotch (opened and heartily tested), I smelled dinner.

Dinner was in a solid middle-class dining room set with a flowered tablecloth, linen napkins and wine glasses. The host was lifted and deposited at the head of the table by his mistress and son-in-law. The louvered door of the kitchen swung violently open. A Caribbean servant with a yellow chignon on her hair came though with platter of ceviche that she spooned with undisguised hostility on everyone's appetizer plate. She soon (too soon!) followed this with a soup tureen she splashed into soup bowls, and disappeared without a word. I looked at our dying host for a clue about what had just happened, or maybe a word or two about the menu, but he had started on his soup with eyes on the spoon.

This was the time to get going, so I said that the magazines I had brought with me were for everyone in the room, I hoped they enjoyed the fresh literature of them, and that, one day, the *Exquisite Corpse* would be renowned, if the God or Moolah favored us. I kind of garbled the word "corpse," embarrassed by the obvious, but the old man's interest was piqued. He looked out of the spoon.

A desultory little conversation flared up, concerning the literary taste present, consisting as I recall, of solid best sellers and articles in the *Baltimore Sun*. The son-in-law also mentioned the Bible, and the mogul's spawn nodded. I said, "Great Book!" The mistress made a sound between *phooey* and *yick*. The dying was silent.

A cold and indifferent slab of poached salmon followed, hurled on plates by the cook, with a hostile force that had increased since the ceviche. I wondered if it was poisoned. During the removal of the mostly untouched fish, and before the arrival of the rhubarb pie, the old man motioned his helpers to take him to an armoire in the corner of the room. From there he extracted a checkbook and a fountain pen, and was taken back to the table. He asked me how much my little publication needed for printing another issue, and I said without hesitating, "Thirty thousand dollars."

The son-in-law gasped, but the old man had already started writing the check. I spelled both "exquisite" and "corpse" for him. I mentally urged him on as his hand began forming zeros: each movement of the pen revved up my silent urging. He had made at least two zeros when his hand stopped and the hand hovered in the air. I felt the eyes of the son-in-law locked on the old man's wrist, holding it with invisible fury. The hand, caught between my pushing it to move and the son-in-law's paralyzing stare, stayed in the air.

"As your accountant," said the son-on-law, without losing his grip on the hand, "I would advise you to think before making a big donation."

I redoubled my psychic force: if Uri Geller could bend spoons, I could surely make a feeble old hand make another zero. Both son-in-law and I looked at each other at the same time. It was War. The War of the Zeros. Simultaneously we returned to the wrist. It had ceased moving. The mogul passed the check to the mistress who took a quick look and handed it to me. It was for $3,000. I had lost. I'd been this close (*makes teensy two-fingered gesture*) to causing the writing of another zero.

No matter. It was enough for another issue of the *Corpse*.

The only shadow over this auspicious beginning was that we made our patron a "lifetime subscriber," and he died shortly before the second issue. We faithfully sent every issue to his mistress's house, until one was returned two years later with the "no known addressee" stamp. The ritzy suburb had become a slum by then.

Corpse Readers, Take Heart

I moved *Exquisite Corpse: A Journal of Books and Ideas* to Louisiana in 1984 when I went to teach at LSU in Baton Rouge. Since its founding in January 1983 in Baltimore, the *Corpse*, as the aficionados intimately call it, delighted not-so-innocent readers and catered to the craven complexes of overeducated aesthetes, while also pleasing the autodidact lumpenproletariat on those long American afternoons by the Kerouakian railroad tracks now known as Starbucks. In other words, we fed the souls of both the jaded and of those too young to drink. We also enraged the literary establishment, garnering resentment, jealousy, damnation, and three threats of never-materialized lawsuits. From the very first issue, the *Corpse* attracted an energetic and sophisticated cadre of writers united by a kind of suicidal fearlessness specific to 1980s America. In 1983, American literature had settled into a cozy bubble of MFA program McWriters buttered with postgraduate NEA fellowships. American poetry was increasingly going back to the aesthetics of the 1950s under the tutelage of impressionist critics like Helen Vendler of Harvard. Alongside prosaic confessional drivel in "free verse," throwback versification calling itself "the new formalism" captured the workshops and the university quarterlies. American fiction began returning to psychological realism and sentimental autobiography. The fury of the establishment at having its nap disturbed by experimental writers in the 1960s and 1970s (and by modernism, surrealism, and postmodernism before that) resulted in the return to a literary landscape H. L. Mencken had once called the "Sahara of the Bozarts."

Taking potshots at this new status quo would have been like shooting fish in a barrel, but for the fact that the new reaction was (and is) huge. This was just fine by the *Corpse*, which relishes a fight the way academics crave prizes. It turned out, however, that fighting was not what the *Corpse* turned out to be about. After the initial skirmishes with some of the more visible capos of the new retrenchment, it became evident that a community of terrific writers existed in pristine disdain of the mainstream, and their works made the *Corpse* an important literary magazine. These writers embraced a variety of aesthetics and were part of different scenes: New York School and Black Mountain poets, West Coast surrealists and eco-surrealists, ethnic accentualists, Iowa actualists, Midwestern abstractionists, Southern minimalists, and San Diego maximalists. The editor's eclectic pleasures were further enhanced by the absence of biographical notes. From the beginning, *Exquisite Corpse* was conceived as a newspaper, to be read for the news within, not for the glamorous bios of recent conquerors of the Amy Lowell Traveling Fellowship plus glam shot. We began on page one with debate and controversy and moved, like Don Quijote, from windmill to windmill. Each issue had its own story pieced together by its contributors exactly like a *cadavre exquis*, the collaborative form that the French surrealists had enjoyed in the 1920s, from which *Exquisite Corpse* got its name. The *Corpse*, like Don Quijote, or perhaps Pantagruel, was also dedicated to the blurring of genres, demolishing distinctions between poetry and prose, lyric and reportage, essay and manifesto. In addition to poetry and a sprinkling of fiction (there was an inexplicable editorial bias against fiction), essays, letters, and art, the *Corpse* published "bureau" reports from various parts of the world, and a great many translations.

The *Corpse* in Louisiana (1984–1998) had two distinct periods: the first (1984–1990) was more or less an extension of the Baltimore *Corpse*, tropicalized by the environs; the second (1990–1998) was the era of the Body

Bag. In its first Louisiana stage, the *Corpse* drew its energy from early contributors to the magazine and material solicited by the editor, with less than 20 percent of its contributions coming over the transom. There was also a nameless and invigorating force emanating from the diffuse hostility of the academic environment which, in those days was (and weakly still is) a bastion of New Criticism reincarnated as Southern-boy hickism. In the second stage, with the addition of Laura Rosenthal's column "Body Bag," which answered would-be contributors directly in the pages of the magazine, there was a sudden influx of young, new, hip voices into the *Corpse*. We were discovered by another generation of literary revolutionists who found in the tone of the magazine a perfect medium for their pop-culture-informed skepticism, expressive violence, and humor. During this time, more than ten thousand literate, amused, hungry readers read the *Corpse*. The audience widened from just writers to readers interested in culture and, to some extent, the *Corpse* became a general culture magazine. *Corpse* essays were reprinted in *Harper's, Utne Reader, Playboy,* and other mass-circulation magazines, and *Corpse* poets started winning awards (!), such as Pushcart Prizes, and inclusion in anthologies like *Best American Poetry.* We didn't feel that such successes created any painful dilemmas, preferring to believe instead that "grown-up" culture had finally tired of academic pieties and found the *Corpse* tonic and necessary. The initial critical attitudes of the *Corpse* became an inspiration for dozens of small magazines, zines, and newsletters. The world was catching up. At this time, more than 70 percent of our material came over the transom from writers unknown to us, but who had caught perfectly the *Corpse* je ne sais quoi. Thirty-two years ago we changed the name of the publication to *Exquisite Corpse: A Journal of Letters and Life,* because we felt that it more accurately reflected our turn toward topics of wider interest.

Academic hostility continued unabated, however, because the retros in charge of the pathetic literature pie resented having any part of their wobbly conformism questioned. The problem with the wimps, Jim Gustafson once said, is that there are so many of them. You said it, Jimbo. Every year they multiply to the point where they cover the sky like a locust plague, leaving room only for their own reproduction. No matter. We have our own sky. And it's a "cybersky." In 1998, tired of mountains of paper, but also fearful of inevitable institutionalization, ossification, poetry fatigue, and literary ennui, we suspended publication of the paper *Corpse,* taking it into cyberspace. The cyber *Corpse* can be found at: http://www.corpse.org. The cyber *Corpse* is still the *Corpse,* but it is more fluid, subject to instant change and, above all, not so labor- and time-intensive for us. And the trees are ecstatic.

L=A=N=G=U=A=G=E

BRUCE ANDREWS

This is the name of the journal of Poetics that Charles Bernstein and I co-edited & coproduced in New York City, from its first modest issue in February 1978 to its fourth "volume" copublished with Toronto's *Open Letter* in 1981.

Let me sketch out a little of its background & implications — all the while aware of how hard it is to claim any accurate representation of the 1970s & 1980s, especially about a journal that seemed to "come out of nowhere" & from a community most onlookers were surprised about.

Memoir is not my forte.

Memories fail, even if they are "officially" "correctible" later, after research in the archives. [Much of ours are now helpfully housed at UC–San Diego.]

Certainly the idea of some recoverable — or worse, essential — "truth" of a referred-to world must give way to a mapping of a network of meanings, a little too fugitive for comfort.

Still: how did we end up doing what we do & did, not only as poets but as editors & practitioners of poetics?

Circumstances write the subtext — perhaps especially when the desire is to create something new or unfamiliar.

A lot later, in retrospect, we become a received idea of what is "established"; yet this success or this "establishmenting" were not the project, nor are we "fully responsible" for the success.

The project was an editorial intervention in Poetics that we thought was called for — perhaps piggybacked onto an intervention into the stylistic menu of the day for Poetry that we (even beforehand) also thought was needed.

But to understand the Poetics effort, we have to insist on its discursive context, & not just on some valiant energized effort to surpass the usual formal constraints of the poetry of the day.

Maybe a first cut would resemble the kinds of things students are invariably told to emphasize in their applications: tell me what is *distinctive* about three things — your *background,* your *interests,* your *plans or aims* for the future.

1. Background

The magazine, a journal of Poetics (rather than of so-called Poetry) stems from relationships among adventurous & rambunctious young poets (largely "baby boomers," born from the mid-1940s to the early 1950s).

The work of these poets came to be called (by ourselves) "language-centered writing" and (by others) L=A=N=G=U=A=G=E writing or poetry, or (my own favorite, with a nod to its availability for being named by outsiders) so-called Language Poetry.

Gradually, among the poets, a sense of belonging & group identity did develop, but not as a strategic effort to "join" or align with some already valorized tendency.

Perhaps this did come later — as critics or editors or teachers try to link somebody to an already written "success story," or poets try to get on board the bandwagon.

But the *L=A=N=G=U=A=G=E* years were a time of making this mobile bandwagon, not of building a fortress or a monument.

With this informal Language scene, it's so hard to bring back a sense of the collective enthusiasm or shared exuberance of this experimentalism.

We weren't so much engaged in problem solving as in producing problems.

And the work (& the thinking & feeling that went along with it) had a *scale* that transcended genre.

The poetry being written, and the past poetry being investigated, challenged most familiar expectations about the *raw materials* that could be used and the *finished products* that might result.

On the first, more "micro" level: challenges to traditional deployments of Syntax and Rhythm opened up (or required) broader explorations of Time; challenges to the usual investments in Transparency and Referentiality led to subtler explorations of Space.

On the second, more "macro" level: challenges were posed to the final result's commitments to Formal Unity and either Narrative Sequence or "all-at-once-ness" (which seemed to push an analogy with the closure, in Time, of the experience of the Reader), & to either Representational verisimilitude or Authorial self-expression (analogous to a closure of Space, for the Reader).

To many of us, the mainstream's more conservative commitments seemed insufferably boring or distracting or irrelevant — compared with the desire to explore the workings of Language & the (social, embodied) production & reproduction of Meaning & Sense.

But how to historically situate this?

One common view is agonistic: you go up *against* the past because it is bankrupt, & so you become reactive.

As if we were merely reactive to the neoclassicism of "official verse culture" or to the emerging phenomenon of so-called Workshop Poetry.

Not really true in our case.

This loose alliance of writers in their twenties was propelled more by their aesthetic & procedural passions than by any reactive negativism.

We found ourselves similarly situated on the fringe (or edge) of several existing currents in nonmainstream poetry (mostly in the US & Canada).

We were huge fans of (& cartographers, if not detectives about) what would be known as Radical Modernism & its most adventurous descendants.

In that period, what seemed hegemonic in this arena was the New

American Poetry (taking its name from the Grove Press publication of Don Allen's anthology) — of the Black Mountain, Beat & San Francisco & New York School groups of prominent poets, mostly born of a full generation before us in the 1920s & 1930s, with their second & third cohorts competing in an implicit pecking order of status, publication, attention.

[It's worth mentioning that this was still playing out largely inside the small press poetry world. In the early 1970s, the biggest names of the New American Poetry were just beginning to shuttle into that mainstream publishing success & canonical status we're now so familiar with.]

Also, by the late 1960s, this lineage is taking clearer public shape (with the critical writings of what has come to be called the Pound/Williams/H. D. tradition) having offered a toolkit to be put to use (& variously added to) by the New American Poetry, with prominent theorizers of its own (for instance, Olson Creeley Spicer Duncan ...) extending what Hugh Kenner called *The Pound Era* (in a book of which many of us had pretty well marked-up paperback copies).

For the young baby boomers of the '70s, outside of the academy, these previous formulations (of the New Americans) did seem comprehensible, using these existing theoretical lenses or paradigms to frame their stylistic adventures.

Yet by this point, the New American toolkit was bulging, with other heritages already being hovered into the mix (Whitman or Dickinson or the European Symbolist/Surrealist traditions or the Objectivists).

It was already in need of re-sorting, if not a full makeover.

What was coming into print & coming our way was distinctive, under-processed & volatilizing: the full record of Gertrude Stein's more radical experimentalism [possibly the one thing most of the so-called Language Poets could agree on is that Stein is the key twentieth-century "writer," let's just forget about so-called poetry for a moment], of the related "Revolution of the Word" tradition which Jerome Rothenberg anthologized, of European Dada & Futurism & Constructivism, of Concrete & Visual & Sound & Performance Poetries (from Brazil to Europe to ...), of the procedures & use of Language in ethnographic materials (Rothenberg, again, a huge resource & inspiration as translating "hunter/gatherer" but also less macho "gardener/redecorator"), of the results & procedures of Minimal,

Post-Minimal, Neo-Avant-garde or Conceptual Art, of the methods of the Cage circle, of New Music composers & free improvisers, of experimental filmmakers, post-Judson movement choreographers, etc.

So, what was now available for being put into the mix (by those of us pushing outside the limits of the New American Poetry's second or third "generation") was not *already fully* theorized.

We had a job to do — which neither our elders nor the English professors were up for.

So the poets, first in the mail (from the very early 1970s, when we were much more geographically dispersed) & then supplemented by community-wide discussion & talks & essays on Poetics, took this on — as a task complementary to our poetry writing & even, to some extent later, as a possible profession or life focus.

Largely through the mail, rather than in school-based or urban "scenes," a dense network of connections got created in the first half of the 1970s.

Plus, there was a connection between the poetic methodology & the social methodology:

Seemingly something about the move away from expectations of transparent self-expression made the writers a little less self-preoccupied, more willing to engage in interchange or collaboration.

Writers got involved in an ongoing dialogue about Poetics, something with the closest (often local, *nearby*) readers of their work & at other times with peers they ended up meeting in person only years later.

The cultural contexts of a poetry "scene" & of a poetics journal end up being nowhere near the same.

For example, "Language Poetics" is often talked about in terms of the development of a "group consciousness" among the "members" of a "Language School."

Basically, with $L=A=N=G=U=A=G=E$, these were all things we tried to avoid — the inevitably grotesque connotations of a "school" & its "groupthink."

Groups are centripetal.

We wanted *L=A=N=G=U=A=G=E* to be centrifugal.

Group identity was not the point.

[Nor was it how to define the basis of *exclusion*. Instead, how could we help establish some sort of integration policy among the egalitarian gatekeepers of a "placeless" community? Of course, the exclusions might appear more striking once the scope of inclusion gets expanded.]

By design, this was a counter-sectarianism — not a sloppy eclecticism.

And this fit our circumstances in New York City in the mid- to late 1970s: the discursive social space of the city itself [or is it, "THE City"] seemed to enable a wild centrifugally tilted experimentalism.

This became especially hard to square with the textual closures of transparent representation or authorial self-centeredness or with the tidy time lines of narrative or epiphanies of self-disclosure.

It was just too c-r-a-z-y.

For that reason, the notion of a Language Poetry having two "fronts," with the East Coast or NY one centered around *L=A=N=G=U=A=G=E* magazine, is false.

In the San Francisco Bay Area (unlike NYC), more of a vacuum in non-mainstream poetry culture was *visibly* being filled up by an emerging "Language" group — who were put more actively on "group defense."

In NY, discourse & poetic experiment could develop more easily "under the radar," without drawing the notoriety that attracts attacks & denigrations (based in part on envy, in part on oppositional politics).

For Charles & I, having moved (or moved back to) New York City in 1975/1976, there's a distinctive whiff of "location as destiny" — or at least as the facilitating of idiosyncratic openness.

To launch a Poetics project, we didn't need to succumb to some well-detailed group consensus or compulsory bohemianism among poets — especially when it came to our investment in serious poetic conceptualizing.

Even (or perhaps especially because of being) without ties to an English department, we were in proximity to arenas of intense involvement in other *arts* and other areas of *inquiry* operating at a national level — instead of subsisting largely in a coterie or tightly knit scene of poet practitioners.

[Those local scenes were often prone to keeping poets just as locked into an identity-expressive-heroic-romantic (& anti-intellectual) stance as any MFA workshop poet today — albeit more "boho," more "street," more ethnically hybrid, etc.]

In retrospect, these were lucky (& enabling) contingencies.

2. Interests

What dissolved some of the isolationism of the small press poetry community were currents of internationalism, historicism, & nonfiction discourse (a.k.a. "theory" or, in downtown jargon, "academic bullshit").

In fact, we could ask: What ended up being the most stigmatizing about so-called Language Poetry: its radically disjunctive, non-narrative/non-lyric writing, or its interest in (high-falutin'/Continental) theory?

The era was crucial — especially in the city: with its almost alchemical condensation of the energy left over from the new social relations & enthusiasms put on the table in the 1960s.

It gave us access to a social vernacular or speech coming "from below," along with the excitements of negotiating such a dizzying quilt of different personal & social textures.

Even so, the poetry was often later perceived as having taken place in much more of a social vacuum, narrowly framed by others as if it were all just a (reactive) assault on contemporary poetic orthodoxy.

Yet: what would be the reason to *take on* the poetic orthodoxy?

Taking on (or, very often, simply ignoring) the orthodoxy is usually aimed at countering a restrictive range of poetry & its powerful "promotional literature" (bolstered, in an elective affinity, by institutional power & $$$) which fosters equally restrictive notions of identity (splayed across certain categories, but still riveted onto valorizing institutions or solid/sticky "tendencies").

But the "enclosures of the possible" in the world of poetry had an analogy or allegory in what was being ruled in or out within a wide social world.

In turn, this helped nudge the journal's project along a more socially & politically ambitious path — at the national level, where these connections or parallels among different social domains could register.

True, any discourse about a unified national heritage was unraveling after the 1970s, but we had at least a vision of a national mosaic or constellation (if not yet a fully global one) beyond whatever was happening in our neighborhood.

[Also, very likely there was something resonant about having grown up, as Charles & I both did, in "national" towns (whether DC or New York) that stoked some of that desire for national (as distinct from local) connectedness. My own training as a scholar of International Politics & US Foreign Policy, or Charles's studies in Philosophy, helped point us similarly *outward*.]

"Language" — what our poetry was polymorphously centered on — was vast enough in scale, eventually even beyond the national — to offer housing for most of our projects & ambitions.

Not as a given but as a question.

What different ways of characterizing it could do the best job of clarifying our literary praxis?

Meanwhile, the "linguistic turn" in other disciplines far outside the poetry world unleashed a flood of relevant critical theorizing.

The late 1970s/early 1980s were especially marked by this postmodern Theory Boom, bringing forward (often in new translation) an incredibly wide range of writing: from the European Marxist tradition, from structuralism & semiotics & so-called post-structuralism, from emerging studies about sex, gender, popular culture, diasporic or hybrid social identities — much of it becoming voguish cross-disciplinary reading for young intellectuals, students, activists, artists.

This range of resonant materials could completely disrupt the complacency of any tightly consensual "local scene": outside of academia, nowhere was this perhaps more true than in New York City.

Instead, we were enticed by the chance to investigate a variety of protocols of understanding & engagement — reminding us that "orthodoxy"
operates not only in the writing of poetry but in any, even vague, sense of
what system of evaluation or grasp sits underneath it.

Like the social system itself, this can be unveiled or contested.

But this wasn't just true in poetry.

Before the trends toward the academicization of many precincts of the art
world, New York City had been the vital center of a cross-media ethos of
constant exchange across disciplines & genre conventions.

It was a poly-arts town, an intermedia town.

We could envisage language as a "medium" (in a modernist discourse of
medium-specificity), resonating with new theorizing about postmodern
visual art or "new music" or dance performance.

Meanwhile, various new practices were getting *pieced together* in dozens
of specific personal projects & distinctive careers, all visibly on display in
the years we were, at first, strategizing & then publishing.

These poly-art procedures often seemed ripe for sharing or appropriating,
even if the specific "forms" did not [— or was it that the significances of
"form" got taken for granted while the significances of "process" (& the
openings they allow for readers) seemed to call for extra critical probing?].

3. Aims

The aims of $L=A=N=G=U=A=G=E$ had almost nothing to do with academia, nor with its enshrining of Poetry as an autonomous (or decontextualized) institution.

Contemporary poetry had not been typically receiving official academic
attention; maybe it occasionally would get covered in journals, but usually
only as an occasion for a myopic (exclusionist) survey of the landscape,
eager to bolster itself with conservative standards derived from poetries
of the (often distant) past.

[This began to change, perhaps a decade later; by comparison, for example, in the discipline of Art History, a willingness to come to terms with more radical postmodern work came a bit quicker.]

So, rather than contesting the current academic version of a contemporary canon, we were digging beneath the past canon (of, say, twentieth-century Modernism) to probe what had been excluded & why; to shift the spotlight, to reveal some hidden procedures of sorting & comparative valuation, enmeshed in networks of power & hegemonic authority.

Some of this went on in person — the comments, the formulation of notions, the gathering of hints & urgencies & sharp questions & dreamier tugs at a response.

But it also pointed up the need, beyond either local talk or the postal system, for a chance to get more sustained critical theorizing about radical poetics into print.

[This task, of course, paralleled the political activisms centered around race, gender, empire, etc. — that sought to use new theorizing to help clear a path toward a more open, egalitarian, praxis & future. In each case, critical writing was needed, building a theoretical armature to support some resolutely independent community players as well as a drastic embrace of idiosyncrasies.]

The agenda for exploring Poetics works off of the particulars of this challenging work of our peers: to shed some light on *tactics*; not to prescribe, ahead of time, some grand strategy based on fashion or "theoretical correctness."

It meant avoiding a narrow exclusionist poetics — that typically results from a justificatory impulse. In a way, the theorizing felt retrospective: aimed at understanding how to grasp or come to terms with our own work & the work that we were already excited by (in the present & past).

It wasn't prescriptive.

It wasn't a guidebook (as we were sometimes charged by our detractors — as if we were just sitting around reading our Derrida & then immediately proceeding to work out its dictates in our poetry).

Perhaps the active mapping was at least prescriptive in its ambition or scope, in the quite expansive breadth of what we were proposing as relevant insights & sources for self-reflection.

But that's a long way from some programmatic or manifesto-like power grab.

For the far-flung "Language-centered" writers, it made sense to raise the question: What sorts of poetic activity had been (already) theorized enough to be understood, to enable the invoking of standards or clear-cut guidelines to move the writing *at least a little bit* into fresh territory.

For instance, by the late 1960s, mainstream Modernism was being dissected in undergraduate English classes; also, contemporary (often defanged) versions of it would receive enough attention in the reviewing press so that *their* standards were graspable.

But our experimentalism couldn't as comfortably rely on previously theorized poetry.

We weren't producing work that was immediately "accessible" based on existing protocols.

[The density of words — & the diversity of worlds — seemed to exceed those protocols.]

Outside of a local scene, this community of poets didn't need a unifying program, but it did seem attractive to open up discussion (beyond our locales) about the sets of distinctions & emphases & shared understandings that could serve as the basis of comparison or enthusiasm.

We needed our own forums for discussion.

But not just "debate" (often just a non-generative clash of fixities) so much as something we both enormously prized: a creative, improvisatory, wandering, self-clouding, self-twisting of thought & feeling in & on & around & about Language.

[One parallel from well outside Literature: avant-garde visual artists in the 1960s were intent on getting out from under a (watered-down Kantian) formalist aesthetic & its belle-lettristic chatterers.

They not only found inspiration from other art-making projects outside their medium (John Cage's wide-ranging impact is notable) but also clarified the significance of their own efforts by engaging in a dialogue with newer philosophical (or even scientific) modes of thought & analysis. And just as much as our homegrown/hothouse hybridizing thinking gradually morphed into respectable academic presentations in the later 1980s & '90s, the theorizing about visual art had already begun to gravitate back to philosophically well-versed nonartist critics & art historians in academia by the 1970s — (the launching of the journal *October* in New York, out of a faction from the editorial staff at *Artforum*, provides a handy example).]

Production

OK, we have these aims & interests.

[This brings up memories of labeling & packaging sessions "with a little help from our friends," of schlepping to offset printers & to the post office (facilitated by odd contingent things like James Sherry's new Segue Foundation getting nonprofit status which allowed for cheaper bulk mailings of the journal as well as of promotional matter), of shameless requests for private donations from people we did not know, of hawking of product at Small Press Book Fairs, of athletic efforts to get the hard-to-categorize journal into a few bookstores here in New York City, etc.]

[A related anecdote: both Charles & I were huge enthusiasts of Richard Foreman's vanguard theatrical works, which often involved his framing of his productions with written essay material. We thought one recent intro piece of his would work perfectly in our magazine if we could just edit it, for length, & reorganize it, which I remember doing — without asking first; then we decided to simply publish it — without getting permission. This insouciant boldness (now reminiscent of Kenneth Goldsmith's curating of his Ubu site) worked out surprisingly well: Richard lived in Soho in Manhattan & frequented Jaap Reitman's hip art-spangled bookstore which we got to carry some copies of the journal. Richard bought the issue including his edited-down piece — but, instead of being "professionally" outraged, he became a huge supporter of our project, which led to close relations & a long interview project with Charles & his introducing the "Language Writing" portion of the New York Public Theater's Language/ Noise Festival (which I helped organize) with terrific enthusiasm.]

Our frames were the postal service, the library, the public reading (where authors sold their books), the occasional bookstore taking things on spec —

(Relatedly, a year or so into our project, we also launched the
L=A=N=G=U=A=G=E Distribution Service, where we advertised a list of
out-of-print poetry books that we would make available as photocopies;
this was, revealingly, a project closely tracking our most basic commitment — to encourage readership as well as dialogue about the vast *scale* of
what was relevant for experimental literary practice in our era.)

The first issue appeared in February 1978 and went out to our initial subscribers — about 200 by the end of the first year — as well as being distributed through a few bookstores.

The first three volumes (years) of *L=A=N=G=U=A=G=E* were typed on
legal-size sheets on an IBM Selectric typewriter, sprayed to prevent smear-
ing, and then pasted into our format by our designer Susan Bee; the initial
run was offset printed, although we often produced additional copies by
photocopying.

We stopped publishing the magazine in 1981, with our fourth volume, a
perfect-bound book copublished with the Toronto magazine *Open Letter*.

In 1984, Southern Illinois University Press published an anthology, *The
L=A=N=G=U=A=G=E Book* including about half of what we had published;
this anthology has been reissued by the press.

[A side note: occasionally the question comes up about the meaning of the
equal signs in L=A=N=G=U=A=G=E. "LANGUAGE" was among a long list of
possible names Charles & I compiled in 1977 — based on conversation with
several of our friends and collaborators. As we began to settle on *Language*,
we did want something to make it stand out both from the generic word &
from the journal of the Linguistics Society of America, not to mention Jack
Spicer's great book. We knew we needed to use some kind of punctuation
or visual mark between the letters. Ultimately, we decided on the equal
signs, without explicitly discussing what those equal signs between the
letters meant. It looked good &, at the time, that was good enough. (Just
this week, I notice the appearance of a GIANT equal sign on the cover of
the new *Postmodern Reader* cover, although admittedly it is: $e = mc^2$).]

Right Now

It is tough to reimagine the 1970s.

I've characterized the project of the journal *L=A=N=G=U=A=G=E* & have tried to sketch in some of the factors that made it possible & that account for its distinctiveness.

How is it going to work, how to make it work?

We are not denizens of English departments.

We are not independently wealthy.

We are keeping close to the ground (our slowly expanding network of interested folks).

There is no bookstore sales/distribution available beyond what is going on in the small press poetry world.

Subscription sales are possible — & in our case, subscriptions developed out of the very same network that made up our list of potential contributors and potential targets of inquiry.

The parallels would perhaps be the beginnings of *Social Text* or *October*, or, better: the start-up of journals on the Left based in academic disciplines but without any institutional support: for example, the *Review of Radical Political Economy* in Economics, *Antipode* in Geography, *Insurgent Sociologist,* or *New Political Science* (the journal of the Socialist Caucus of the American Political Science Association: I was on the tiny editorial collective of this during the years I also coedited *L=A=N=G=U=A=G=E*).

Centerstage, in each of these Left journals, were endless debates over format & fanciness (often including costly compromises that would make the journal "classy" enough to get journal distribution yet would risk financial ruin if everything did not work out maximally).

Grant money might eventually come available, but the prospects were a little dim.

We took the risk-aversive route, keeping to a DIY tradition of self-production (which involved doing all the data input [we used to call it "typing"] ourselves, the proofreading ourselves [I am perhaps obsessively/narcissistically proud of there being no noticed typos during our entire four-year run: the unheard-of journal without an errata slip *ever*], doing the layout & design ourselves, doing the mailing ourselves).

It would be interesting to see what prescriptive implications for the future we could tease out of this experience:

For instance, what are the chances of a similar journal getting off the ground in today's context?

How much of its distinctiveness is a period phenomena, now long vanished?

Now, the *background* as well as what would be typical current interests are profoundly different. Literary materials (especially from the multiple "pasts" of Modernism) that could be layered into the "mix" of a new Poetry tendency seem to have become pretty thoroughly available — in print or back in print.

Before the 1970s, there had been enough *missing* in what had been available to open up some striking changes in what would seem stylistically or procedurally attractive. [Examples: lots of Stein, Zukofsky, Loy, Riding, Reznikoff, Gillespie, Khlebnikov, Shklovsky, Celan, de Campos].

These materials called for discussion as a prelude to being in any way incorporated into ongoing writing practice.

The discussion was crucial — take our feature on Stein, as a modest instance — because, in their era, these tendencies had not been given elaborate critical or theoretical treatment.

Three decades later, this is much less the case.

[A revealing exception might be the still-needed effort to make available large archives or databases of avant-garde or experimental work from the worlds of film, performance, music, visual art, activism.]

[Right now, a closer parallel might be an "undermanaged" flood of modernist poetries from outside the usual US/British canons — & the uses of language (or presentational procedures) within those heritages. Even so, arguably, the theories & concepts needed as a basis for discussion of these *global* (modernist) *languages* have already become well monitored & familiar. Also, they may have gotten entrenched enough in the academy for the poetry community to have all the guidance it needs, when it comes to grasping the significance of what is now available for influence & inspiration. More likely, some elaborate *sorting* of this now dramatically over-whelming body of poetries is called for, but not so much the independent working out of their theoretical implications. This sorting (& translating) might now self-consciously take place *in relation to* the already existing poetic tendencies with which they resonate, rather than as building blocks for drastically different new tendencies or startling new perspectives.]

At present, in what we could (very roughly) call the world of experimen-tal poetry, we have even more diversely mixed local communities — still clustered around a few large US cities & a number of university scenes, but now perhaps even more inflected by political thematics & community concerns & both art world & popular culture involvements outside the usual poetry viewfinder.

[An example today would be Vancouver, Canada: arguably, in the 1980s–90s, the site of what most closely resembled a "second generation" Lan-guage Writing scene, now caught up in much more locally particularized social & political involvements in the struggles against globalizing "neo-liberalism."]

[Also, today we have forms of so-called conceptual "poetry" or writing praxis that oppose (or claim to transcend, or leave in the dust) not only mainstream neoclassicism & workshop poetry, but also earlier radical Modernism as well as the New American Poetry and even the Language project as they negotiate a changing techno landscape as well as art world opportunities.]

Another issue is today's greater dangers of exclusiveness & exclusion, along with the reinforcing (or reification) or group identity.

Likely this occurred *less* within an older small press poetry world made more pluralistic by its self-management (compared to a newer poetry world made more hierarchical either by the dominance of mainstream publishers & their journalistic apparatus — or, now, by a scholarly estab-lishment in today's English departments).

[Maybe the letter hierarchy feels exclusionist to, for example, today's "workshop poets" compared to today's so-called Language Poets; & per-haps *their* exclusion becomes a breeding ground for hostility to the (now, academic) success stories, in a twist or reversal from the anti-academicism of the New American Poetry (which did, also, promote their group solidarity). One parallel, perhaps, for the so-called Language Writers would be a feeling of exclusion from the dominant practices of creative writing workshops, which have become so enormously more powerful since the early 1980s when $L=A=N=G=U=A=G=E$ finished its run.]

Also, the small press poetry world has by now ceded much of its sovereignty or self-governance to the English departments (at least in the US), with both their helpful institutional support & their unhelpful domesticating conservatism operating as an outside filtering device.

Plus the "Theory Boom" (along with its highly politically charged agenda) has largely subsided.

The power of the Creative Writing Programs & of so-called Workshop Poetry has increased — with one notable effect: a reduction in the felt need for conceptualizing the writing of poetry in either historical or theoretical terms, in fact within any framework much beyond personal self-expression or credentialing.

Meanwhile we hear all about the end of the book, or of taken-for-granted literacy, the decline in enthusiasm for challenging reading material, the hand-wringing about the lost era of sustained & focused attentiveness by today's youth, etc.

The frame now for a serious formatting of poetic inquiry would be different.

It would be much less that of the library, the bookstore, the public reading, the extensive archive of private correspondence.

Instead, it would now very largely be the Internet — that wild, ever-expanding data set.

The geographically located "scene," & the public reading as a privileged site where a community could take shape around a particular mode of writing: these are pre-web notions.

Now, given the flood of information, for an adventure in Poetics, you'd need more than an informal community organized through the mail (along with two or three face-to-face scenes); you'd need full-scale reliance on the social networking potentials of the net &/or on "official" institutional support.

So, it's not coincidental that these alternatives track pretty well with the trajectories of the hugest (& most ambitious) success stories of recent years on the US experimental poetry scene: the SUNY Buffalo Poetics Program, with its Electronic Poetry Center Listserv & website, the huge archives at PennSound, UbuWeb, Eclipse, not to mention vibrant blogs, websites, collective autobiography projects & ambitiously crafted individual "careers" taking full advantage of today's dramatically transformed media/tech landscape.

Spearheaded by some of the most active players in the communities that paid attention to so-called Language Poetry (& to *L=A=N=G=U=A=G=E*) those parallel developments keep opening up a future for our particular story.

The centrifugal pulls continue.

The radicalism continues.

Publishing Is Personal

REBECCA WOLFF

Once an editor rejected a poem of mine from a small but influential magazine with a page-long typed note suggesting I rid the poem of the pronoun "I" and try again. I got mad at him and started a magazine instead in which I made room for all the personal pronouns and their endless efficacy: "I" is a metaphor for "you." That's how I get by.

I can't talk about *anything* without talking about myself.

Lately money is all anyone talks about. I've been waiting a long time to talk about money. Money is a metaphor for ectoplasm.

So how do you like my titular riff on that old saw about how the personal is political? From this it follows logically that since publishing is personal, and the personal, political, then publishing is political. The imagined opposition to such airtightness would say no, publishing is impersonal. Publishing is business, is industry, is making books and books are, ultimately, for sale. Publishing is making things to sell. Making things to sell is impersonal. The impersonal is.

We here all know what it means to read. It is the opposite of writing. It is an agreeable hole we throw ourselves down to make contact with the Others. When we read we read alone but in the activity of neurologically forgetting where we are and who we are we become intertextually riven, hatched, attached. I lose consciousness when I read, except for that intramural publishing consciousness which is acquisitiveness.

I explain my son's autism to my son by metaphor: I tell him we are each traveling in a bubble—consciousness, selfhood, fortunate or unfortunate—and that our efforts as humans are all to roll our bubbles up to others' bubbles and bounce against them. But we are each fixed in our centrality inside our bubbles by mysterious forces no one can satisfactorily explain no matter how hard they try.[1] It's a bit like bumper cars but more concentric—like a hamster in a see-through plastic ball, whose

1. Unless it's all capitalism.

perpetual motion fixes itself. I tell my son that people with autism have bigger bubbles than most other people—those with severe autism have huge bubbles, daunting distances to navigate, while someone like him has a bubble that is just a bit larger than the average—and that there is more space between "him" inside his bubble and the outside of his own bubble, more space that he has to trouble, encounter, be mediated by, be translated into, in his effort to encounter the outside of another bubble. I tell him all this while he sits in my lap in the cushy chair in the corner of my kitchen in the house I recently bought with money my parents gave me, where I live with him and his sister, my daughter, but only half the time because they live with their dad the other half. Their dad with whom I parted because I found true love, and afterward could not truthfully return to the other kind. It's been difficult, the transition out of married life, family life, financial and partnered and living arrangements, but in the end of that story I find myself brilliantly realized and activated, and I would recommend it to anyone, the leaving and the finding. I would recommend it; I would publish it.

A certain abjection, part and parcel with ejection from the life that I had known in which my security depended in large part on the efforts of another, was allayed by the application of a large deposit into my bank account by my parents, who are, in my book, rich, though they worked, and still work, as property managers, for their money and live carefully so as to maintain that money, and though they violently reject the label. To someone of their generation—born in the mid 1930s—a "rich" person is one who does not, did not, work for their money; does not need to make careful decisions. The question of whether I, Rebecca Wolff, am personally "rich," has troubled my identity as a publisher from the start. When that trouble would have started if I had never started an independent press; at what point I ought to have, would have, might have turned the inward gaze on my outer resources ... these are luxurious questions!

Over the years I have been given a lot of money by some very rich people in support of my publishing activities. I mean, *Fence* has been given a lot of money in support of *Fence*'s activities. (*Fence* is a metaphor for me.) Historically, those who found literary journals and literary presses are enabled to do so by the lack of limitation of the possibilities they have heretofore known. They have not been told *no* by the world very often, and so the financial prohibitions of literary publishing—this perplexing situation of making invisible art objects via mass production, making art out of such prosaic things as word-objects and letter-objects and parts of speech, material everyone knows how to use just like toddlers make splatter paintings and toilets make examples and color is *everywhere*—are not prohibitive. They are fun obstacles to surmount with the writing of sweet, sweet checks. I would think it would be very fun to be rich in that situation in which one's peerless passion for art is matched only by one's ability to pay. Fun for everyone.

This has never been my situation. But I once had the fortune (great, good ,or mis-) to be paying $400 a month for a rent-stabilized apartment on Lower Fifth Avenue in New York City, an address so posh, ceilings so high, that sans any transparency regarding my actual financial details it signified exactly the situation in which most would expect to find a literary publisher. George Plimpton, Jean Stein, James Laughlin, Gertrude Stein, family *money-money-money*. My parents were the building's managers, and they rented me an apartment. I made my rent temping in offices. Nonetheless my address and my publishing moxie presented a total package to those who cared to check out my package.

It has attracted certain fortune and I'm sure it has made it harder for me to attract certain other fortunes. Money likes money, but money only likes money that knows how money lives, what it eats and what it drinks and how it talks and walks. I'm rich, but only by comparison and because I accept the label because it is closer to the truth than to say I'm not. I don't live like a rich person—I do my own laundry and I clean my own house and I can't afford much child care and I must not lose my job. However, before my marriage my parents purchased every used car I ever drove into the ground. They paid off my student loans the day I graduated. I accrue debt like a regular person but I shake it like a rich person. When my parents pass on they will leave me half of whatever remains and I will be, in my book, rich.

That is my working definition, in this current cultural context, of a rich person: One who has certain assurances.

When I want to publish a book, or a poem or story or text in this magazine, *Fence*, it is because I am pleased by that writing in a special way that has to do with its lack of compromise with the mysterious forces.[2] The writing is flagrant and defensive and provoked and responsive. Despondent and indicative.[3] I am pleased by it and I want to share, to spread, to not shut up about it but to promulgate and propagate its trails and implications, make indelible the inscription of the conditions that made it possible for that writing to take place. But why do I figure myself in that place of power? Who do I think I am? Who died and left me a publishing empire? Who jokes about the word "empire" anymore? Not me.

Who takes this on, this honor, this called-out role in the roll call: Will

2. I guess the same ones. But it is mysterious.
3. John Lennon: "You can indicate anything you see—'I dig a pony.'"

you be the one to identify and select and fashion a relevancy? Will you juxtapose and proximate and associate freely within a hierarchy of effort? A recent poem, "Kill List," by a man with the name Josef Kaplan, seems to tabulate some modern poets—living ones, all within the age range of the contemporaneous, twenty-five to sixty-five or so—and say whether they are "rich" or "comfortable." Why he ignores the poor, the indigent poets is beyond me, but it would seem to indicate that the poem is attempting in some super-crude way to say something about the effects of privilege on contemporary poetry. Some of the poets on the list might self-identify as members of the avant-garde; most are well within the rims of the cocktail *Fence* has had a good hand in muddling. One thing this poem is especially good at is gesturing wildly at a bunch of categories, or aptitudes for categorizing, or kinetic categorization—it just basically begs a whole lot of questions. And you know beggars can be choosers.

Fence has never had much to say about an avant-garde, except to posit by example that the terms of any writing are worth examining, including those of any self-described avant-gardist—how fantastic and laudatory it seems to me now (when it used to seem misguided and comical) to think that with one's attitude toward text production one is advancing at the forefront of indispensable dispute, furthering a cause worth dying for. I hope I understand the potentialities of an artist's—anyone's—commitment to an idea: it can be, or seem, worth dying for. It should be that all of us would be willing to die—to die on the page or to advance on enemy ideas with intent to kill—to make things better than they are for others. For the greater good, a poet must not feel unequipped, or helpless; must not learn more than the average helplessness.

The closest I come as an editor to invoking a concept of an avant-garde is to declare, when provoked—usually in the context of trying to explain to a lay person (and to declare that there is such a thing as a lay person when it comes to poetry is actually to include a term within a definition of that term) why poetry is so hard to fund—that *Fence* is constructed in part to support the continued production of writing that furthers the art form. I used to say "exigency," by which I meant to indicate the aura around the words that Emily Dickinson saw and I see too, or I see one too. But what is that aura composed of after all but right response to material conditions? Response to oppressors, to pleasures, to impulses and sensory occasions and the precedents no one else could imagine. Fat, young woman in shorts prone on an Amtrak seat, midafternoon, foot rapidly jigging—she might have left her children behind this morning in Canada. That might be why she cannot stay upright—she was up at dawn to drop them off at her mum's. *Farewell.* I'll send money home.

It so happens that I have made assumptions, assumed positions, and been said yes to, and worked hard to put myself in a position to have the privilege to publish: to give people power. Power to the people to further the art form. It is in my power to bestow power, to share it. But first I had to get it for myself. It so happens that jobs and money and security and leverage and influence and primacy come to those who publish, the more they publish, or are published. To publish: The verb is transitive sometimes and I think only in academia is it not. I publish writing by writers. Writers are "published"; scholars "publish."

Publishing is political, but I did not think so at first. I did not know that. I did not know that everything was within material reality. I had not read or been exposed to Marxist thought. Or I had but I hadn't grasped that political thought stood out in importance from any of the other thought I had been exposed to, the personal thought, the Buddhism or Existentialism or Decadence or what have you, a level playing field. I knew publishing as a business, by virtue of its producing a product. I followed a line of reasoning which one often encounters as an obstacle to efforts at finding donors to give money to organizations whose primary purpose is publishing books, the line that is followed by those who do not see that publishers who specifically choose to publish what I call, archly and demurely and perhaps ineffectively "very contemporary writing," are committing themselves to an unpalatable art form, just as surely as are those whose charitable efforts are to present video art or movement art or performance art or to the preservation of significant artifacts of those arts.

One very rich person came my way a few years ago, a man who had amassed a quantity of wealth over a long period, starting very young. He was about my age. He was a trustee of a museum in London. He bought up collections of rare editions and Philip Guston paintings and floor-through apartments. He had wanted to buy a publishing house but after meeting me at lunch one day—this is really how it happened—he shook my hand and offered to instead become *Fence*'s "publisher." We had never had one before; I had always just called myself that even though usually the title implies a personal financial accountability I could never have taken on.

I thought the first thing we should do with our new relationship was to publish, in *Fence*, a short interview between me and him in which he would speak frankly to me about what it is like to wield such an instrument as great, massive wealth. A financial instrument. What is it like to be a patron of the arts, specifically, to be in the position of materially enabling or empowering or affirming the creative work being done in the world by artists and writers? Just what on earth does that feel like? Aside from: So Much Fun.

He didn't want to talk about it. By comparison.

He wanted *Fence* to have more subscribers, a quantifiable goal, and he wanted *Fence* to have a "higher profile"—an unquantifiable, yet related goal. I want *Fence* to have more readers. It is all for the writers. I'm a writer too. I'm a hot mess. I keep my head under water sometimes.

To talk about *Fence*'s money is to speak of my money. Not exactly a power trip. Not exactly a power grab. And it doesn't have to be that way: for a long time I insisted on the distancing, the extraction of my personal life from that equation. I took pride in, and trumpeted, even in grant applications, my professionalism. Once or twice I've lost an author to another press during moments when my personal life, including my obstreperous, imperious, autistic son who cannot get along with anyone for more than forty-five minutes, was so compelling and needy that I could not get a book out when I said I would, could not spare a minute for an author on the telephone—but on the whole I have made a convincing case for my ability to depersonalize or make impersonal the hours of my days. And in fact I used to sneer at publishers who could not get with that program, who could not make the books come out on time, could not work within the structures of the larger publishing world, the deadlines and catalogs and advance promotional metadata. To publish professionally necessitates a work ethic that does not afford itself the luxury of noncompliance. As we are laborers.

And even now to say that *Fence c'est moi* is to collapse the fragile material structures—tents and lean-tos and sukkahs—that allow me to seek out donations and provide tax exemptions to those who make them, the legal status as a corporation that makes it impossible for an angry contributor to sue me, personally: It's a tax shelter, *Fence*. By virtue of that status I seek tax-exempt donations.

This Being 2015

ANDER MONSON

This being 2015 and the age of the much-ballyhooed death of print, I am wondering whether I should be pontificating on whether or not the print journal is dying or, worse, according to the many of us that still love the feel of a printed book or magazine in our hands, dead. I am wondering if I should be writing this in Macromedia's (now Adobe's) Dreamweaver, the software used for composition and design for the magazine *DIAGRAM* (TheDiagram.com) that I founded in 2000 and continue to edit and design. I am not, partly because that software is not well suited to composition of longer pieces of prose, and also, this being written for the paper page, it seems more suitable to use software designed to compose for that page. I'm not particularly interested in poking the dead-horse space of whether or not the book is dead (it's not; don't worry; calm down everyone; the book is a durable technology). The idea of the literary magazine—what it contains, where it's found, how it's composed, published, distributed, and read—is certainly recalibrating for the age of the electron and instant gratification. Fifteen years ago you couldn't find a handful of good literary journals publishing original content online. Now it seems that, particularly for poetry, though increasingly so for prose, too, the most exciting magazines are publishing online, and I am happy to celebrate *DIAGRAM's* fifteenth year of publication.

In 2000, my one-year tenure as editor of *Black Warrior Review*, the University of Alabama's graduate-student-run literary magazine, run out of a couple of offices on the third floor of Manly Hall in Tuscaloosa, Alabama, ended, and I wasn't sure what to do next. *Black Warrior Review*, named not as a nod to the Black Power movement but to Chief Tuscaloosa, who was killed, and his body dumped, in the Black Warrior River in the city that still bears his name, was an education in running a large organization of a journal, the oldest continuously published student-run literary journal in the nation, as the literature we distributed to potential subscribers and donors constantly reminded us.

Distribution is part of the problem, as any literary journal editor will quickly tell you. How to get what you're sure is your greatness to the readers who will love it? Literature is a slow thing, often designed for the turn of centuries rather than the monthly rotation of mass-market magazines on bookstore shelves. The age of the Internet has coincided with the downturn of the bookstore shelves, too, and even before that was obvious to most of us, dealing with distributors who delivered copies of *BWR* to bookstores was its own logistical nightmare. Editing, designing, and printing the artifact was a pleasure, but trying to find our way to readers was trickier. In 1999 or thereabouts, *BWR* joined the space of Web Del Sol (WebDelSol.com), a loose bazaar-style network of many literary journals and readers. The next year, under my editorship, we started debuting exclusive, online-only content via the *Warrior Web* (*WW*), our online arm. We published two issues of the *WW* before I handed the editorship of both *BWR* and *WW* over to the next student editor, who promptly scuttled the project. This made obvious one of the many downsides of publishing literature online, that one day it might exist and find thousands of readers nationally and internationally, and the next, it might be gone, without so much as stacks of back issues or remainder copies in distant readers' hands to attest to its existence.

This was exactly what the old guard suspected, many of whom were lodged in academic programs that refused to recognize an online journal as a legitimate venue for the publication of serious—meaning lasting, long-term—work. That publishing online wasn't like publishing at all. It certainly didn't count as a publication toward tenure, except at a few forward-thinking universities. The National Endowment for the Arts (NEA) then refused to count online publications as qualifying publications for their yearly coveted grants in literature. And certainly no yearly anthology, the *Best American* series, the Pushcart, or the O. Henry Prize, would include work published in such a transient space. It would be like anthologizing poems written on dry-erase boards.

That year in the *BWR* office I had access to copies of many of the literary magazines published each year in America, particularly the ones safely ensconced in and supported by creative writing graduate programs, which seemed to constitute the majority of the prestigious and serious literary magazines still extant. I admired journals like the independent *Fence* and University of Massachusetts's *Jubilat* both for what they published as well as how they published it. Part of what made magazines like this appealing and attractive, and differentiated them from the *Georgia Review*s of the world, was their design sense, which created a different sort of reader experience. Instead of staid—or classical, if you prefer— typography and wide margins constraining fields of prose and poetry unbroken by columns or pull quotes or whatever, a magazine like the great and now-defunct *Chain*, edited by Jena Osman and Juliana Spahr, suggested that you might have to rotate pages to read the text, that you could expect an art object, forward-thinking design mirroring edgier content.

At that time there were still only a very few literary publications of any sort publishing original work online, though the Internet was nearly a decade old. Some magazines popped up on personal websites, on Angelfire .com or Geocities.com pages that spawned pop-up windows with flashing text and ads. A few academic journals had slight websites with long, unmemorable URLs buried deep inside their universities' digital nests. Some editors published themselves or didn't bother to respond to submissions. Some forgot to renew their domain names and had them poached.

Not that the professionalism of a literary magazine is the only benchmark by which we might measure its interest or significance, but that lack of professionalism was one thing among others—transience, bad design, poor editorial standards, lax response times, wack brand, no vision—that kept most of the few all-online publications from being recognized as worth a writer's or a reader's time.

Happily there were a few great online journals. One was *Born Magazine* (BornMagazine.com), which retired (their words) in 2011; it used the web to pair artists and authors and create multimedia works that would never have been possible outside of digital spaces. There were electronic mixed media collages, sound art, interactive digital artworks, rhizome.org, *Poems That Go*. Most of the theorists who studied and talked about electronic literature still believed that hypertext was the future. Most of the great literary sites online bordered the art world and privileged design.

The idea for the magazine—and I prefer to call *DIAGRAM* a magazine, or sometimes a journal, when I am trying to impress someone—was born out of a collection of old dictionaries that I was in the habit of collecting, partly for the quality of the illustrations. At the time I had been taking a letterpress printing class, studying classical typography and the history of letterforms and alphabets, and spending time in the special collections section of the university libraries that held a large collection of amazing artist books. I had been collecting these dictionaries for reasons I could not articulate. I'd buy them in pleasantly ramshackle stores like America's Thrift Store (née Alabama Thrift Store), fascinated by the sheer physicality of both store and book. I loved—and still do—the dictionaries' bulk, their weight, the moldering paper smell of their pages, but mostly I loved the illustrations for their own intrinsic value. The illustrations, occasionally engravings or etchings, would have involved substantially more work to make than the quick scans in the newest *Webster's*. What struck me about the best of them was what happened when you took them out of context. I couldn't draw or make any real sort of worthwhile visual art: that much had been obvious for some time as I dodged art classes. But I could scan images. I used a couple scanned diagrams and images from these dictionaries in a failed poem.

I started buying other old books with odd images and diagrams: engine repair manuals, amateur radio guides with schematics for building your own ham radio kits, outdated biology and medical textbooks. All this stuff—all these lovely, studied drawings and diagrams—were caught in the old media of defunct publishers, outdated editions, factual errors, pages eroding in landfills. This was awful. This was also great. Quickly I realized I couldn't keep everything, and I'd have to cut them up, keep the images and the indices, which I found lovely but wasn't sure why. My girlfriend, then fiancée, then wife cocked her eyebrows at this accruing, stinking mess of books that bowed the cheap pressed wood shelves we could then afford. Every time we went shopping, there were more coming back with us. Buying old books was in some ways a practical choice: we also bought and used old furniture, usually perfectly good, that our cats would tear up with glee. We bought other books online and sold them used on websites like Half.com and the early eBay. Some months we made rent reselling found books. But my collection got bigger and odder, even as I trimmed out the pages that didn't interest me, and scanned the remainder.

I liked the feeling of having these images digitally, infinitely manipulable, easily deployed in whatever text or page or space I wanted. The best images took on their own importance when decontextualized. No longer were they subservient to the prose they accompanied or were meant to illustrate. No longer aperitifs, the images could become entrées. This was pretty cool. Several of them attempted, improbably and spectacularly, to diagram or depict things that were seemingly beyond diagramming or depiction. The structures of guilt. The quantification of how much clothing you wore in units of clo (1.0 clo was a fully dressed individual in coat and hat; 0.2 clo was a woman in her underwear). They were funny. They were strange. Disturbing. Beautiful. Tragic. They were great. This was what literature does too, I thought. In that huge stack of literary magazines that I looked through weekly in the *BWR* office, I saw only a few publications that published the sort of work I was writing, that I was reading, that I believed in and wanted to read: work that spanned or elided genre boundaries or was ambitiously hybrid, work that included images or design elements, or actively pursued strangeness. *Chain* published a lot of concrete poetry, which wasn't really my thing, but which often made interesting moves. *3rd Bed* came out around then, publishing good work, and is now long since defunct. *Quarter After Eight* published some great prose, but without any real sense of apparent design or direction. But I could count on one hand the journals that were doing what I thought of as the important work of publishing important and ambitious work.

Of course in retrospect there were probably plenty of places that published these works; I just didn't know of them. It's for the best. Editors of journals have to start from a place of egotism served with a side of myopia. My taste was self-evidently better than the taste of the staff at *BWR*, I assured myself. My taste was obviously superior to other editors of other established magazines and their established writers. It was stupid, but it was useful. If you don't think you bring something new to the world, why bother doing anything at all, much less putting the time and effort into founding a literary magazine? And once it's founded, how do you keep it going, especially without a budget?

So I started a journal. Or actually I bought a uniform resource locator (the long way of saying URL, one of many gloss words that disguise what exactly the Internet consisted—and still consists of—complicated systems of representing and connecting amorphous sets of data, which require methods of mapping language to numbers in order to locate the millions on millions of resources accessible online), TheDiagram.com. The journal would be named *DIAGRAM*, though Diagram.com was unavailable. I thought briefly about Diagrammatic.net, but the .net seemed obscure. (To this day, *DIAGRAM* is often referred to as *The Diagram*, which continues to irk me: I understand the logic, but the journal's name is and always has been *DIAGRAM*, no "the," all caps.) I designed a couple pages, using scanned and found images from my collection. We would republish schematics along with original writing and art, six issues a year, all online.

I called Heidi Gotz, a poet friend of mine who was actually in my second writing workshop ever, who I remember being critiqued for her "virtuoso" prose. I asked her if she wanted to be the poetry editor of an online journal. She said sure, count her in. She had some questions about rights, working at the time as a permissions editor at a textbook publisher. We talked through it and through *DIAGRAM*'s identity, what it would be, what it could be. It seemed like it was a good enough idea. Another friend from Knox, Steve Franklin, said yes when asked to serve as fiction editor. He would only stay with us for a couple issues, sadly. Maybe a year. In the absence of being able to connect physically with staff, to see them more than periodically, it is difficult to keep people connected and on task, to keep them involved in the journal as much as they need to be. Editors have lives. Families. Jobs. Having no revenue stream for *DIAGRAM*, we aren't paid. The work keeps coming. We get flamed by pissed writers. Is it worth it to keep going? Sometimes it seems like it's not. For Steve, it wasn't. For the rest of us, it is, for our own reasons. Another comrade from graduate school, Lauren Slaughter, took over as fiction editor. Heidi continues on as co-poetry-editor. And now our staff's expanded, involving former exemplary students and writers and friends, to a sizeable, if relatively autonomous (we don't do much micromanaging—one secret to keeping things going without too much friction) fifteen active editors.

Design is a big part of what makes *DIAGRAM*. The advent of desktop publishing software and scanning technology, along with software like Dreamweaver and Photoshop, had made it far easier and cheaper to design, produce, and print nearly anything on paper, or on the Internet, than was possible before. The cost of producing print magazines (*BWR* had a yearly budget in excess of $50,000) was obviously a factor. I did not have the money required to produce a print magazine that would be as beautiful of a print object that I felt it had to be. But I could design something for the web that could echo some of the aesthetic criteria that I loved in print, and produce and publish it myself, quickly, professionally, and send it almost anywhere as close to instantaneously as the protocols of TCP/IP, HTTP, and the technologies of the networks that carry and switch packets of data allow.

We did the first issue quickly, working mostly from solicited work. I started a small press, New Michigan Press, at the same time, and we advertised a chapbook contest, offering $500 for the winner and publication. NMP remains the official publisher of *DIAGRAM*, and continues printing chapbooks and limited edition broadsides, along with periodic *DIAGRAM* print anthologies.

Don't get me wrong. I love the feel of books. The continuing utility of that technology is amazing, and will surely endure for another millennium if human culture does, but, like many of my friends and contemporaries, I am a product of a culture rapidly becoming addicted to quickness. Instant gratification and linkability, networkedness, the feeling of now, of liking and being liked: these were what the Internet and its accompanying culture had to offer us. The web felt like a particularly good medium for the short lyric—a pause to read and consider in the clicking and surfing. A bite. A substantial bite, certainly, and one that you can hold on to for a long time, but a small thing. What is a poem, I wondered, but a bit of the world, a moment taken out of context?

In the last decade it has become obvious to everyone that publishing has been changing. The ways readers might find their way to the work we published in literary journals were shifting, often online. Yearly published indices seemed impossibly old-fashioned compared to search and the near-instant gratification that the web offered. Some journals have moved to even quicker gratification, publishing original work irregularly if quickly, using blog software and templates, or tweeting 140-character poems daily. Speed was important, but not everything. After all, publishing takes time. Even online publishing, if you want to do it right, takes time. Publishing isn't providing content. Publishing is an intellectual and emotional conversation, a slog through constantly shifting aesthetic criteria, hoping with every individual submission (and we get thousands every year, as do many journals) to be wowed from the first line. And we needed to compete with other great journals to get the submissions we wanted. We solicited some. We considered simultaneous submissions; even as many print journals frowned on the practice, simultaneous submissions seemed an inevitable consequence to us. From the beginning *DIAGRAM* considered and encouraged online submissions (though we also continue to read hard copy if writers prefer it). We advertised (and continue to advertise) that we try to respond to all submissions within a month. We sent print contracts for accepted work. We had a masthead. We began a rigid publication schedule—six issues a year, every other month. We had an ISSN. We were indexed by the *American Humanities Index*. We sent prepublication galleys to authors. We were listed in *Poet's Market*, *Short Story Writer's Market*. We joined the Council of Literary Magazines and Presses. We were nominated for the Pushcart Prize and for the yearly prize anthologies. We aspired to be as stable as an online journal could be—certainly much more stable than many print journals that have disappeared into archive and memory. We've been here fifteen years. We aren't going anywhere.

DIAGRAM has persisted, I think, because of its visual and textual identity: it is recognizable and fairly stable in both design and content. Most issues use black and red on white, print-page-like backgrounds. The typography is fairly conservative (at least until all web browsers can do advanced typography, classic and simple makes the most sense to us), and jives well with the images we present. All issues have a diagram or schematic (or sometimes just an image) as their table of contents. There aren't a lot of moving parts. We only rarely use Javascript, Flash, or complicated programming. Our issues include diagrams—mostly those found by myself or our staff, but increasingly writers and artists have submitted found or original schematics. But much of the reason *DIAGRAM* has persisted is because of my own obsessions, with the out-of-print books and defunct magazines that keep finding their way to me, sometimes from friends, other times from readers in Australia or San Francisco or Japan who find something great and send it our way. Much of the reason we're still here is because there are many like-minded readers out there, evidently, who find what we do as beautiful as we do.

In the age of everything shiftable and editable on the web, which is to say in the age of impatience and impermanence, it's worth thinking about the role of art—and in particular, literature—and what it means to publish a poem or a story in a journal that happens to be distributed via the Internet.

A week ago I got an e-mail from a contributor asking if we'd be willing to change a word in a poem we published six years ago. I wrote to tell him, nicely, that we would not. Admittedly we are an online journal, infinitely editable, and it would be technologically trivial to make the edit and be done with it. We'd just have to tweak some HTML, upload it to the main site and the mirror, and it would be done. But that devalues the idea and the act of publishing, and this is how an online publication is different than blogging or self-publishing: publication is an overt act of making one's work public. By publishing a poem, you give up control (mostly) over how it's presented, how it's published. You give up the right of continuing to make changes to it—at least in the place it's published. In publication, writers become authors, public figures with all of the legal considerations that accompany that. Though *DIAGRAM* is not properly an artifact as a book is, and if you were to unplug everything, *DIAGRAM* wouldn't exist except as data on hard drives and in browser caches or in printouts for those readers who print out the journal to read and keep it, we consider the journal to be a stable, digital object. From the beginning we thought it important to acquire first North American serial rights, the same rights the *New Yorker* would acquire. This was clearly confusing for some writers who assumed that they could submit work for reprinting. Because we are online, for the first five years we took pains to make clear that an online journal was in every way as material, as real, as durable, as professional, as much an art object, as any print journal. The medium of the journal— whether dried pulp or electrons—is immaterial. We sent duplicate print contracts that required a signature. In fact we didn't print the contracts on ordinary paper but on laid paper, or stiff, 100 percent cotton archival paper with watermarks. We were overly material. We wanted to be felt. The materiality of the contract was meant to echo the apparent material-ity of the digital page. It was something you could hold on to. It said that *DIAGRAM* is a formal space. A permanent space. A stable one. We don't just print: we publish.

To clarify, we make edits after the fact to correct typos or errors (or if legally compelled for some reason; this hasn't happened yet but I can imagine the possibility). This is one of the pleasures of electronic publica-tion, after all. At an author's request, we will occasionally edit bios and the notes writers write on their work. Later, we'll remove e-mail addresses— those nice little feedback loops that we encourage authors to provide, so that they can get the quick pleasure of receiving an appreciative e-mail—at the author's request. But those texts are ancillary. They're incidental to the art (though I can think of a few times when the notes on the pieces or the bios were part of the artwork or art act—and this changes the calculus). My feeling is that when we publish a work of art we are making a contract not just with the writer, but with readers, present and future, that we will continue to maintain the work we publish in perpetuity. This is what a journal does: it persists. It makes official, public. It acts as a record. It must be stable.

And it is stable—cached in many places online and in thousands of readers' browsers. It is indexed. It is archived. It is printed off and read over coffee (as we're told periodically by those who prefer to be able to spill drinks on their reading).

A couple years in, because of our love for the book artifact, we produced the first of our occasional print anthologies for the New Michigan Press. These anthologies—there are four, including a playable tenth anniversary deck of poker cards—generally collect our favorite works from a couple years of *DIAGRAM* online, the texts that work best in a print form, add new found schematics from the archive, and are published as books using digital print-on-demand technology. This technology is increasingly difficult to tell from offset printing. As anyone invested in publishing books will tell you, the ability to print on demand is changing publishing, too, especially for smaller publishers. University presses increasingly keep their backlists in print this way, and I'm sure this is going to be the future of the backlist.

Return to 2015. *DIAGRAM* is in its fifteenth year of publication. This decade has witnessed every major literary journal rethinking their approach to the web. Nearly all accept online submissions. All have websites. Quite a few have blogs, Twitter feeds, Tumblrs, Pinterests, and whatever else. Most publish at least excerpts from the print magazine on their site. Many, like *AGNI* or *McSweeney's*, publish some work exclusively online. Online publications have found their way into *Best American Poetry*. *DIAGRAM* has had Notable Essays in *Best American Essays*. Clearly people are paying attention to this work online. The feedback loop is fast and powerful. You publish, people read, then they let you know what they like. Many print journals are increasingly well designed and produced, taking advantage of the book as object. They're branded. They're made over. There are lessons to be drawn here from the music world: vinyl's resurgence in response to the mp3 and the obviation of the CD is due in large part to the physical— and social—experience that a record can offer that the mp3 (and the CD, always a substandard artifact) cannot. Some journals have or are apps for Android or iPhone. Twitter feeds. Blogs. They use social media. In the age of the aggregators it's sometimes hard to tell what a journal is at all. All this is to the good. I'm glad to have so many great places to read, listen to, send, and otherwise experience works of literature and art. I'm glad to see our hit total for a year of *DIAGRAM* crest above four million. I'm sure other online journals are doing well too. The university-supported print journals are starting to see their budgets cut, or in some cases, go to zero. They're having to rethink their commitment to print. Some will cease publishing. Others, like *TriQuarterly*, have transitioned well to the web. Maybe others will become, like *McSweeney's*, even more rarified experimental print objects. Who knows what's next? I don't.

DIAGRAM feels old. It's always felt old, though. It's embraced the old, and tried to recontextualize it in the new, to offer lovely things in new packages to new readers. But it hasn't deviated from what I'm sure is at the heart of every literary enterprise: a desire to publish work that excites us and that we think might otherwise not get published. Most of what we do is grounded in the old: black and red on white. Words on a sort of paper, or at any rate, a sort of page. For future editors of future journals, I'd leave off by briefly noting that a journal is—and always has been— mostly just a gathering of the like-minded in our pages and in our pixels and the place in which they meet, as contributors and editors and coders and readers and haters, whether gathered in a room and reading furiously or e-mailing twice a year to checking in bimonthly as we punctuate the increasing frenzy of our lives with a poem or an essay. The Internet may not have a memory exactly but we do. And we remember all of you.

Part 4:
The University
Magazine

War of the Words: Fighting for a Journal and a Genre

LEE GUTKIND

Hard to imagine, but there was a time when most writers were not affiliated with universities. They were much more a part of the world—driving taxis, selling insurance, teaching high school, thinking that you had to experience life in order to write about it. (Or the more fortunate few were living on trust funds or the good graces and hard labor of spouses.) But the establishment and growing popularity of creative writing programs in the 1980s and 1990s became a lure and a safe haven; why struggle for health insurance and a certain amount of praise and prominence? Teach the craft and huddle under the protective academic umbrella where young wannabes idolized you, for as long as possible.

I don't mean to sound condescending here regarding English departments and the academy; this is the road I followed in my life and it has served me well. Selling shoes and driving a truck during the day and subsequently creating advertising and public relations campaigns, while writing a novel at night while in my twenties, was not an easy life. I tried it for a half dozen years, and I learned about people and the worlds they inhabited, and that strengthened my writing and my passion to make a mark in the world.

But I do wonder if I would be writing this today—and perhaps not writing at all—if it wasn't for the support of the University of Pittsburgh specifically and the academy generally. Not that I appreciated everything about life in the hallowed halls of ivy, but it made being a writer easier. It gave you a platform, a home base and an audience to try out ideas on—and colleagues to drink beer with, smoke dope, and cheat on wives and girlfriends. But it was also very difficult to be a part of this world, especially as an outsider. These guys could play rough, and do it in such a subtle but debilitating way, that a guy like me, coming from the wrong side of the tracks—no PhD, no academic pedigree—could be ruthlessly frozen out.

This is an excerpt from Lee Gutkind's memoir in progress, *Creative Nonfiction: The Fine Art of Literary Fist-Fighting*.

It's been said many times before and is so unfortunately true of faculty members in English departments: Never have so many fought so hard to achieve so little.

As far back as the early 1970s, the debate about teaching creative writing—and especially creative nonfiction (then the "new journalism") writing—was intense, mean, and often nonsensical. I remember once, at an English Department faculty meeting, the then editor of the university newspaper, *Pitt News*, went to see the department chair, requesting that the department offer a new journalism course. Back then I was teaching part-time an expository writing course—but in this guise I was introducing Tom Wolfe, Gay Talese, Hunter Thompson, et al.—and the students, especially from the student newspaper, were turned on. The idea of immersion got them going, for one thing, experiencing life and then using fiction techniques—dialogue, flashback, etc.—to make their work cinematic. They wanted more.

So the editor—his name was Bill Gormley and today he is an author and professor of public policy at Georgetown University—made an appointment with Walter Evert, the chair of the department back then and proposed something like the "Basic New Journalism 101" that I would teach. It was actually what I was already doing in secret, but this would allow me to come clean and could lead to other nonfiction courses that were more advanced, specialized, and challenging. Evert explained that he lacked the authority to approve, let alone encourage, such a course so out of the mainstream of contemporary literature. But in the spirit of free speech and openness reflected in the early 1970s, he would allow Gormley to make a presentation to the faculty at its next meeting. This was long before the department authorized a creative writing program.

I will never forget the scene. Gormley was a little guy, with straight brown hair hanging in bangs down his forehead, bespeckled, and he stood, almost dwarfed by the podium, reading from the sheaf of notes he prepared, about the history and relevance of the new journalism and its many practitioners to a totally silent collection of Birkenstocked, ponytailed professors. There may have been a few questions—I don't remember—but after Gormley's presentation, a big, balding, flat-nosed guy named Don Petesch stood up, carrying one of those massive flat-bottomed leather briefcases that folded out like an accordion so that you could carry around half of your library, as well as lunch and dinner. He plopped the case on the table beside the podium and, facing the bespeckled Gormley, who had retreated to one of the back rows, began pulling out books—Faulkner, Thurber, Fitzgerald, Thomas Wolfe, ad infinitum—holding them up in the air and providing us all, one by one, with a succinct description of its literary value and inherent brilliance, and then, slamming them down on the table beside his briefcase, *kaboom, kaboom*, until the massive briefcase was empty. And then, peering across the room and addressing Gormley, he said something to the effect of, *Until you and the other* Pitt News *staffers read all of these books and learn to appreciate and understand them, this department should never support such lightweight work of what you think you are calling writing that is "new" in journalism.* Like I said, I don't remember the words—but that was the gist of the finale of his illustrious presentation.

Listening to Petesch pontificate was actually too much for many of the other members of the department, and they all burst out in debate over the books he had selected as classics—not in any way having to do with the subject at hand, typical of the English professors; they would pontificate about anything, as long as someone would listen. And admittedly Petesch's incredible rudeness also annoyed them. There was really no reason to treat an undergraduate who had had the courage to present an idea to the department in such a dismissive manner, especially the editor of the student newspaper who could wreak revenge on Petesch or the English Department should he choose to; *you gotta give the kid some credit, even though, maybe, his idea was worthless.*

Finally, Walter Evert stood up to tone down the rhetoric and move to another subject, by reasoning: "After all, gentlemen, we are interested in literature here—not writing." We few writers paused for a moment to allow that inherent wisdom to sink in. There were, by the way, many women in the room who snickered but also held their fire.

So this is the atmosphere in which creative writing programs existed— were forced to exist—an insignificant minority in a large and fractured department looking to remain prestigious and viable in a growing, changing university. They—the lit profs—were willing to tolerate courses in poetry and fiction writing. But journalism ("God forbid—you gotta be kidding me!")—journalism and literature in the same breath? How dare you?

Well, Bill Gormley dared and the faculty backed off after a while and the following year I was permitted to introduce a new journalism course called "The New Nonfiction." As bad as the term nonfiction was, according to my colleagues—("Nonfiction is a 'non sequitur!' How can you describe what you do as something you don't do?")—it was better than the "J" word. *Journalism*, fodder for the masses.

Like I said, a quarter century ago creative writing programs were rapidly being established in the US, mostly in English departments, comprised primarily with poets and fiction writers and a scattering of playwrights. On a graduate level, nonfiction was totally glossed over; undergrads could take essay writing or expository writing course electives, like the one I had been teaching, but without concentrations and majors. Since non-fiction was not poetry or fiction, it was not considered literary, and if you wanted to write in a nonliterary manner, that was okay. But there were other places for that kind of low-end stuff: Technical writing, PR writing, or basic journalism. Nonfiction was formulaic, like plumbing.

I won't say that my poetry- and fiction-writing colleagues in creative writing programs across the US opposed adding a third genre; they were mostly ambivalent. They were part of these programs as a shelter from the outside world so that they could write in peace and not have to hustle for part-time jobs, so if you didn't bother them, then you could write or teach anything you wanted, even Sanskrit, even if it was nonfiction! They wouldn't take the time to complain or doubt or debate—as long as it didn't threaten their own comfort and position.

But the more contentious word was "creative." The traditional journal-ists hated "creative" because to them it meant that you made stuff up—lying, exaggerating, etc. But the academics in the English Department also found it threatening. "Why can't my work be considered creative, too?" they whined and they argued. Why were their essays on Milton or postmodernism referred to as criticism, while my prose about traveling the country on a motorcycle or hanging out with major league baseball umpires (two books I had written in the 1970s) was artistic and literary and creative, for God's sake? This wasn't fair.

The debate went on in our department for years—literally—and it may well still be going on. And it got to be very bitter. The MFA in creative writing for poetry and fiction at Pitt was established in the 1980s, while an MA in nonfiction came about a bit later—perhaps the first advanced degree in nonfiction in the world. A couple of us began campaigning for a nonfiction MFA, and at that point, the nonfiction writing students were harassed, intimidated, and threatened by literature and composition pro-fessors. One woman actually resigned her teaching assistantship under the constant pressure and torment. Simply put, the English Department was a very dark and dour place to be if you wanted to be different and do something new, for it was all such a threat to the Petesches of this clois-tered world.

If you look back at our history and the information explosion that was precipitated by the Internet, nonfiction as the predominant literary genre was actually inevitable, but the resistance of the academy at that time made the outlaws and interlopers like me angry enough to fight and per-sist and conquer by thinking out of the box with a worldview and mar-shaling the power of the people. The very fact that I was not part of the academy, actually, that I was an interloper and what people would some-day call an entrepreneur, and that I couldn't care less about tenure or about maintaining the status quo allowed me to force the transition faster than it would have come about naturally.

During Wartime

Here are some of the things that happened, the small skirmishes and the bigger battles that were fought, in no particular order, as *Creative Nonfiction* the journal moved from idea to reality. This was at a time when I thought that the journal would be an integral part of the creative writing program at Pitt, helping to launch and support the MFA—and build a lasting community of nonfiction writers.

Anyway, I came up with the idea of the journal and presented it, as best I could at the time, to two colleagues; they were supportive to the general extent that I could explain what I was trying to do or accomplish which was not easy, since I did not know exactly what I was trying to do, except establish a literary journal publishing creative nonfiction exclusively. After that, I figured, circumstances, opportunities, would drive and guide me. I should say that to the extent that the genre or the journal have become successful in the subsequent years, that's been my entire modus operandi—less of a day-to-day plan and more of an ability to be flexible, act instinctively, and take advantage of whatever idea or asset seems most tempting and promising, which can be two entirely different things. I had some names of writers I put together who I thought might be interested in contributing and decided to write them, as soon as I figured out exactly what I was doing.

I went to the English Department chair (Walt Evert was no longer in power, but to be honest, I can't remember whom I talked with about start-up money). I did make follow-up requests from a longtime successor, David Bartholomae, who would also later decline, insisting that creative nonfiction was not significant, was a fad, didn't belong in the English Department. Bartholomae, a leading figure in the world of composition, whose textbook, *Ways of Reading*, was to eventually be used in composition programs all over the world, was not a fan of the idea of teaching creative nonfiction, which he called "tendentious," a word I had to look up. Creative nonfiction was not one of the "ways of reading" of which he approved. In 1995, in an article in the journal *College Composition and Communication*, published by the National Council of Teachers, he wrote:

Should we teach new journalism or creative non-fiction as part of the required undergraduate curriculum? That is, should all students be required to participate in a first person, narrative or expressive genre whose goal it is to reproduce the ideology of sentimental realism—where a world is made in the image of a single, authorizing point of view? a narrative that celebrates a world made up of the details of private life and whose hero is sincere?

I don't have an easy answer to this question. It is like asking, should students be allowed to talk about their feelings after reading *The Color Purple*? Of course they should, but where and when? and under whose authority?[1]

Clearly, Bartholomae then believed that students should not be permitted to think or feel for themselves—without a professor of composition to monitor them—and protect them from "sentimental realism."

Smith and Bartholomae referred me to the director of development of the College of Liberal Arts, to whom I made a presentation and who also, as expected, declined. Creative nonfiction, as Bartholomae had made clear, was simply not a serious discipline for a liberal arts college; it belonged in a journalism department. But the University of Pittsburgh disbanded its "J" school in 1961. That was that.

Anyway, I had a few dollars remaining from money I had raised to start a writers' conference—all genres, not just nonfiction—so I approached one of my former undergraduate students, Paul Mathews, whose family had a printing business in town, explained my idea and asked if he would help by printing the journal, if I ever got it put together, just for the money I had. We're talking maybe $1,000–$2,000. I figured I could supplement the rest out of my own pocket because I remained convinced, no kidding, that once the journal was produced, the department would endorse and support it—despite the obvious ideological resistance. Paul was a good guy, a quiet, hardworking undergrad who had once been an intern for the Pitt conference. Over the course of the previous ten years, I had put on maybe a half dozen conferences—something also that was pretty unusual back then. And it turned out that the conference idea would be increasingly fruitful in helping establish the genre and the journal. Today there are conferences everywhere. Paul had left Pittsburgh for Boston after graduation to work for the *Boston Phoenix* but he was now back in town helping with his father's business—but he remained fired up about the publishing industry and got very excited about the literary journal concept for creative nonfiction. He would do anything conceivably possible— whenever I was ready, he said.

I took the list of names I had gathered—about 170 folks whom I suspected had some interest in nonfiction—and wrote letters—real letters— explaining what I wanted to do and asking for advice, comments and, most of all, submissions. I got some nice return letters, telling me what a

1. "Writing with Teachers: A Conversation with Peter Elbow," *College Composition and Communication* 46, no. 1 (February 1995): 62–71, at 69.

great idea an all-creative nonfiction journal was. And people sent submissions. I think I got about *forty* in all.

I won't say that most of the manuscripts sent my way represented bad writing, whatever that is. I mean, lots of bad writing comes across the transom of any literary publication, but over and above all of that, what people sent as nonfiction—what they thought the term meant—even creative nonfiction—was difficult to fathom. We got some poetry, for example, because the poems were true, the writers said, or, more often, submissions with poetry interspersed with prose. That was the "creative" part, the writers said when questioned. (I am talking now not only about the first issue, but the first couple, where people began to realize that we were a live and functioning market.) We got lots of fiction, writers explaining that, for one thing, the stories were based on fact, and so more or less, true. So why not just call it creative nonfiction? And then, of course, there were writers who just sent us whatever they had in their files and drawers—lots of newspaper clippings—stuff unfinished or rejected a dozen times by other publications. This continues to happen, of course, but less so over the years, I think, because most writers writing bad stuff simply blog it and forget it these days. Quality is secondary to the search for publication and the genre doesn't matter so much now.

In the early 1990s, genre mattered more—especially this creative nonfiction thing. The debates were all over the place. As I said, traditional journalists despised the idea for various reasons and academics were rather ambivalent, figuring out how to either destroy it through ridicule or employ it to their own advantage. We were making headway in my English department, however; we got a faculty line for a nonfiction position, in addition to mine, and then, suddenly, dozens of unemployed literature and composition PhDs who had written newspaper articles or op-ed pieces at some point in their lives and had no place to go in the academy, were proclaiming themselves master nonfiction writers and applying for the position. These "imposter" issues we don't need to deal with much anymore; the overwhelming presence of creative nonfiction as a genre (and a publication) is now fact, and while the exact meaning of the term remains somewhat cloudy and imprecise, I think we can say the same thing about fiction and poetry; it is what we say it is. The art defines itself.

I am not going to go over all of the pieces we published in the first issue, for the TOC is available on the *Creative Nonfiction* website, but I want to mention three that stand out in my mind: First, Natalia Rachel Singer, then an assistant professor at St. Lawrence University, sent a manuscript based on a talk she gave when she was applying for the St. Lawrence position. It's a great essay, very informative and personal at the same time, which is what we then and now believe is the balancing factor of creative nonfiction, but it was the title that caught my attention and turned me on so much because of the statement it represented. It was like a proclamation, a definition of doctrine: "Nonfiction in the First Person: Without Apology." It knocked my socks off, it was so apropos! I know Wolfe and Talese and Mailer and God knows how many other hotshots were saying this to the world, nothing new, but Natalia was making this statement to some very judgmental folks—opposition, not only at my university, but in most universities and English departments in the US. This was something I too could have said and did say, frequently, to as many people who would listen, but it was much better coming from someone who was not such an avowed true believer. So we accepted and published this Singer essay with pride and excitement.

Michael Pearson, like me, a lone wolf in a writing program, teaching creative nonfiction, more or less, at Old Dominion University, did not submit a manuscript; rather, he wrote a letter offering to interview and write a Q and A with the *New Yorker* writer John McPhee. Pearson had interviewed McPhee once before for an academic article he had written—so they were acquainted. I needn't tell you how special McPhee was and how his very name on our cover would elevate the journal and the genre. For one thing, he was a *New Yorker* writer—and he was the author at that time of twenty-four books. And with rare exceptions—such as William Howarth's brilliant interview and profile of him in the first *John McPhee Reader*, McPhee rarely discussed his work or his approach to writing. So this would be a gigantic coup for the journal if Michael could make this happen— and he did—with incredible panache because when Michael arrived at McPhee's office, tape recorder in hand, for his "20 Questions," McPhee told him to put his tape recorder away. "You will get a better story without a tape recorder. Besides, the question and answer format is the most primitive form of writing, you realize. Writing is selection. It is better to start choosing right here and right now."

So Michael had a conversation with McPhee and wrote a profile of the writer—whose work I admired more than anyone else's, along with Gay Talese's—which we published in that first issue. "Profile of *New Yorker* Writer John McPhee" was right on the cover. This was a triumph—and a road of connection not only to the high and mighties in the academy, but the traditional journalism folks as well. McPhee was a master of fact, who rarely wrote in the first person—the "I" referring to himself was nearly anathema. A journalist might contend that Natalia Singer was self-obsessing—but not the great McPhee.

So the first issue of *Creative Nonfiction* was on its way to make an impact that would change everything in and out of the academy with an exclusive McPhee interview leading the way. So Paul Mathews printed the issue—for peanuts. We put it in the mail—176 copies all told, of people who subscribed and others we hoped would subscribe, crossed our fingers and held our breath. What we did was terrific—but humiliating—since we fucked up.

Who is this "we?" and where is this taking place? Mostly, my wife, now my ex-wife, Patricia Park, was with me pretty much all the way at that point. Patricia is a nurse, an avid reader, and a great editor. I am happy to be still working with my ex-wife on *Creative Nonfiction* after all of these years, even though we have gone in different directions in our personal lives. She is probably the only person besides me who remembers what we did to the Mary Paumier Jones's essay "Meander," published in that first issue. Maybe even Mary doesn't remember, but I tell you, it was humiliating.

The essay was a very short piece, basically about essays and how they meander, subject to subject, idea to idea, seemingly without connection, twist and turn like a winding river and then somehow, based on the skill of the writer, converge, to make a point. It was the first essay in the first issue of the journal. So it was very important—what the first-time reader of the first-time journal would see and read for the first time! So picture this: We work so hard soliciting, editing, and choosing manuscripts on our dining room table, my two-year-old son, Sam, watching impatiently, sometimes throwing food and acting like the toddler he was. We proofread carefully—no mistakes for the first issue will be permitted; there's too much at stake. We gotta be perfect. We send the manuscript to Paul and it *was* absolutely perfect—or so we thought. He sends us back proofs and then, subsequently, galleys—and we read and read and read and then we go to press. We get the magazine shipped to us—1,000 copies. It's thin, I know, 96 pages—no ads, cheap paper, nine essays. But we think it is beautiful and we can't wait for others to think so, too. We hand-address 176 manila mailing envelopes and slip the issues inside, lick the flaps and the stamps and lug it all in a couple of cardboard boxes to the post office, and sit back and wait for the response.

That night I cannot sleep, tossing and turning and worrying, and I go back downstairs to the dining room to look at and admire the first issue of *Creative Nonfiction*, my vision fulfilled, with a green cover and our look and logo at the time—which stayed with us for 36 issues—a paper tear in the upper left hand corner. I was very proud—and I loved it, after all the trauma and aggravation, it was here; it was real and I did it! I pick up the issue, admire the names of the authors on the front—just like all of the literary journals at the time were doing, even though, in most cases, no one ever heard of these people. Michael Pearson's work was on the top: "A Profile of *New Yorker* writer, John McPhee."

I opened the issue, flipped past the TOC and began reading "Meander," and then suddenly I realized somehow, someway, that something was so wrong: Three paragraphs, a significant chunk right out of the middle of the essay, was missing. Gone. Mary Paumier Jones would be livid. And my credibility in the academy and in the journalism community—would be shot. I would get it from both ends. I was a lame duck at that point—and *Creative Nonfiction* had lost all of its esteem and credibility was how I was feeling. This was the beginning of the end—at least I thought so for a few weeks until Patricia, Sam, and I, and perhaps a thousand other literary types of one sort or another landed in Tempe, Arizona, for the next annual meeting of the Associated Writing Programs.

Victory? Maybe.

I had been to AWP events before. They were quiet, casual, and fun with maybe a couple thousand people attending in all. A good group. People mostly knew one another and it was a great time to get together and share war stories about colleagues, publishers, etc. These days it is very big and crazy—a total opposite. Creative writing has turned into a big business now on the college and university level—tens of thousands or writers and wannabe writers swarming convention centers and hotels attending pedagogy and craft sessions, drinking too much wine and beer and networking like crazy. Looking for jobs. Looking for an editor to publish their poems. Looking for a one-night stand.

But it was more manageable and a lot more fun twenty years ago. Anyway I had been to a few of those conferences in the 1980s, as I say, and it was then as it is now the biggest event in the creative writing academy world—and because it was that, I had made a promotional plan around it. I decided I could make the biggest bang for our buck by officially launching the first issue of the journal at AWP. And to help bolster its image and impact as the voice of the emerging genre, I designed a panel on creative nonfiction—the first ever at AWP, previously dominated by poetry, fiction, and drama. Ironically, the AWP that year, 1994, took place at the Radisson Tempe Mission Palms Hotel (now called Tempe Mission Palms), sponsored in part by Arizona State University, which is where I now teach and live part-time. I had no idea whether anyone would show up for this panel—"Creative Nonfiction: How to Live It, Write It and Define It." And again, it was a proving ground for my theory that creative nonfiction was the way in which many writers have always wanted to write, if only they had a place to publish or a classroom to learn more about it, or a community to discuss or debate it. Or a name—an official label—to give it.

I signed on some good, supportive people to be a part of the event, beginning, of course, with Michael Pearson and Natalia Rachel Singer. Jane

Bernstein was also included—author at the time of a novel and this wonderful memoir, *Loving Rachel*, about her family's struggle to understand and make peace with her daughter's developmental delays. We met and talked before the panel to make certain we were on the same page, related to our presentations, joking all the while that we might be talking to ourselves. No one would show up, either because they didn't know what creative nonfiction was—or that they thought they knew what it was and were appalled by the thought of it.

The morning of the panel I made certain I steered clear of the designated room and kept myself occupied with other matters. Even though I was the moderator and the initiator of the event, I intended to be, if not late, then right on time. Not early, for God's sake, because I feared standing there with my fellow panel members watching an empty room not fill up would make me crazy. So I walked around town, drank an extra espresso at the nearby Starbucks with my heart literally pounding with anxiety. Patricia and Sam would be at the table at the book fair displaying and selling the journal. At that point, a few people had come around to look us over. There were only a few sales, but a lot of interest. Which was encouraging.

Anyway, to make a long story short, I waited until the last minute, like I said, and then hurried to the conference room absolutely petrified that no one would be there. But I couldn't get in. I had to push and shove to get through the door, explaining to those fighting for seats that I was the panel moderator. The place was packed. People were flopped on the floor everywhere. It was amazing. Many of the attendees knew exactly what we creative *nonfictionites* were all about and others were intrigued by the idea, thinking that they all along had been writing and reading this stuff or wishing they could write this stuff if there was a place to publish it—an eclectic, curious, and enthusiastic mix.

In my introduction to the panel, I made a pitch for the journal. I tried to be sincere and passionate. Now there is a potential home for your narrative nonfiction work, I told them, an exclusive place. It is the new journal I started. *Creative Nonfiction*. Come and peruse it at the table at the book fair—buy and subscribe and give to the cause. Your commitment now is crucial. Patricia and Sam were at the table ready to show and sell, I said.

After the panel, the conversation continued with people jamming the podium and in the hallway in front of the room, as we cleared out, making space for the next upcoming event. People were all over the place, incredibly excited and it was hard to break away—and I did not really want to break away, if truth be told; I was enjoying this feeling of making a connection like never before. Like coming out of a dark alley, having wandered aimlessly, seeking an exit—a tunnel of credibility. I can't tell you what emotion I felt more at that time: elation or relief. Either way, it was great and glorious.

When I got back to the book fair table, most of the copies of the journal that we had shipped to the hotel had been sold. The event, the panel, the launch, had all been a combined big hit. Like I said, my emotions were mixed. I knew that something very good had happened and I wished that all of my doubting colleagues in Pittsburgh had been around to witness it. But it didn't matter in the end. The genre and the journal were on its way to lead the way to establish something significant to and for writers and readers.

Back to Mary Paumier Jones and "Meander" and the missing paragraphs. The only thing we could figure to do, except for apologizing up and down to author and readers, was to have the essay reprinted and mailed out to our subscribers with a note of apology. Thinking about it now, it was no big deal. Now we would put it online. But that night, when I had been unable to sleep and discovered our error, with so much riding on the hopeful respect and momentum to garner that was at stake, I was unnerved. Until that moment I did not understand how much I wanted to make creative nonfiction, genre and journal, happen. Become a significant voice and change maker. It was to become, more or less, the prominent part of my life's work.

Decent Company between the Covers

CARA BLUE ADAMS

When I joined the *Southern Review*'s editorial staff in 2008, the magazine's offices were housed in the Old President's House, a charmingly ramshackle historic building at the heart of Louisiana State University's campus with an arched entryway, ancient, gnarled live oaks shading the lawn, and a tarmacked roof. It was possible to crawl through a large double-hung window and onto this roof, where one could sit reading in the Baton Rouge sun. We sometimes brought out folding chairs. Other times I used my cardigan as a blanket. (This was, I soon learned, both a pleasurable way to read manuscripts and likely to result in sunburn.) I was given a huge, empty office on the second floor with big windows and its own bathroom.

The office contained a desk and a computer and a chair, and stacks and stacks of papers left by the previous tenant, stacks I was supposed to some day organize and send to the archives in Hill Memorial Library. The papers comprised previous issues' marked-up manuscripts and correspondence from the magazine's authors, the blue-penciled detritus of seasons past. The furniture and stacks of papers sat like little islands in a sea of unused space. Our business manager told me to make a list of things I'd need and she'd order them, using the state's archaic and highly regulated purchasing system. Picture Bartleby the Scrivener here as the system's animating intelligence, or maybe Kafka. My vast, empty office—it was so full of potential! So I made the list, and we ordered a few things, including a stapler and a mouse pad, but most items, it turned out, we could not buy. We couldn't buy a desk lamp, because the office came with an overhead fluorescent light, and Louisiana purchasing regulations deemed that sufficient; we couldn't buy a wall clock, because my computer told the time and Louisiana purchasing regulations deemed that sufficient; and we couldn't buy a curtain for the bathroom, because this too was prohibited by Louisiana purchasing regulations—why, no one could say. Maybe the regulations took the position that the glass was a sufficient barrier between the person using the bathroom and the outside world.

And so you see the miracle it is that something as utterly improbable as a literary magazine could exist at a state institution at all—because such institutions believe in what can be generalized and regularized, in the minimum, in the scalable, in the anodyne, in saying no rather than saying yes, in what might be defended rather than what deserves to be loved, and this is exactly what literary magazines resist.

How did I come to work in this cavernous office, wondering why the state of Louisiana didn't want the bathroom to have a curtain—or at least didn't want to participate in getting it one? The story stretches back to my first day of high school in Brattleboro, Vermont, when the vice principal and a family friend came into homeroom and put a staple-bound pamphlet-style publication on my desk: a school-run literary magazine called the *Dial*, named after a famous old New York modernist journal which in 1922 published T. S. Eliot's "The Waste Land." Ezra Pound and Marianne Moore had served as editors for that *Dial*. This one was overseen by a long-suffering but cheerful public high school English teacher.

I joined the staff. We weren't as good. In fact, at meetings I would chew on my pencil and marvel at how *bad* the work we received was, how juvenile. An odd boy named Tim who wore his dark hair long, middle-parted, and tucked behind his ear and who spoke with a vaguely British accent was also on the staff. Given to wearing suspenders, Tim was the kind of boy who had grown up in Vermont with eccentric hippy parents who didn't allow him to watch television and who considered Dickens light reading, which is to say the kind of boy to whom I could relate. At one point, I told him that I despaired of finding anything worth publishing. "We do have to publish *some*thing," he told me, at once both droll and pragmatic.

But I did eventually find a poem I liked, to my surprise and delight. It wasn't perfect, but it had a real point of view and a series of arresting images drawn from the rural New England world we inhabited—snow, mountains, deer.

Hope: that thing with feathers, singing from the muddy depths of the slush pile.

We weren't making literary history, true—unlike the authors of the original *Dial*, our authors were not handing over work bound for the whisper-thin, cream-colored pages of the Norton—but we were forming a community, both within and around the flimsy Xeroxed pages of our little production. And this, I saw, was the point: to wade through the pages that were failing to do what art can do, giving each piece and each writer the benefit of the doubt, and to find and release to a larger audience the stories and poems that began to succeed.

This launched me on a path of dubious repute but much pleasure. I went on to attend Smith College in bucolic Northampton, Massachusetts, inspired in part by Sylvia Plath's chronicle of the place in her journals, where I edited an undergraduate literary magazine called, unsurprisingly, the *Siren*. The editor had a tattoo of a sentence in a black san serif font that began on the back of her neck and trailed down her spine; once early on in our acquaintance she wore her hair up and, catching sight of it, I asked what the sentence said. She angrily announced that it was "private." Editorial meetings focused on feminist theory. Sappho was invoked. So was Gide. One intense conversation revolved around the politics of the word "clitoris."

I was hooked—deeper than I knew.

At the University of Arizona, I became fiction editor for *Sonora Review* and learned to work with authors in an editorial capacity that went beyond Xeroxing, and at AWP glimpsed the dazzling array of little magazines being published today, which seemed a private and momentous discovery. A whole underground world, flourishing like pale, tender wild mushrooms! I scooped them up and loaded my suitcase. Once done with my graduate studies, I was invited to become assistant fiction editor for *Cutthroat*. We read manuscripts on weekends in my living room on North 2nd Avenue, drinking the cheapest decent dark-roast coffee available at the Tucson supermarket: Café Bustelo in the yellow-and-red Spanish-language can which read "Siempre Fresco, Puro y Aromático Como Ninguno." I did this for free, and happily, and might still be doing it today had I not seen an advertisement for a managing editor position at the *Southern Review*.

Gradually my cavernous office in the Old President's House filled with donated goods: an embroidered loveseat done in a flower pattern and two worn Oriental rugs in deep reds and blues donated by a retiring English professor, an ugly but comfortable Laura Ashley–print puffy chair, a curtain I bought myself. Beyond the door to my office sat our resident scholars.[1] Poet Jen McClanaghan hung above her desk a hideous cat poster printed on canvas that had been mailed to her by her mother. The poster possessed a glossy sheen. Hordes of cats lounged in menacing positions, and inexplicable red blotches were spattered on top, suggesting blood. Around this poster Jen mounted small plastic cowboy figurines. A battle played out in front of nine sets of watchful feline eyes.

1. The resident scholar program brought talented emerging writers to the magazine for two-year stints to write, teach, and edit.

So here I was, twenty-nine years old and an editor at the *Southern Review*, a magazine as storied as the original *Dial*. I felt the weight of that history every time I looked at the gray wooden bookshelves outside my office sagging under the many volumes of the magazine's first and second series.[2]

The *Southern Review* had begun, the story went, in February 1935 on a sunny Sunday afternoon when James Monroe Smith, then president of Louisiana State University, dropped by Robert Penn Warren's house and asked Warren if it would be possible to launch a good magazine on campus. Yes, Warren replied, "if you paid a fair rate for contributions, gave writers decent company between the covers, and concentrated editorial authority sufficiently for the magazine to have its own distinctive character and quality." He and Cleanth Brooks founded the magazine with an annual budget of ten thousand dollars. Writers were paid a cent and a half per word for prose and thirty-five cents a line for verse. The *Southern Review* quickly became identified with New Criticism, the legacy of which governed my education at Smith, and the Southern Agrarian movement, though it was never merely a regional magazine in taste or in fact. Warren and Brooks opposed the increasing industrialization of the South and were close to the Agrarian movement—indeed, Warren had contributed an essay to *I'll Take My Stand*, the movement's manifesto—but their interests in founding the magazine extended well beyond this question. As Lewis P. Simpson notes in his essay "The *Southern Review* and a Post-Southern American Letters," the prospectus preceding the magazine's publication stated that "the chief aim of the quarterly would be 'to define large issues' and 'to attempt interpretation of the contemporary scene.'"[3] The prospectus made clear that Brooks and Warren sought "a cosmopolitan authorship." It was within this context that they aimed in part "'at presenting and interpreting Southern problems to a national audience and at relating national issues to the Southern scene.'"

The magazine was promptly hailed as an important player in the literary world. The *New York Times* called the magazine "a leading literary quarterly." *Time* raved, "Superior to any other journal in the English language."

Decent company between the covers? Well, yes: Wallace Stevens, Randall Jarrell, Ford Madox Ford, Katherine Anne Porter, and Aldous Huxley.

2. The *Southern Review*'s first series ran from 1935 to 1942 before ceasing publication during World War II. In 1965, the journal was revived under the editorship of Lewis P. Simpson and Donald E. Stanford.

3. *The Little Magazine in America: A Modern Documentary History*, ed. Elliott Anderson and Mary Kinzie (New York: Pushcart Press, 1978) 89–90.

And that's just the first issue.

The list is long and incredible: W. H. Auden, Eudora Welty, John Berryman, Thomas Hardy, Nelson Algren, Federico Garcia Lorca, W. S. Merwin, Allen Tate, Pablo Neruda, Theodore Roethke, Maxine Cumin, Peter Taylor, Walker Percy, Wendell Berry, Ted Kooser, Wole Soyinka, Elizabeth Bishop, Nadine Gordimer, John E. Wideman, Rita Dove, Joyce Carol Oates, William Gay, Toni Morrison, Ernest J. Gaines, Mary Oliver, Alan Cheuse, Billy Collins, Amiri Baraka, Charles Simic, Philip Levine, Claudia Emerson, Eavan Boland, Seamus Heaney, Amaud Jamaul Johnson, N. Scott Momaday, Andrea Barrett, Larry Brown, James Lee Burke, Ron Carlson, David Kirby, Jake Adam York, Yusef Komunyakaa, Natasha Trethewey.

Mavis Gallant. Paul Valéry.

And even, you guessed it: T. S. Eliot.

On those bookshelves outside my office the magazine's evolution was apparent in its covers, which went from monochromatic to monochromatic with a white dot-matrix-style etching of a live oak, given by staff the affectionate moniker "the mushroom-cloud tree," to contemporary full-bleed images.

It was daunting, this history. Daunting and thrilling.

Because we had such a small staff, when I began as managing editor, I did a bit of everything. Daily the mail arrived at my desk, envelopes date-stamped by interns or student workers and carried upstairs in a milky-white plastic US mail bin. I would sort these envelopes, culling the obviously unpublishable and pulling out work with incredible first lines to read immediately. Mostly, I read and commented on manuscripts: the good, the bad, the in-between, toughest of all because they demanded rereading as you asked yourself, *Is it you or is it me?*

Beyond reading manuscripts and weighing in at editorial meetings, I was responsible for editing all the prose. My *Chicago Manual of Style* grew dog-eared. I wheeled the dictionary stand with *Webster's Third* into my office, as we had not yet switched over to using the online version of the dictionary. The house style sheet was five pages of typed notes with mysterious examples and abbreviations, and a conglomeration of Post-it notes on the assistant editor's computer. I would sneak into her office and jot down what she'd written. She often said she would type these up, but six months in I realized I'd better start my own house style sheet, developed from preferences she expressed on manuscripts or explained in conversation.

Neither had the magazine begun using Track Changes in Word to send edits; I would instead count down the lines, and write editorial letters to authors beginning, "On page 5, seventeen lines from the top, you write..." I was also responsible for stripping code from prose documents to be sent to our designer, using the Reveal Code feature in an old version of Word-Perfect. WordPerfect had long since stopped being supported for Macs, so to use it I had to partition my hard drive and install Windows on one side. The blinking red rectangular cursor on the pale gray screen reminded me of the temp job at a shipping company I'd held after college. The shipping company had used enormous old beige computers that appeared to have been manufactured in the 1980s; running Windows on those computers was out of the question. They were strictly command-line beasts. In my airy office I would scroll through the text of each prose piece to locate and delete stray bits of formatting code, printing and rereading the story or essay once I'd finished cleaning it up to make sure I had not also deleted a letter.

Gradually, I began to prevail in some of these discussions about technology. I introduced Track Changes. We began to use the online dictionary. WordPerfect, however, remained.

This is in part what is important about the university magazine, I was seeing: the conversation between past and present, the luxury of having a staff to lavish attention on the selection and production of pieces of art that have no duty to be commercial. If I sometimes wished we could leap forward in ways that were not possible, I also relished the connection to the *Southern Review*'s history and, more than anything, the ability to make decisions free of any pressure aside from the aesthetic.

My office became furnished, lived in. It grew homey. I read on the loveseat by the window in the sun or in that ugly, comfortable chair.

In 2011, I became coeditor. We merged with LSU Press and moved offices. In many ways my daily life was the same, but now I made final decisions about what work to publish and my editorial assistant went through the mail. I traveled to conferences to represent the magazine. I wrote to authors to invite them to send work. I missed much about the old building, the old life the staff had shared in it, but the autonomy was rewarding and my relationships with our authors deepened.

The LSU Press building was old and lovely and situated on Lakeshore Drive, its wide porch lined with classical Southern columns, the interior marked with domestic architectural features that signaled the building's past as a sorority house: window seats and closets containing clothes drawers. My new office featured French doors and built-in bookshelves. I now had all the furniture I needed. I covered the drafty floors with my rugs, hung white curtains, replaced the flowered love seat with a black leather one. My *Mississippi Review* "Love Is Strange" posters, designed by Frederick Barthelme, found new spots. The block-print images were reminders of the strangeness of love—and art. An orangutan holds an apple. He peers at the viewer with somber eyes. Two men in old-fashioned wrestling uniforms embrace in an ambiguous way that suggests affection and violence, one lifting the other aloft.

I held the coeditorship until this past June 2013. Leaving the magazine to accept a faculty creative writing position was difficult, but I missed the classroom and I wanted more time to write, and so I said goodbye to the *Southern Review* and packed up the office and turned over the keys to the LSU Press building and to my French doors. But not to the desire that led me to pursue editorial work in the first place—that, I kept.

Looking back I am struck by the correspondence. All the letters! They flooded in and filled that empty office with their voices. More than one morning as I sat drinking my coffee and reading the mail I felt like the Dear Abby of the literary world. "Perhaps you remember me ..." one began. "We met at a reading I did at Antigone Books in Tucson in October of 2008. Lydia Millet read with me." Many confessed personal losses, tragedies, failures of confidence: My mother died of cancer and so I am writing this memoir. I am in jail. Can you send me reading material here? I can't send you postage but I would appreciate it. This essay may not be any good but I am trying. I was praised for my writing in high school but began drinking heavily and found I had no time to read or write. I got sober this year and started writing again. Here are two poems. This is the seventh story I have sent to the magazine and it will be the last.

Often the writer strove to establish a personal connection: We had dinner in a group in Boston and you encouraged me to send. I met you last autumn at a conference and you encouraged me to send. My friend so-and-so is your friend and she encouraged me to send. My friend so-and-so met you once and he encouraged me to send. I read an interview with you and felt encouraged to send.

Dear Cara Blue Adams. Dear Editor Adams. Dear Ms. Adams. Dear Ms. Blue Adams. Dear Ms. Blue.

One of my favorite correspondents was Albert Goldbarth, whom I met in Denver at the annual madhouse occasion of AWP. He was talking to Ander Monson in the hotel bar. While I can't say with certainty it was Strata, the stylish, sleek bar at the Hyatt Regency, I believe it was; regardless, it was a bar cleaner and more corporate than most bars literary writers frequent, and Ander's signature energetic shock of curly hair was the more distinct. Knowing Ander, I said hello, Albert introduced himself, I said I was a fan, and we were off and running. I invited him to send. He did, and his poems were accepted by the magazine, rekindling a relationship that had begun in 1997 with the publication of his poem "The Time Machine" and promptly gone dormant. Albert does not use computers, and claims never—never—to have sent or received a single e-mail message. He is strictly a US Postal Service and telephone call kind of guy, and so our correspondence took place in analog. The seal of one missive, sent in a plain white letter-sized envelope, features a drawing of Albert's: a friendly snail cradled by the arcing slogan, "Save snail mail!"

Albert Goldbarth's charming typed letters: surely these belong in a museum. His letters to me begin "Dear Cara Blue Adams" and migrate to "Dear Cara" and finally to "Hey, You." He uses heavy cream stock or plain white printer paper on top of which he photocopies a cartoon panel. One such letter features a stylized Godzilla looming over the skyscrapers of New York, which Godzilla has begun to topple. In the bottom left corner flees a blond with wavy hair, dainty arched eyebrows, and a heavily lipsticked mouth open in an 8 of surprise. This particular letter is dated simply April 9 and begins, "I hope all's well and hoppin' and boppin' in Baton Rouge." Albert goes on to ask about a paragraph he had sent for inclusion in his essay "Annals of Absence," material he terms "'extra fixer-upper material.'" His typed signature reads:

Best,
  Goldbarth

In the space between *Best* and *Goldbarth* he has signed "Albert." The "A" is a big oval made of a curve and, inside, a loop. The "t" sweeps around and goes flying off toward the right margin.

First we accepted three of his poems. Then, the essay, later featured on *Poetry Daily*. The edits had to be sent by post. His response was delayed in the Louisiana mail—notoriously unreliable—and did not arrive for weeks after he entrusted it to the Kansas post office, necessitating a few semi-frantic phone calls and duplicated efforts. He hadn't made a copy, because why would he? So his notes were gone. But we worked it out, discussing over the phone questions like whether to use "layman's texts" or simply "lay texts," and the essay appeared in the magazine.

It's beautiful: ambitious, succinct, heartbreaking. You should read it.

Dear Sir. Dear Sirs.

Can you help me rehabilitate myself? I get out next month and I need a job.

Another of my favorite correspondents was Christine Sneed. Her story "Student, Teacher" absorbed me one clear, cool Saturday morning in March as I read submissions in my rented apartment on Belmont Street. This was shortly after I began at the magazine, when I was still spending my weekends trying to "catch up" on the slush pile. In the story, a movie star named Alex Rice returns to college, bringing along his bodyguard and enrolling in an English class taught by a professor who is at first unnerved by Alex's presence, and then, as Alex fails to attend class, by the bodyguard, who continues to appear. Upon reading the last page, I was so happy, so swept away, I had to go for a walk and think about the characters. I advocated passionately for the story at our weekly editorial meeting—being the managing editor, I did not yet have final say on such decisions—but we passed. It was scooped up by *Pleiades*. The manuscript joined Scott Nadelson's "Dolph Schayes's Broken Arm" (*Ploughshares*), Kirstin Allio's "Icarus" (*Witness*), Smith Henderson's "Number Stations" (*One Story*), and Mary Jones's "The Father" (*Brevity*) in my file of submissions I wish we'd published.

Christine appeared in our pages not too long after this with a story called "Beach Vacation," and when I became coeditor, I accepted two more stories—"Relations" and "Flattering Light"—which went on to become the first two chapters of her stellar debut novel *Little Known Facts*. Bloomsbury sent me an advance reading copy that failed to arrive. I planned to go out and buy the book, but Christine inquired, and upon learning my copy hadn't made its way to me sent me one herself, a UK edition, reporting: "It went media mail because the USPS has raised its first class rates—now everything over 13 oz is priority mail. This book is pudgy too—more than a pound. But still cute." I gobbled up the book. I vowed to teach it someday, perhaps in a graduate seminar. When I opened my Sunday *New York Times* to see Curtis Sittenfeld's review of the novel on the front page of the book review section, I yelped in joy. Christine had written earlier that she knew a review would be appearing, but said, "I have no idea who the critic is or if this person liked it. I hope so because I will have to hide my face in anguished humiliation of he/she doesn't." She needn't have worried; the review praised her prose as "intelligent and graceful" as well as "strangely hypnotic."

Unlike Albert, Christine uses e-mail. Her e-mails were sharp, insightful, funny, full of questions about me and my life and vivid and amusing bits of reportage from her own. But she also mailed notes. Christine is, I learned, a giver of sincere compliments and gifts, the kind of person who remembers what you say and puts the knowledge to use to make you feel known. She passed along news of writer friends, political observations, reading suggestions. Where Albert had cartoons, she used stickers to add color and humor. Upon learning I had rescued a collie-spaniel mix from the Baton Rouge shelter, she decorated an envelope with a scene made of stickers: a black-and-white dog eyeing a fire hydrant. A lime-green owl with red wings perches on the front of another envelope, his claws wrapped around a branch she's drawn and leafed with green, silver-veined ovate leaf stickers. Enclosed in a third envelope were more stickers, butterflies and flowers, a whole springtime shimmering from between clear plastic sheets. On a quiet, gloomy day at the office, a day like many days when my hand was cramped from marking manuscripts with blue pencil and my eyes sore from stripping computer code to ready work for the production department, it was the best surprise.

Well, not quite the best. The best was always new work from her desk.

The intimate pitches: "a brief narrative focusing on a personal masturbation experience." The intimate material: a memoir in translation featuring a scene in which the narrator has sex with a chicken. Bill Lychack's SASE, the return address written in a neat blue script-print hybrid: "grim news from the *Southern Review*."

(I accepted that essay, so no grim news was mailed.)

Attention: Cat Blue Adams.

Tamas Dobozy I read in the *PEN/O. Henry Prize Stories 2011*. He was at first reluctant to send; he worried it wouldn't work out, which would be uncomfortable, he said, and he'd rather know his work had made it through the slush pile screening process and was therefore worthy of real consideration. I insisted. I accepted the first story he sent me, a very long piece about expat Hungarians living in Toronto called "The Beautician." The *Washington Post* went on to call it "likely to become a classic" in their review of the collection in which the story appears, *Siege 13*. The book itself was widely praised.

Lori Ostlund I read in the same PEN/O. Henry. Maggie Shipstead I read in *Gulf Coast*. Holly Goddard Jones in *Epoch*. Barb Johnson when I picked up *More of This World or Maybe Another*. I queried them all. Many of my queries were directed at women. As the VIDA count demonstrates, editors need to be especially vigilant about seeking out female writers; I felt this weight especially at a magazine with such a traditional history and such a masculine line of editors, where Jean Stafford had been the office secretary. But plenty of women sent on their own. Lydia Conklin and Jaquira Díaz and Farley Urmston I read first at my desk at the *Southern Review*.

Peter Levine's work I initially encountered in the pages of the *Cincinnati Review*. After reviewing the issue for *NewPages* and making special mention of his haunting story "The Seldom Brother," I invited him to send work to the *Southern Review*. He wrote back with a story, saying how nice it was to hear a voice from what can feel like the void. We published three of his stories, two of which appeared in his first book, *The Appearance of a Hero*. This summer Pete and I attended a workshop and drank vodka tonics together at the Sewanee Writers' Conference, a turn of events I would not have imagined when, fresh out of graduate school and teaching as a lecturer, I read and admired that first story of his.

Quebec. Florida. Virginia. California. New York. Scotland. Egypt. Qatar. So many voices, new and old.

"Hey Cara Blue—old pal, VT brother Leath here. I sent you this story last winter but like a fool I sent it outside of your designated submission period."

"I recently had an enlivening conversation, while holding a mannequin, with Cara Blue Adams, and I hope you'll pass on my good wishes with this submission."

"I miss you and Nick and all of my fellow waiters."

News arriving from all parts. "I've got a contract on the house in Italy, Texas, and so hopefully maybe that chapter of my existence is drawing to a close, at least in the physical sense." "I hope your summer is going well. I moved to Idaho." "We're in high-gear Muse preparation now." "I hope you are enjoying Louisiana. Vermont is, I swear, trying to thaw."

I've come to think of this literary world we're all in together as a surprisingly small one, but a world in which a conversation of gigantic size and importance is taking place—a conversation about writing, and what matters. What does it mean to be human? we ask. *This*, we answer, and *this*. How are you living the writing life? How are you making it work? As best I can. It plays out among writers, editors, and readers in magazines and in e-mails and in letters, across states, across countries, across history.

It's a conversation I hope to be a part of my entire life.

It's a conversation I love above all else.

It's a conversation—the conversation—we are left with when all the noise our culture produces, all the static in our lives, dies down and we can finally really listen.

You can hear it, can't you?

Good. So can I.

Alaska Quarterly Review and the Literary Tonic

RONALD SPATZ

F. Scott Fitzgerald had a passion for the Gin Rickey and Edna St. Vincent Millay for Between the Sheets. Much has been written about writers and their alcohol and the creative mystique of it all. So shouldn't Alaska's national literary magazine have its very own signature cocktail too? We thought so. In 2013 *Alaska Quarterly Review* (*AQR*) unveiled the "*AQR* Literary Tonic," a zesty yet balanced drink made with local ingredients and the support of an Anchorage distillery. The occasion? The launch of *AQR*'s fall and winter 2013 edition.

Had you been there you would have seen a full house of supporters, the ubiquitous glow of winking smartphone screens, a silent auction, a jazz band, readings from the issue, the launch of *AQR*'s YouTube channel featuring the premiere of a video-poetry collaboration, and a dramatized photo essay. If it sounds like a dynamic, fun evening, it was—a tonic of sorts for all involved: an invigorating book launch with the help of local businesses and volunteers.

It is accurate to say that the literary market, like the broader artistic market, is evolving rapidly. Readers, supporters of nonprofits, and consumers of the arts are inundated with choices. Whether we like it or not, literary magazines and artistic ventures must adapt to this reality. We must engage the community from multiple perspectives, by using social media—Facebook and Twitter—and events, such as book launches, art gallery openings, readings, and collaborations with leaders in the performing arts. We have to use all of the tools in the toolbox to catch their eyes and ears if we want to make more connections and expand our audience.

And, yes, we must do this to generate revenue. As funding sources dry up for the arts, and many other fields, financial support is a central challenge to achieving artistic vision. Is fundraising antithetical to creating art? In many cases, yes, and in all cases it is an incredible drain on scarce time and energy. But, crass as it is, we have to find ways to increase revenue to support the operation of the magazine. It's up to us to use our creative power to turn this pernicious challenge into an opportunity for engagement and inspiration.

Alaska Quarterly Review's journey began as an idea on a sweltering hot day in Missouri in June 1980. I was busy packing for my move to Alaska to take a tenure-track position at the University of Alaska–Anchorage. In the background was NPR's broadcast of the National Press Club and the guest was the governor of Alaska, Jay Hammond. I wasn't listening that closely but at a certain point I realized Governor Hammond was reading one of his own poems. I was surprised that a politician would like poetry enough to share it at the National Press Club and delighted that one would actually write it. And the governor of Alaska was doing just that. I felt right then that in addition to the magnificent and wild environment, there might be a deeper artistic spirit in the Last Frontier that would value and sustain creativity. Indeed, Alaska was (and still is) such a place, where the individual has opportunities to make a real difference. In such a place, I thought, a national literary magazine could take root and thrive.

When I arrived in Anchorage, I quickly confirmed my prior research that there were only sporadic and mostly very local amateur literary publications coming out of Alaska. Most focused on Alaska's majestic and extreme setting, flora and fauna, and the lifestyle of the rugged pioneers. I saw almost nothing in these publications representing the rich and diverse Alaska Native cultures and no meaningful attempts to bring the richness of broader literary traditions to Alaska. I saw a compelling need for a national effort, rooted in Alaska, that would work to discover, nurture, and provide a forum for new and emerging writers, to give attention to the noncommercial work of established writers, and to serve as a bridge between Alaska and the national and international literary community. I pitched the idea to my colleague Jim Liszka in August of 1980, and we founded *Alaska Quarterly Review*.

My controlling vision was to create a national magazine that is strongly influenced by Alaska—the place and people and cultural traditions—without being provincial. But the ambitions were even higher than that. *AQR* would *be* a work of art, issue after issue, a forum for writers whose noncommercial work would challenge accepted forms and modes of expression. Ultimately, artistic risk taking—from the point of view of editor and contributor—would be highly valued. Focusing on finding the new voices in individual pieces within genres or crossing genres would be the primary target. Collectively (and very selectively) developing ambitious thematic projects to publish as whole books would also be a goal. One example is *AQR's Alaska Native Writers, Storytellers and Orators* edition, deeply rooted in Alaska's living history, celebrating the first people of Alaska's uniqueness and rich cultures. *Kirkus Reviews* described it as an "omnibus of poems, oral histories, folk tales, and stories by Native Alaskans, many appearing in their original languages with translations on facing pages (with) very extensive commentaries to what remains a largely unknown world."[1] *The Expanded Edition* is a 400-page stand-alone book. Between the two editions, the book has been reprinted six times. In another book, *One Blood: The Narrative Impulse*, we explored first-person singular without distinguishing between fiction and nonfiction. This deliberate blurring of the genres is appropriate because in many indigenous cultures the stories of fact and fiction have a comparable flexibility. "By choosing not to classify stories by genre," I wrote in the editor's note, "we ignore the boundaries between fact and fiction. Although the purpose of each story is unchanged, the *truthfulness* of the story is enlarged. A story presented in this framework brings the reader closer to the story's heart, closer to its original narrative impulse." Nevertheless such an approach is risky because it runs counter to reader expectations.

Within *Alaska Quarterly Review's* regular series of editions, we often publish various types of special literary features. Among them, the photographic essays we publish probably distinguish *AQR* the most from other journals. These special sections uncover universal and yet deeply personal and intimate stories ranging from one family's love and loss in Richard Murphy's "Cancer Journal" to pressing issues of global consequence far from America's radar in Pulitzer Prize–winner Nikki Kahn's "AIDS in Guyana." They give exceptional depth, magnitude, and scope to large questions. Indeed it is the universal aspect of the photographs and narratives that reveal the immediacy of the personal impact of these global subjects. Heidi Bradner's eighty-page courageous and unrelenting photo essay is an example. The piece covered both sides of the tragic civil war in "Chechnya: A Decade of War." Another example is the 140-page proactive tribute to the lives and memory of Tim Hetherington and Chris Hondros in "Liberty and Justice (for All): A Global Photo Mosaic." The scope of these works is rare these days in any publication and difficult to achieve financially and technically. We pushed the boundaries, asked the tough questions, and brought to light new voices and new connections.

Throughout all of this, from inside the literary kaleidoscope was the intense rush of artistic creation and idealism—powerful forces driving the

---

1. "Alaska Native Writers, Storytellers and Orators" (review), *Kirkus Reviews*, May 10, 2010: https://www.kirkusreviews.com/book-reviews/ronald-spatz/alaska-native-writers-storytellers-and-orators/; accessed March 30, 2014.

production of each and every edition. This motivation buoyed *AQR* in the face of the business plan monster—that uncouth and frothing reality of bottom-line revenue and market share, sometimes robed in the elegant and medieval regalia of the academy. Nevertheless, despite new challenging realities that are accompanying the dramatic paradigm shift in publication, it is foolish to think that this changes the fundamental goal of publishing *noncommercial* literary art of consequence.

After more than thirty years of publication, *AQR* is recognized as one of America's premier literary magazines and a source of powerful new voices. *AQR* publishes short stories, novellas, novel excerpts, plays, poetry, photographic essays, and literary nonfiction in traditional and experimental styles. By identifying and showcasing important new work, *Alaska Quarterly Review* continues to serve as a frontline crucible for developing America's literature and, ultimately, that literature helps forge America's culture and identity.

Work is submitted to *AQR* from all around the world, and from that large pool of new and emerging voices, the work that ends up in the pages of *AQR* is work that is fresh and compelling in traditional and unconventional styles, and often because of length or complexity or crossing of genres, just won't be seen or read anywhere else. Consequently, reading each *AQR*—as the collection of works that each issue represents and as a work of art in itself—is an experience readers won't get *anywhere else.*

At this writing, *Alaska Quarterly Review* has published sixty-one book-length double issues—all with national and international distribution. A number of the issues are in multiple editions. Over these years, works initially published in *Alaska Quarterly Review* have been selected for America's most prestigious awards anthologies including the *O. Henry Prize Stories, Pushcart Prize, Beacon Best, Best American Mystery Stories, Best Creative Nonfiction, Best American Fantasy, Best American Essays, Best American Nonrequired Reading,* and *Best American Poetry.* Additionally, *AQR* has been featured at the Frontline Club (London, UK), VII Gallery (New York City, NY), Fovea Gallery (Beacon, NY), *The Book Show* (Australian Broadcasting Network), The Verb BBC Radio 1, CHON-FM (Yukon), *NPR's Writer's Almanac, Harper's Magazine,* National Endowment for the Arts' *NEA Magazine* and *ART Works Blog,* and the Poetry Foundation's "American Life in Poetry." Most recently, *The New Yorker* gave *Alaska Quarterly Review* unique recognition by featuring a sixteen-page excerpt from *AQR*'s fall and winter 2013 issue.

These are just some of the highlights over three decades of consistent quality that led "*The Washington Post* Book World" to call *Alaska Quarterly Review* "one of the nation's best literary magazines." Matching this consistent quality with pressing boundaries and searching out new voices, we hope to live up to the description *AQR* received in *The Sunday New York Times Book Review*: "fresh treasure."

How does all this happen? First and foremost is our guiding philosophical principle, our unbreakable rule. We publish high-quality work that fits our mission; we don't publish our friends or publish writers based on their reputation. We never forget that our job is to serve writers and readers and not the other way around.

On a practical level, the magazine happens *on a shoestring* in the face of serious challenges. Working within an academic institution is blessed with academic freedom—something that is very powerful and not to be taken for granted, and for which we are every day very grateful. But the *bureaucracy itself* is exceptionally challenging. Sometimes it seems a miracle of sorts that we are even able to persevere. Notwithstanding *Alaska Quarterly Review*'s regional, national, and international acclaim, *AQR*'s intrinsic value to the university is questioned and misunderstood. As a result, despite its centrality to the university's mission in research and creative activity, *AQR* has not had an increase in base funding in twenty years.

The sustaining force of our success is the generosity and service of various volunteers over the years. They have helped us at every key juncture. My editorial team also benefits from editors with extensive experience with the magazine. Stephanie Cole, Senior Affiliate Editor, has served voluntarily as *AQR*'s top-level screener since 1986. *AQR*'s lone, part-time staff member Robert Clark, started his work for us as a volunteer in 1992. He serves key dual roles as Senior Affiliate Editor and as the day-to-day operational manager.

A couple of years ago Don Ball interviewed me for the National Endowment Arts *ART WORKS BLOG* during our thirtieth anniversary year and got me thinking about the past three decades. Over time, *AQR* has created a body of work that spans works emerging from the oral tradition to those that explore and expand the boundaries of genres and styles. *AQR* has taken risks—devoting entire issues to individual works, or developing special features expanding boundaries of genre or style, and bringing new voices to light.

AQR has published book-length works exploring the full range of the story in "Long Stories, Short Stories and True Stories." In "Intimate Voices, Ordinary Lives" we explore stories of domesticity; and Arnold Nelson's exceptional book-length exploration of language, literature, and culture: "How to Write a Good Sentence: A Manual for Writers Who Know How to Write Correct Sentences."

AQR has discovered and promoted voices that may not always be heard in the dominant culture and have something important to convey. Siberian Yupik artist and writer Susie Silook's "Ungipamsuuka: My Story" is an innovative, heartbreaking and raw memoir-as-drama. New poetry by Tlingit poet Robert Davis Hoffmann and Iñupiaq poet Joan Kane were featured in chapbook-length sections. Don Lago's novella-length essay "Storm Pattern" explores Edwin Hubble's search for the ideal location for the world's most powerful telescope that brings him face to face with the Navajo "Storm Pattern" rug, which presents the Navajo vision of the universe. And most recently, Andrea Bruce uniquely tackles what *The New Yorker* called a "study in duality" in her compelling photographic essay "Afghan Americans: Diptychs."

Alaska Quarterly Review has consistently published new and emerging writers, young and older (that is, writers who have begun the journey much later in their lives). Some of our authors have come to writing only after they have retired from careers that did not afford them the time and opportunity to truly reflect in such depth, such as John Gamel, a professor emeritus of ophthalmology. He moved from academic articles to creative nonfiction after retirement. His latest *Alaska Quarterly Review* essay, "The Elegant Eyeball," has been reprinted in *The Best American Essays*.

It is satisfying that *AQR* also has been a launching pad for new works that have evolved into books and garnered significant international acclaim and influence. Sarah Shun-lien Bynum, now a well-known fiction writer, was first published ("Talent") in *AQR* and later featured in *The New Yorker*'s 20 under 40 fiction issue. Kate DiCamillo, who also published her first story ("This Is Me, Lona Bretweiser, Leaving the Amusement Park of Love") in our pages has continued to delight readers of all ages ever since, winning two John Newbery Medals along the way, and publishing a best-selling novel that was also made into a motion picture. Heather Sellers's essay "Tell Me Again Who Are You?" on the subject of face blindness also had a wonderful trajectory after we published it. I sent it over to *Best Creative Nonfiction* and it was recognized there. Heather expanded the essay into a book *You Don't Look Like Anyone I Know* and that book received widespread notice and media attention and was widely cited, including in Oliver Sacks's book *The Mind's Eye*. Heather wrote me a note after the Sacks book came out saying, "I won't ever forget who got me down this path."

This past fall I was asked by the English department of a very prestigious university to evaluate a candidate for tenure and rank of associate professor. It turns out that the candidate was another writer whose very first story was published in our pages. What started in *Alaska Quarterly Review* blossomed into a multifaceted, ascending career as a serious and versatile literary writer. Soon after her publication in *Alaska Quarterly Review*, her stories began appearing widely in literary journals and magazines followed by a cluster of books and the awards and acclaim. This is a pattern that has repeated itself *many* times over. It's not always the *very first* story or poem or essay that we've published, but often *early work* that shapes a career.

It is also satisfying to discover that new voice—perhaps one that is compelling, but also imperfect, yet deserving to be heard. For me, it does not matter whether or not that piece will be the part of a long and illustrious body of work or a singular publication. If fate has it that this is the writer's one and only special song to sing, this is not a strike against publishing it. At *AQR* that song is important. I know some of my peers would not agree, but I think this sense of mission sets *AQR* apart and we're proud of it. Ultimately, the measure of this unwavering commitment is this: the lion's share of all of the pieces *AQR* publishes comes to us *unsolicited.*

What drives me is simply this: creating art is essentially a moral act. The artist is the mirror, the conscience, the provocateur, the translator, the individual demanding attention to the compelling questions, and the literary magazine is itself a work of art, produced as a collaborative endeavor—a process akin to conducting the symphony or the making of a film or directing a play. Rightly the focus falls on the individual works first, as one shines the spotlight on a star performance in the film or play. In the end, however, that performance is part of the larger context and influenced by the collaboration with the editor. The editor, like the symphony conductor or the director and the producer, *makes the choices that only an artist can make.*

New technologies have made publication and dissemination easier and more democratic (and chaotic too) than in the days of the ditto master. Yet, one thing has stayed the same—the foundational collaborative artistic relationship between the editor and the writer. This is crucial and sometimes overlooked. However, as writers of all stripes swarm the gates, we need to be grateful that there are many gatekeepers—from the literary magazines to the major publishing houses—which makes it much more likely that good work will be not be ignored. Furthermore, having gatekeepers, especially ones with real rigor and standards, elevates work that emerges from the process.

Collaborations are not only the domain between the editor and the new and emerging writers. Another kind of collaboration is represented in the special features we created with major writers like Tracy Kidder, Jane Smiley, Richard Ford, and William H. Gass including multifaceted presentations of their work and conversations about craft and literary vision. Likewise, our contributing editors including Elizabeth Bradfield, Billy Collins, Olena Kalytiak Davis, Stuart Dischell, Stuart Dybek, Nancy Eimers, Patricia Hampl, Amy Hempel, Jane Hirshfield, Dorianne Laux, Pattiann Rogers, Michael Ryan, Peggy Shumaker, Benjamin Spatz, and the late Maxine Kumin and Grace Paley, all significantly helped *AQR* cast our literary net wider and deeper. Nowhere is this truer than when we created our *Alaska Native Writers* anthologies with editors Gary Holthaus, Nora Dauenhauer, Richard Dauenhauer, Patricia Partnow, and Jeane Breinig. Nora Dauenhauer is a Tlingit linguist and writer; Jeane Breinig is a Haida scholar. All have extensive experience in Alaska Native cultures and oral and written literatures.

This creative process has memorable surprises too. One instance in particular comes to mind. Grace Paley was working on an essay for *AQR* in late 1993. We had discussed it a couple of times over the phone. When the manuscript arrived at *AQR* via fax, printed out on our ancient thermal paper, we found it all rolled up like a biblical scroll, partly typed, mostly handwritten and barely readable from faded or missing type. What a moment of, yes, awe, to *discover* that scroll in the plastic tray attached to the machine! I felt exhilaration and responsibility. I knew the paper was sensitive to light, to touch, had a tendency to discolor and the text invariably would fade and disappear. For just the briefest instant I thought, *What if her words disappeared? What if we lost—the world lost—this amazing essay?* Quickly my focus returned to the business of transcribing the essay titled "Six Days: Some Rememberings," which, after we published it, went on to be recognized in *The Best American Essays, The Pushcart Prize* anthology, and to take on a life of its own—as many works first appearing in *AQR* invariably do. For those interested, Katha Pollitt does a wonderful reading of "Six Days: Some Rememberings" on the PEN America website.

Stephen King's explanation of why he selected Cary Holladay's story "Merry-Go-Sorry" for an O. Henry Prize—a piece first published in *AQR*—distills how fiction and, I think, all literary art centers us and why it matters. "Good fiction," he wrote, "shows us the inside of things—a community, a job, a relationship, the human heart. Great fiction can sometimes show all of these things working together; it lifts us briefly above the event horizon of our own day-to-day existences and gives us a dreamlike (and godlike) sense of understanding what life itself is about." Collectively too, when looking back on the body of work *Alaska Quarterly Review* has produced, we have stayed true to our mission—each issue a fresh literary experience—one that challenges, moves, and ultimately offers readers opportunities to see in new ways.

And here we are—more than three decades later!—doing what the Council of Literary Magazines and Presses calls (and what will always be) the "backstage work of American Literature." It's important work. But it's not fancy or glamorous. Each day we begin anew, adjust the scaffolding, check the lights, assemble the manuscripts, and start from the very beginning.

So friends, please stand with me, right here in this humble place, as I propose a toast. Here's to all the literary magazines past and present and to their literary editors and contributors who weave and have woven an integral part of the living literary fabric of America; here's to all of our readers and inspirations; here's to the bean counters and bottom-line true believers too; and here's to *Alaska Quarterly Review*'s literary tonic with fresh lime, perfect ice cubes, and with just a touch of lime foam. Let's raise our glasses to *why we create*—to the invigorating, refreshing, restorative, and transformative nature of art! *Bottoms up! Cheers!*

Making a Living and a Life in Little Magazines

CAROLYN KUEBLER

It was news to me, when I moved to Minneapolis just after college in 1990, that publishing could be a creative enterprise as much as it was a business. The people behind presses and magazines like Chax, Detour, and *Conduit* were as language-mad as any poet (and in most cases *were* poets), and larger publishers like Coffee House, Graywolf, Milkweed, and New Rivers were strong proof of how an individual's passion for and taste in new writing could not only produce singular books but could blossom into a real business creating real jobs. These latter presses were the establishment, and yet they weren't at all what I had in mind when I rejected, as an idealistic college graduate, the idea of a job in that New York monolith known as "publishing," where I assumed I would end up like Bartleby before the age of thirty. After an internship at Milkweed Editions, which introduced me to the people and the process, I realized I could very happily work in publishing—nonprofit literary publishing, that is. Of course the same thing also occurred to half the other recent college graduates in the Twin Cities, and though it was true that some people made a living in independent publishing, it wasn't true for many. Restaurants and bookstores were still more useful for collecting a paycheck, and a paycheck was still, of course, the only ticket to an independent postgraduate life.

I was working at Borders Book Shop—a much-coveted job at the time, as Borders was thought to be the serious book person's alternative to Barnes and Noble—when I discovered the books of Dalkey Archive Press: *Ava* by Carole Maso and *The Fountains of Neptune* by Rikki Ducornet, in particular. These extraordinary books opened up new possibilities in fiction to me, and I sought out more, looking for Dalkey's distinctive black-and-white covers and that squared spiral logo on the spine. When I wrote to the director, John O'Brien, to see if they had any posters or other promotional items we could use in the store, he wrote back saying, literally, "Where have you been all my life?" They didn't have promo items, but did I want to apply for the job as their marketing director? Though Normal, Illinois, wasn't my ideal location, I was thrilled when I landed a "real" job with a press I admired, and moved there in 1994.

I didn't know what a marketing director would do exactly, and marketing directors at Dalkey had, at the time, a notoriously brief tenure, but I was determined to make it work. It didn't take long for me to realize that it was nearly impossible to get any attention for books that most people considered dense or difficult or strange. Newspapers and magazines had very little space for considering authors like Arno Schmidt and Gilbert Sorrentino, and even the Barnes and Noble that opened up right there in town hadn't bothered to order copies of even the most popular Dalkey titles. After six months I decided that no, this wasn't working, I was miserable, and I returned to Minneapolis. I was working again in a bookstore, this time the Hungry Mind in St. Paul, when Randall Heath, who had just finished a studio art degree at the University of Minnesota, suggested we start our own publishing outfit. I was hesitant; did the world really need another small press when so many good books were already out there struggling for attention? But we started talking about it with our friend David Caligiuri, who'd just left a job at Coffee House, and the more we talked, the more appealing it became. At first we thought we'd start by publishing some out-of-print treasures, a kind of "rediscoveries" series, and we had in mind to start with *Call Me Ishmael* by Charles Olson, but the project took off when we landed on the idea of a book-review magazine.

To me this made complete sense and was sure to work: newspapers were only reviewing mainstream titles, even the alternative weeklies didn't think there'd be enough audience for some of the books I wanted to review for them, and there just wasn't a good venue for engaging with the most interesting new books in the way they deserved. How did people even find out they existed? The *New York Times* wouldn't tell. The publications that did exist for reviewing were closed to the books I wanted to review and closed to reviews by someone unknown to them. There was a very limited platform for discussing books outside the big sellers, which I generally didn't care much about, and yet there was so much going on in independent publishing that even publications like the *Hungry Mind Review* seemed not to notice.

This was the age of the zines, and anyone with desktop publishing software could produce one. It was also before the Internet took off as a publishing vehicle, before blogs and Amazon reviews. What we wanted to do was bigger than a zine—we would include the voices of many in our pages, not just the editors, and we wanted eventually to be paid for this, to be a part of the indie establishment—and because of design programs like QuarkXPress and the sudden ubiquity of fast and cheap e-mail communications, it seemed breathtakingly possible. The three of us, with our various skills and passions, could make this happen. We'd create our own meaningful jobs, not in service of someone else's vision, but in service of our own.

We brainstormed about the name for days, until we finally hit on "Rain Taxi," which I loved in an instant. With that name we were off and running. The magazine would be serious but the opposite of stuffy. There was a great sense of freedom and possibility: finally I didn't need to ask others what I could write, how long it should be, would they please publish it—I could decide this myself. I could decide which books were worth reviewing and who would write about them. We were on fire, talking to all the readerly and writerly people we knew and asking them to spread the word about our project. In addition to reviews, each issue, we decided, would also present a list of independent bookstore favorites (sadly, a look back at the stores in that feature is like looking at a reliquary), an independent press profile, essays on not-new books, and the occasional tongue-in-cheek piece, like a review of *Peef the Christmas Bear* (a book with phenomenally high sales at the time) and a profile of a literary escort (a personal chauffeur to authors who came through town on book tours). We'd also include extensive interviews with authors we loved.

For the first issue, I called Rikki Ducornet in Denver. Could we interview her for this start-up magazine? Sure, she said, would you like to come for lunch? I don't know if she knew we were nowhere near Colorado, but we said yes, and Randall and I drove the thirteen hours down there for one of the most enchanting interviews we'd ever have, and met someone who would turn out to be a great friend and supporter of *Rain Taxi* for years to come.

Establishing a business model for *Rain Taxi* was less intuitive but would be just as important in defining its image and reach. We knew it wouldn't be profitable—those other presses and magazines were registered nonprofits for a reason—but we had a lot to learn. It was Don Olson, the Twin Cities indie magazine distributor, who explained to me the economics of bookstore sales and convinced us that we should make the magazine free of charge. If the point was to get the word out about books, then you wanted as many people as possible to get the magazine, and bookstore sales, he said, would be at most "icing on the cake." You wouldn't recoup your expenses that way, ever. Better to have a high circulation and sell ads. Since we'd been assuming bookstore sales and paid subscriptions would be the cake itself, this changed the game plan a bit. But after a few nervous phone calls, we had Consortium, the Hungry Mind, Milkweed, Dalkey Archive, Copper Canyon, and a few other advertisers on board, which pretty much covered the cost of that first print run. Randall convinced his parents to make up the rest, and to donate the fee to incorporate as a 501(c)(3).

We were then set up to apply for grants and foundation money when the time came, but to start off we decided to print thousands of copies of the magazine on newsprint and make them available free in bookstores and cafés across the country.

Once we had a pretty firm lineup of reviews and features, we set a date with the local newspaper printer, the cheapest way to print several thousand copies. As we got closer to the date, we realized how much work and know-how would go into this. PDFs were not yet in use, and to get the Quark file ready for the printer there was another production step involved, which took extra time and money. The color processing was particularly tricky, but Randall navigated through all of that without flinching. We also didn't realize how much time it would take to dot the i's and cross the t's. Watching David copyedit was a crash course in professional-level editing (there was a lot more to it than being a whiz at the Test of Standard Written English we all took in high school), and watching Randall work the QuarkXPress was a crash course in desktop design. But when the first cover came together I had a real sense of the magic that would come out of all that work.

That once-distant printer date came up quickly. We were firmly committed to meeting the deadline, but we'd have to keep working every day after work and into the night to do it. David started to get cold feet about the project. It wasn't exactly what he wanted—book publishing was still his main idea and this magazine sideline project was taking over—and he didn't want to work on the schedule it demanded. He had other things going on in his life. He decided to resign before the first issue appeared. It was distressing to lose one of the main forces behind the project so early, and he'd already invested a lot of himself into it, but the first issue contains his editorial hello and goodbye.

Randall and I, however, were enjoying every minute of it (minus those ad-sales calls), and there was no slowing us down at that point. We really did end up spending many late nights, and often all night, getting each issue ready for print. But it was a renewable energy, fueled by the satisfaction of seeing the magazine come together from nothing to something you could put your hands on. Picking up those first boxes of newsprint from the plant was a tremendous thrill. I don't even remember how many copies we printed at first, or what bookstores we mailed them to, or how we got all the boxes up all those stairs and then out the door again, but I remember the beauty of that colorful saturated newsprint, of seeing our hard work take form. I wanted to read it over and over, to pore over the layouts, to admire the perfect placement of the book jackets and the table of contents and all those little details that make the difference between a bunch of Word files, a bunch of people talking, and a real publication.

One of the local writers contributing reviews to those first couple of issues was Eric Lorberer. Not only did his reviews need no editing and always come in on time, but of everyone involved he was the most enthusiastic about the project and seemed to have the most to give. When Randall and I received an invitation from the local NPR station to be on *All Things Considered (ATC)*, we invited him over to our apartment and tested out some ideas of what we might say. (It turned out that *ATC* was most interested in asking, Are you crazy? Why start a print magazine about books when the Internet is where everything is going?) We got on so well with Eric that we asked him to be our third board member—every nonprofit needs at least three to be legal—and he agreed. And about five minutes later, or maybe it was days or weeks, we asked him if he wanted to be a co-editor, an equal on the masthead. He was managing a B. Dalton bookstore in a mall at the time, so this was a welcome outlet for him, even if it was all after-hours work. I continued at the Hungry Mind, Randall continued at Half Price Books, and we scrounged as much time as we could to do this magazine, day after day, working in that tiny attic apartment with the requisite dormers and intense summer heat and low ceilings that we'd bump our heads on late at night. We set strict quarterly publication deadlines for ourselves and always met them, though that first year or two we could only do that by staying up all night and driving the file to the production center early in the morning. I remember falling into a delirious sleep after returning from dropping off the file one morning and waking with a startle: *Did* Moby-Dick *have a hyphen or not? I think I put a hyphen in it. Or did I?* I had, and it was okay either way, but the all-consuming intensity of the work was making itself felt.

The three of us had democratic ideals, no tyrants or monomaniacal egos here, and we did everything as equals. We made assignments as a group, we'd sit at the kitchen table and edit each piece line by line together, and we'd gather around the computer when it was time to design each individual page, giving Randall our suggestions (*move it this way, no, that*). We'd hand the phone around in a circle and go down the list of publicists at publishers, big and small, and cold-call them for advertisements. We wanted for each one of us to have the same level of satisfaction and investment in the project, every part of it.

But it was all a bit much. Our apartment became overrun with books, and we were hitting our heads on the ceiling more and more. Anytime we traveled, we spent most of our time and energy going to bookstores and convincing them to carry *Rain Taxi*, and every book we read, every free minute we had, was dedicated to some aspect of *Rain Taxi*'s development. We could see the magazine fairly easily breaking even in terms of cost, but never in terms of labor.

Advertising was tough to get and added up slowly. It was time to enter the grant game. Luckily in Minnesota there were some private foundations we could turn to (foundations that helped account for the wealth of literary publishing in the Twin Cities), but of course getting grants would mean doing something in addition to what we were already up to. For our first grant, from the McKnight Foundation in 1999, we devised a reading series, which would bring in an accomplished author from out of town to read alongside a local emerging writer and thereby build community and encourage local authors. We held these readings at art galleries, and the authors often stayed with Eric and Kelly Everding in their guest room. Arthur Sze was the first author to come to Minneapolis for the Rain Taxi Reading Series, and his reading at the Weinstein Gallery, and his abounding graciousness, remain among the highlights of those years. The reading series turned out to be a lot of work but also energizing; getting people together in person, rather than just in words, added a dimension of community and another kind of pleasure to the enterprise.

Those first grants gave us more confidence and a little more cash, though of course they also meant more expenses and more work that had nothing to do with editing the magazine. Once we had established ourselves with publishers and reviewers, the magazine actually became the easy part; we knew how to do it and knew it would work. A few years in it occurred to me that Rain Taxi was very much like a real job, but I wasn't getting paid and it didn't look like I ever would. Except for the reviews, publisher profiles, and author essays I wrote for Rain Taxi, I wasn't writing enough, either. I was thirty years old, and I didn't want to devote my entire life to this if I wasn't also creating my own work. So I started to back off. I applied to the low-residency MFA program at Bard College, thinking I could keep things going back at home but also devote some real time and energy to writing fiction, and spent two months for three consecutive summers in Annandale, New York. I then became possessed by the need to move to New York City, write, live a different life. I ended my time as an editor of Rain Taxi at the end of 1999, though I continued to write reviews and will always subscribe and support it. (Not only was Eric the right person for the job back in 1996, but now, nearly twenty years later, he's still the editor and director who keeps Rain Taxi going.)

In New York I landed a part-time job right away, through a connection from Rain Taxi, as an in-house copyeditor for Publishers Weekly, which paid twice as much per hour as my job at the Hungry Mind. Soon I was offered a full-time job as associate book editor at PW's sister magazine, Library Journal, just across the cubicle divide. It was wonderful to have a job, to be paid to be an editor. There was less freedom than at Rain Taxi, but also more freedom: I didn't have to work around the clock, and I could live in New

York and pay my own bills. I also worked with a group of thoughtful and dynamic people—book review editor Barbara Hoffert was a marvel—and I still loved editing and shaping other people's words, and contributing reviews of my own. And it was New York City, which in itself was exhilarating, though of course not without some serious drawbacks—the expense and time required for just getting by, for one. Commercial publishing had its downsides too: At *Library Journal* there was constant pressure for speed, and those 200-word book reviews got pretty formulaic after a while. And when an editor would quit, they'd often distribute that person's workload, opting to hire another ad-sales person or more management instead, as if the magazine's content itself were incidental (which in that business model essentially it is).

When in the autumn of 2003 an advertisement appeared in the classified ads of *PW* for the managing editor position at *New England Review* at Middlebury College, I wasn't looking for a new job but this one sounded too good to ignore. Did they actually hire people to work at literary magazines? I'd assumed that university-sponsored lit mags were staffed only by faculty; I didn't know some of them hired editors as well. But I'd known the *New England Review* for years. We carried it at the Hungry Mind and Borders, and it was always available in the Minneapolis Public Library and at St. Mark's Bookstore, the places I went most often over the years to explore lit mags. Plus it was published by the college I'd graduated from more than a decade previous, and I knew some students who'd helped read manuscripts for T. R. Hummer, the editor at the time. I didn't have any experience editing a literary journal per se, but the job called for someone who could be involved in all areas of production, distribution, and publicity, and also to read and evaluate manuscripts, particularly fiction. It was exactly what I wanted. I knew from *Rain Taxi* that I enjoyed what I'd once considered the incidental side work of publishing—the copyediting, the layout, the negotiating with authors, the planning and organizing and get-it-done work—and I was excited by the prospect of selecting original fiction for publication. The job description seemed like it had been written just for me, and after a couple of interviews I was lucky enough to be given a chance.

One of the questions I asked the editor, Stephen Donadio, when he called to offer me the job, was, To what degree does the college support this magazine? How serious are they and what do they get out of it? I didn't want to move to Vermont and give up my job at *LJ* just to find that it was a temporary gig. He said that those were excellent questions and he didn't have the answers exactly, but he could tell me that the administration had approved the full-time position and that the magazine had been under the full sponsorship of Middlebury College since 1987. That was good enough for me. My husband, fellow writer/editor Christopher Ross, was able to take his freelance work with him, so we got a car, packed up our stuff, and moved to Vermont in the spring of 2004. I wasn't thinking too far ahead at the time, and would not have been able to imagine that in about ten years' time I would be appointed editor myself. I was just happy to be able to throw myself into the work of a literary magazine again, but this time with a two-hundred-year-old employer to back me up.

Working at an already established literary magazine is not the same, of course, as starting your own; there's a larger vision to tap into and contribute to, and a history and staff to support you. At *New England Review* I joined the editors already in place—Stephen Donadio, a cultural omnivore and professor of literature at the College, and longstanding poetry editor C. Dale Young, the stunningly accomplished doctor/poet. Also helping out was a small hand-selected group of readers—many of them poets and fiction writers themselves. For the first few years I was at *NER* we also had the benefit of a full-time office manager, Toni Best, who'd been working for *NER* since it first came to Middlebury, could nearly do the record keeping with her eyes closed, and had a long institutional memory.

While the staff at *NER* is remarkably tenacious, the world of publishing and literary magazines itself is constantly changing—electronic distribution and rights, printing and web technology, submission practices, subscription dips and rises. And though *NER* is the establishment in terms of literary magazines, for me there's still that DIY feel to the operation, with the constant juggling of responsibilities, the variety of work involved, and the personal investment. There will always be more to do and better ways to do it. In addition to reading thousands of submissions, setting up the website and e-news, haggling with printers, and finding artists for the cover, I've taught a winter term class in literary magazine publishing and started up an internship program, with new Middlebury students coming into the office every quarter. I've also come to rely on and enjoy the larger community that *NER* is part of: the other members of CLMP and its listserv, the subscribers who come and go, the authors who submit, the students at the college, and now with our NER Vermont Reading Series, the writers here in our midst. But for me one of the best things about working as an editor at *NER* is that I've learned to read in a new way. When I pick up a manuscript, I have to be completely open to the unknown; there's no publisher's name behind the work, no agent vouching for its quality, nobody's seal of approval, just me and the words on the page. I've had to get over my personal taste to evaluate a work on broader and less personally subjective criteria, and to test my limits. And it turns out I like reading even more because of that, and I have greater respect for a wider range of writing styles and practices.

I fully understand that it's a privilege to be paid to work as a literary editor, but I also get that it's real work and I take it seriously. The beauty of a start-up is that it's run on passion and idiosyncrasy. The beauty of working at a stable magazine with a consistent staff is the depth of the pool of writers we can draw from, an earned respect by people who compile things like *Best American* anthologies, an established network of subscribers, and especially the time it affords us to work with writers closely and to see their progress over the course of years. I think this is one of the great benefits of being able to work as an editor professionally and not just as a side project. I've been able to see a story or essay that's not quite working come back several months or even a year later revised and hitting it just right; I've seen writers whose work I've encouraged but rejected come back next time with something spectacular. I've also seen writers go through periods of struggle and difficult and stop writing altogether; even more happily, some of them come back.

In the ten years that I've been at *NER*, I've seen the magazine itself go through periods of struggle and renewal as well. Changes in publishing technologies, most obviously, but also in economic climate. There was a particularly difficult moment in 2009, when, because of financial troubles related to the market crash, Middlebury College came very close to closing down the magazine. I knew all along that we couldn't take our position at Middlebury College for granted, but I was still shocked when the college publicly announced that it would discontinue publishing *New England Review* by the end of that June—or, as amended by the president, Ron Liebowitz, it would end the relationship if *NER* was not operating in the black by the end of 2011. To me that meant a certain death to the magazine as I'd come to know it. I'd been in this business long enough to know that it's the people energy that makes things happen, and it's the people energy that costs money; it's quite possible to make a mission-driven magazine break even, but only if your staff works long hours for free and you don't pay authors. To have any paid staff, funding needs to come from someplace else. The most common suggestion people had for us was to just stop printing and go online, as if that would solve everything. By doing that, what we'd cut in expenses we'd also cut in revenues, and we'd be at pretty much the same place but without a print journal as part of the operation. It also wasn't clear what "ending the relationship" meant exactly, though we knew that whatever happened to *NER* in the end, it wouldn't be up to the editors. Even a magazine like *Rain Taxi*, as a 501(c)(3) with the requisite board of directors, is not the editors' magazine; it's up to the board—and in *NER*'s case that's the President and Trustees of Middlebury College—to decide its fate.

The deadline for *NER* to break even by the end of 2011 is a few years behind us now, and the college, encouraged by our progress, has decided to continue publishing the magazine without any major restructuring. We fared much better than some others. Around the same time, Northwestern University terminated *TriQuarterly's* staff of two editors and handed the magazine over to the M.F.A. program to run. Utah State University cut the budget and staff for *Isotope: A Journal of Literary Nature and Science Writing* to the point that the magazine ended altogether.

We had to make some changes in order to keep from going under, but we had the gift of time, which these other magazines did not. I added grant writing and fundraising to my responsibilities, increased our internship program for students, started up a reading series for Vermont writers, and revamped our website to be more accessible and lively, those last two with the indispensable assistance and vision of Christopher Ross and J.M. Tyree. Some of what came out of the budget ultimatum has been good for *NER*. We were encouraged to work with other departments of the college, and so have been helped enormously by the fundraising department, which added *NER* to its list of priorities. The communications department offered some design assistance, the department of information technology helped with the website, and we continue to keep close ties to Middlebury's other literary programs, especially the Bread Loaf Writers' Conference. We were also able to secure NEA funding for some of our work. Overall, Middlebury College, with its broad-reaching educational and intellectual mission, its graduate programs and language schools, is a good place for *NER* to be.

Another significant change—and a more immediately positive one for me—came last year when, after Stephen Donadio decided that he would step down after nearly twenty years as editor, I was named editor in his place. Only the coming months, and hopefully years, will show exactly what this change will bring, but at the very least it means I'll be working in this field for a while longer—and now with even greater sense of possibility and purpose. I'll miss what Stephen brings to the daily operations— his unfathomable literary and cultural knowledge, his editorial discretion, and especially our ongoing conversations. But I'll also enjoy the autonomy and the ongoing collaboration with the rest of the staff: C. Dale Young will continue editing poetry, and I've been able to enlist J. M. Tyree as an associate editor in nonfiction, and longtime readers Jennifer Bates and Janice Obuchowski in fiction. These editors are paid by small stipends, driven mainly by an abiding interest in and love for the work, while still many others work for *NER* as volunteers.

Little magazines necessarily go through changes, financial and otherwise, and they continue to thrive only by some combination of skill, luck, love, and ambition. But what remains steady, what's at the heart and center of it all, for me and for other editors, is that constant connection with literature in the making. Whatever literature is—and we know it when we see it—it's always the motivation behind what we do, what we're all doing in this world of lit mags, paid and unpaid, stable or start-up. When I pick up a copy of the new issue with its gorgeous cover and all those voices neatly assembled inside, when an author likes the edits and a reader likes the words there, and even when I struggle to code a poem for the web or format a list for bulk mail, I know I'm seeing real literature make its way into the world. Even as I back off from some of the day-to-day concerns to focus more on the big picture, the purpose and passion that have always fueled the work will remain the same. In editing *NER*, I know I'm helping to bring the words—in that idiosyncratic combination that manages to convey something complex and intricate and personal—from the writer's mind out to meet the mind of another, and I know that in caring about this enough to do it against the long odds I'll always have the good company of other "little magazine" editors—past, present, and future.

Part 5:
Today's Magazines and the Future

About *At Length*

JONATHAN FARMER

I didn't set out to make a magazine for long work. I didn't set out to make a magazine at all.

It was Dan's fault. I've never known how to tell him no.

And so when he came to me saying we should start a literary magazine, even though I told him it was a bad idea, I didn't tell him no.

Instead, I told him I didn't want to do it unless we could publish the kind of thing we'd be proud of—stuff that was so interesting or valuable that we'd want to put aside whatever we were reading at the time and read this instead, even if we had no role in publishing it. I said this thinking that it meant no. Dan[1] accepted, thinking otherwise.

A few weeks later he came back to me with a question: what good work is being written but not published? After more than ten years of intermittently dumping money into this magazine—lots of money in the early years—and with no hope or intention of ever getting money out of it, I'm amused that it started with a question out of Business 101: what need (want, really) is the market (so to speak) failing to serve? I think it's telling, too, that we identified a gap in the lives of creators rather than consumers. We needed writers to make a magazine, and as with many institutions, a part of our initial motivation was the desire to create that institution. As far as we could tell, even the few publications that would consider long poems and novellas at that time published with a nearly Olympic infrequency. Stepping into that absence meant we could exist.

The first issue showed up at the office where I was working—maybe three boxes in total. Something like a year spanned the initial idea and this object, which had come up through a basement mailroom 47 floors below and, earlier, through customs, on its way from Canada to New York. Dan had dropped out of the project (he later agreed to come back on as a fiction

---

1. Dan, by the way, is Dan Kois. He remains one of my dearest friends and now serves as my editor (and the editor to hundreds of others, too) at *Slate*.

editor), but by then I'd already lined up the writers (two of them) for that first issue, and I was ashamed to go back to them—they'd given me the work as a favor. I was done with grad school, surprised at my own silence, surprised that there was no next validation, and working as a long-term temp at a great-big corporation. I was in New York but too shy and too vain to go out and meet other writers. I was making more money than I needed to pay my relatively meager outer-borough bills, and I had no idea what to say I was. I felt like I needed to go ahead with it, even though I had no idea what I was doing—and if I had any illusions to the contrary (which, of course, I did), the first issue cleared that up.

It looked like shit.

And there was almost no one waiting for it. We had maybe 60 subscribers at that point, almost all of them friends and family, many of them people I knew would never actually read it but were still kind enough to plunk down $20 for four issues, the number I assumed (incorrectly) we would publish in one year.

But it *was* a hell of a read. Two pieces—a novella from Michael Jayme Becerra and a long poem by James McMichael, both of which I can still go back and read in amazement. We'd met my original standard for the magazine.

We'd met it because I was lucky enough to know a few people. Jim had been my professor in grad school. Michael was a classmate there. I knew what they were working on and asked if I could have it. And even though I was in no position to bring new readers to either piece, they said yes, also out of kindness, and in doing so they offered us a little bit of credibility, a way of telling potential readers and other writers that this was something worthwhile.

Two years later—maybe a little more—*At Length* was dead. I was exhausted: financially, emotionally, even physically. Once we had finished an issue, the boxes would ascend through the same mailroom on up to the same office and I would drag them down into the subway and back to Queens. I'd sit in my apartment slotting them into envelopes, apply the address labels I'd printed out at work, then heave them to the nearest post office, which wasn't very near.

The magazine looked much better by then, but there still weren't very many subscribers—fewer than 200, I think. I felt ashamed that I wasn't finding an audience for the writing I wasn't paying for, even though I believed (I still believe) that it was always as good and sometimes much better than anything anyone else was publishing. Anne Winters's "An Immigrant Woman," for instance. The poem still holds me in a complicated mix of terror and marvel, and at this point just reading the first few lines is enough to reinstate the terrible stakes of its achievement—its monstrous achievement:

Slip-pilings on the Brooklyn littoral
—the poles still tarry, flimsy; the ferry terminus
with its walledup doors wan doorshapes
on eroded sills. Downstream, the strutwork
of the Williamsburg cable tower
threw its cool shadow half a mile inland
over tarpaper seams, gantried water butts,
and splintery tenement cornices milled
with acanthus and classical grasses
of nineteenth-century dream-slum fantasy.[2]

I hadn't found readers for this. I felt like a failure. I quit.

I quit, after five issues, with most subscriptions unfulfilled. I quit with no advance notice. Our art editor (we had added art by then) had already lined up the sketches for the next issue. She was pissed. I felt ashamed.

A few years later, I was in a used bookstore with the person who would become my wife, someone I'd met just after I put the magazine to sleep and who only knew about it from my rare and embarrassed references. Rooting through the poetry section, she noticed a copy of *At Length* and handed it to me excitedly. I almost threw up.

The magazine should have done better. It shouldn't have died; I shouldn't have killed it. And the thing is, I knew that someone else could have done better with it. Someone could have marketed it. Someone could have gone out and made connections and developed events and created merchandise and gone to conferences and created "buzz" and made it exciting and appealing and brought in way more subscribers and interns and all the things it needed to survive and find the readers those writers deserved. But I couldn't—or didn't. And I hated that.

I didn't really want to restart the magazine when a few friends started suggesting it to me—starting, I think, with Dan, who had refused to take down the website in the years after I stopped publishing, leaving up the note about a "hiatus" and the excerpts from the five issues we'd published. Someone—I don't remember who—suggested bringing it back as an online magazine, which I didn't like; I'm just old enough to be uncomfortable reading online, and the hurry I feel in front of screens seemed incompatible with reading valuable long work. But the reasons in favor started piling up. We could make the text easy to print. We could add sections like music (an idea suggested by my friend Ehren, who didn't realize that he

2. *At Length Magazine* 1, no. 3 (Summer 2004); the poem was published later in *The Displaced of Capital* (Chicago: University of Chicago Press, 2004).

was saddling himself with responsibility for creating and running a music section) and photography. And I still needed something to be.

But there was still so much about the actual work of it that felt dreadful. It was Caroline — to whom I was probably engaged by then — who figured out that part: bring in someone else to do the things I didn't like.

And so I did. In fact, I brought in lots of people. Without doing anything more than knowing a few people, I had come to know a lot of people by then, since the few people I knew at first were very good at meeting other interesting people. And so with less money to my name, unable to pay anyone, I was able to find an art director and a web designer and a managing editor and a prose editor and a music editor and a photography editor and a community manager, and some of them stuck around just long enough to get the thing started and a couple are still working on the magazine today. But they were all people I was proud to work with and they all enjoyed doing things I couldn't do — couldn't, at least, do well.

There wasn't any grand vision. I made the roles appealing to all those talented people largely by promising to stay out of their way — and then by keeping that promise. The one thing I could offer was a space, but this was the Internet; space is practically free. It's only because the space was defined by the work of lots of other talented people that it became an interesting place for them to do their things — the very things, that is, that were making it an interesting place for the rest of us to do the same. We were lending each other the credibility we could generate by working toward something other than credibility — much as those first two authors had done with the magazine's first issue.

But we were doing it, at least partly, on faith. We were and we continue to be scattered geographically, each of us in a different space overflowing with jobs — multiple jobs, in some cases — and families and creative projects of our own. We encounter other editors' creations and selections for the most part in the same way our audiences do, by reading and viewing them once they're live on the site. Our publishing schedule is determined by who can get something ready when. We're a single magazine in part because we say we are, because that same logo makes its claim on every page; because every URL starts with the same fifteen characters; because that first idea, *length,* is in the name and logo and URL and still runs through all of our work — a presence with unanticipated benefits: because each piece we publish is its own issue, coordination is much, much simpler.

I'm telling this story in this somewhat unflattering way because it's true — and it's a part of the truth we maybe shy away from; the way our publishing comes out of our lives and times in ways that are plainer than the often-invisible and always-present forces of culture, bias, privilege and the like that they are inextricably involved with—and those, of course, are part of it, too. The work of sharing literature includes a lot that's extraliterary, including our own failings and selfishness and insecurity—mine, for instance. And it of course comes out of our good fortune, too. It takes a lot of that.

When I asked our prose editor, Belle Boggs, what I should write about in this essay, she immediately said "community." Meaning, she explained, the way the magazine depends on our creating a community—creating relationships—where none existed before. Our authors, for instance. Until recently, we didn't accept unsolicited submissions. There just wasn't time. (There's still not, but we've decided we need to do it anyways. Belle and I now schedule month-long open reading periods as frequently as we can.) For most of our life online, we've found prose and poetry by hunting down the writers we admire and asking them to send us work. Beginning from one kind of relationship—*I read and value your work*—we reach out for another. As with all attempts at a new relationship, this can be awkward. Sometimes, we get silence in return. And sometimes that person will send back a poem or story that we don't want to publish, which is, even with the kindest of authors (and most of them are extremely kind about it), painfully awkward.

If we say yes, though, that's the moment when a real relationship begins, the one I cherish. While I don't edit every poem I publish, I do edit most. I start out delicately. Unlike prose writers, poets are often unused to being edited. I don't make acceptance contingent on accepting changes; I'm wary of accepting an ideal version of a piece that may not exist, and given how complicated the relationship between poet and poem is, I don't want anyone to feel coerced into considering changes. I ask: Would you be interested in considering some suggestions? If they say yes—and, amazingly, I think everyone I've asked has said yes, at least to considering— then something strange and (at least for me) delightful begins.

I enter into an imaginary relationship. I enter into a relationship with the person I imagine wanted to make this poem and the poem I imagine they wanted to make. And I do so by giving that person and that poem everything I can. As I explain to all my authors, I do so in full awareness of my failings—not necessarily awareness of what they are but that they exist, and that they are numerous, and that they include blindness to many of my failings. I can't know in advance which of my suggestions will be projections of my own biases and idiosyncrasies and which, if any, will create actual benefit for the real person who wrote this—for the poem she or he would value sending out into the world—but I do my best to listen and consider *this* poem, to understand what it's for and what it values, and then I offer anything I can think of that might help. My job, I tell them, is to give them everything I can that could be useful, theirs to decide what, if anything, is. And I always make clear—all of this begins from admiration. This is a poem I already love and want share with anyone who arrives at our site. You don't need to change a word.

And it *is* the beginning of a relationship, sometimes a very rich one, sometimes one that will entail many more rounds of edits. I know it's the start of a relationship because I can see my own personality at work—that same mix of insecurity and vanity, caution and cockiness, that defines so many of my interactions, especially at the outset. The same mix, in fact, that led me to make a magazine instead of actually going out and meeting other writers when I got to New York, even once the person whose idea it was wasn't doing it anymore. And as always, this is where the magazine's vision begins. The magazine is hard to define because it's easy to remake. We publish one story, poem, interview or essay at a time, and each editor is free to work with each author, photographer, etc. to make whatever those two people decide is worth making and sharing. Each piece then finds its own audience, and for the time of those encounters, the magazine is what happens in the relatively prolonged exchange between artist and audience. Patterns emerge, of course, but I hope that we are always able to revise them based on whatever new opportunity for meaning we find.

Ultimately, ideally, we are engaging in the kind of relationship that Frank Bidart calls in his poem "To the Dead," paraphrasing *The Little Prince*, "the love of / two people staring / not at each other, but in the same direction." And there is something in that which feels as honest and as rewarding as anything I know how to do.

However we find the author or the author finds us, though, there's still no money for the work. Possibly because I'm still so bothered by the audience we didn't find for the writing we published in the physical magazine, I'm adamant about not charging for anything on the site. We don't sell ads. We don't have contests. Our sole revenue stream is still my pocket—though we're working on that now so that we *can* eventually pay those people who let us publish their words.

Hopefully, we *are* providing them with something like what I first offered to our editors—a space whose value they increase by entering into it. But that feels insufficient. If the vocation of writing has more to do with a voice—a voice responding to a sense of being called to speak—than an income, it is nonetheless true that (a) most writers struggle financially and (b) money is still one of the hallmarks of value in our culture, and the failure to pay seems to neglect both the writer's value and the writer's need—to neglect the writer him- or herself. As an online magazine, we are taking part in a shift that has made it easier to celebrate writers and dis-

cover their work while also making their work more disposable, less protected, easier to consume, harder to distinguish and harder to commodify
in ways that don't reek of commodification.[3] Not all of that is all bad, but
to the extent that we can, I think we have an obligation to resist devaluing
the very words we put onto our site to say: this is important. Give it time.

But we are doing so outside the institutions—most often universities—
that have often supported literary magazines, and at a moment when
many of those universities are getting out of the business of most things
that don't look at least a little bit of business. Universities are less interested in being patrons, and so are patrons, for that matter. Government
funds are disappearing, too. Meanwhile, new magazines, many of them
very good, are proliferating, as are the Kickstarter campaigns and other
appeals for small donations that are supposed to make community arts
projects more reflective of their communities—communities which tend
to be made up of the same folks who are watching their previous sources
of money dry up. The rules are apparently changing, and what it means to
be a writer—or, at least, to be *valued* as a writer—is likely changing along
with them, but I have no interest in leading the charge. We're working on
securing 501(c)(3) status. Once we have it, we'll start looking for funds
wherever we can find them—and then pass all those funds along to our
contributors, minus the small amount we need to pay for web-hosting and
a few other essential functions. Just as *At Length* was never meant to be a
business, my role in it was never meant to be a job. But because it is both
an identity and a relationship, I want to do it as well and as compassion-
ately as I can. And so we'll find a way to pay.

Meanwhile, we'll also go on, in other unfunded ways, trying to reach the
audiences who might value this. It should go without saying, but maybe
it does too often at this point: the primary audience of any publication is,
well, its audience: the people who do or might read it. The work we do with
our authors must be about those real and potential readers, even as they
remain even more imaginary than our authors—the someone this piece of
writing conjures. The joy or difficulty of reading. The person we might find
so we might serve. In the Bidart quote above, whether we acknowledge it

3. That shift also has to do with what it means and feels like to read literature online.
When we first started publishing the print magazine, if an established journal put actual literature on its website, it was either spillover or a very small sample. The web was,
in essence, a place to sell a magazine and, by an extension, a place to build an audience
for your website so that you could, again, sell the actual magazine. Online magazines
seemed for the most part to be either marginal or experimental, and almost invariably
they seemed cheap. Many writers—many of my favorite writers—resisted being on a
website. It seemed cheap. The object was missing—the familiar cues to meaning and
concentration. There was less validation there—as well as less control.

or not, the direction we are looking is the direction of a reader, wherever—and whoever—he or she might be.

It was easier to understand this when we were a print magazine. The readers had names and addresses that I kept in a spreadsheet. I placed one copy of the magazine with one story and one poem in one envelope for each reader. They mailed in checks, and though no one ever said so, those $20 meant that I owed them $5 worth of reading in every one of those mailings. Now, they are a fraction in a number Google Analytics provides. This poem or that essay or that interview regenerates in the transmission between a server and a screen, neither of which I have ever seen or really understand. In some ways, it makes me hungrier for their presence—for our ability to create them by creating something worthwhile for them. It also means that the relationship is more provisional. The person who finds or is found by this piece may never encounter the next. And so we go on making them up, hoping that somewhere in that process we are creating another relationship, however enduring or brief, that's worthy of their time.

There's plenty of prognosticating to be done—publishing is changing, fast. But I'm not the one to do it. Maybe because I have such a terrible memory, I've never had a knack for imagining the future. I do imagine, though, or at least hope, that it will still have to do with a Janus-faced relationship with audience and reader, wherein serving one is also an act of serving the other. And I hope, too, that it will entail an enlarging of our communities, not because literature needs large audiences—we turn literature into a fetish when we make it into a cause—but because all of our communities, in order to be meaningful, require us to be more imaginative about each other, about who our others are.

More than the changes brought about by new technologies and shifting economic rules and realities, what interests me is the work being done, at various stages of the process, by organizations like VIDA, Cave Canem, and Kundiman—groups that are insisting on different and more equitable relationships in our cultures of writing, publishing, and reading. Like pretty much everything in our lives, these are marked by an overlong and ongoing history of blindness, bias, human frailty, human cruelty, and far, far worse. It is both our obligation and our opportunity to speak to and hear from each other more broadly than we have. Doing so allows us to access a larger and deeper talent pool, to encounter a richer and more varied host of pleasures and styles, to learn more, see more, imagine more, draw from more, and exist in fuller relationship to a fuller version of the world. It makes us better and, hopefully, also makes us at least fractionally more just.

As a straight, white, male editor who grew up in an almost all-white culture, I have to work to be aware of my biases. But literature is, I think, an effort at interpersonal imagination—finding new ways to speak to and about each other, to please and challenge and sing to and entertain and argue with each other, to engage and engage *with* each other, and I believe that the work of inclusion is fundamentally literary work, imaginative work. Finding, selecting, and standing next to each new author, looking out at the invisible, still-imaginary readers we might summon—I want to be part of that.

Summoning the Bard:
The Twenty-First-Century
Literary Magazine on the Web

REBECCA MORGAN FRANK

In 2003, *The Believer* hit the stands, joining the still new *McSweeney's* (b. 1998) and *Fence* (b. 1998) in a wave of journals created by a generation of writers hitting their thirties. Fellow poet Rob Arnold and I had just graduated from Emerson College's MFA program, and we were charmed by the style and attitudes of these journals and excited that a new era of magazines seemed to have arrived. One day I looked up from a copy of *The Believer* and said to Rob, "Why do prose writers do all the cool stuff? We should start a magazine."

There was some impulse behind those magazines that made us want to join in and create something different, something that felt more in touch with the changing culture outside of literary institutions. But we were also coming of age as poets in Boston, a city with a long and respected literary tradition and a wonderful range of magazines and writers whom we admired. We felt an affinity for the aesthetics of magazines that were as old as we were, such as *Ploughshares* (b. 1971), where Rob was a reader and would later become managing editor, or the neighboring *AGNI* (b. 1972). We eagerly read, and dreamed of being published in, long-standing journals like *Virginia Quarterly Review* (b. 1925) and the *Kenyon Review* (b. 1939). We wanted to find a way to meld tradition and innovation, and Rob had the idea that starting an online magazine was the direction for us to take.

Memorious was born a few months after *The Believer* incident, at a Cambridge reading of oral collaborations by Joshua Beckman and Matthew Rohrer. We asked them if they would be willing to let us publish some of the audio collaborations in an online literary journal we were founding. When a CD came in the mail a week later, we realized we had to follow through and make a magazine.

Back in 2003, online literary publishing was still the new frontier, seen as an arena separate from print publishing, and so we began the adventure of asking other people for work to publish in our foray into the unknown. The heart of the issue was an interview that Rob conducted with Robert Creeley, and we successfully solicited prose from Steve Almond and J. T. Leroy. (Little did we know we were starting out in publishing as part of a widespread literary scandal, when in 2006 J. T. Leroy was revealed to be a middle-aged woman from the Bay area rather than a transgender twenty-something who was a former child prostitute and drug addict.) We solicited poetry from both strangers and poets we knew. It was a miracle, I thought at the time, and still think, that people trusted us with their work for that first issue.

In the beginning, there were only the three of us: Brian Green joined Rob and me as our webmaster and fiction editor. As we designed the magazine, I played the role of Luddite. This was easy, because at the time I was one. But it was also useful. I wanted to create an interface that was simple, that recreated to some degree the feel of a print journal and offered navigation that was like the simple act of turning a page. I wanted older generations of poets to feel comfortable reading us and publishing with us. I wanted the look to be clean, avoiding the clutter of so many websites. My cofounders had the skills to make this happen, and they could test it all on me, while I, like any cranky Luddite will, let them know the troubles I faced. Through this process, Brian and Rob envisioned and executed our then unique and easy-to-navigate design.

In winter of 2004, in the Enormous Room, the same bar in Central Square, Cambridge, where we had solicited our first work, we launched Issue 1 of *Memorious*. We had no idea what we were getting into, which made us like everyone else who has ever started an independent literary magazine. Obtaining good content and getting ourselves on to the web was not enough to make us succeed; we needed to prove ourselves and promote the magazine. As we began to face the reality of what we had made, and the responsibilities of developing it, we looked for models not just in long-standing print magazines, as well as newer ones like *Post Road* (b. 1999), but to online magazines like *failbetter* (b. 2000), *Blackbird* (b. 2002), *La Petite Zine* (b. 1999), and *Drunken Boat* (b. 2000). For we were setting out on the sometimes frustrating path of persuading people to distinguish between mission and medium. We are a literary magazine by mission; we face the same issues of any new magazine. At the same time, our medium brings not only new possibilities, but new limitations, most of which are based in the general public's misconceptions about the web. At the time we founded *Memorious*, the perception of online journals was steeped in a lack of understanding, foresight, sometimes even common sense. Even after ten years, some of these misconceptions prevail.

One of the most curious misconceptions is the belief that digital magazines are ephemeral. Writers were at first reluctant to submit, or sent their weakest work, because they believed the magazine, or maybe even the web, wouldn't last. The reality is that some magazines live and some die, regardless of their medium. Is it more permanent to leave behind a few copies tucked into the shelves of used bookstores and peoples' basements, or to be archived on the web? Do more online magazines die than print magazines? It is hard to say. But if you count transient magazines posted up with WordPress as the equivalent of the old Kinko's Xeroxes, I think the differences might not be all that significant. A lot of folks start bands in their basements, some even make it to booking gigs. But reaching a broader audience and keeping the band together are entirely different endeavors.

Daniel Nester and Steve Black's essay in *Bookslut*, "Here Today, Here Tomorrow: On the Lifespan of the Literary Magazine," provides some interesting data about the failure rate of literary magazines founded between 1980 and 1995 and reviewed in *Library Journal*. The lives of the journals were tracked on databases, but of course these reviews were not of online magazines, and to my knowledge, no one has tracked the life span or failure rate of online magazines. I do wonder what we mean by failure, beyond its clear practical use in the study, which is that a journal has ceased publication. Many online magazines, such as Jim Berhle's *can we have our ball back?*, have ended, but arguably not failed. Berhle contributed significantly to the literary magazine landscape, paving the way for us by simply publishing terrific poets.

On July 15, 2003, Jim Behrle wrote on his blog, "I'm thinking of killing *can we have our ball back?* In the conservatory. With the rope. And this isn't so I'll get a bunch of e-mails saying, 'No, no, Joy Division, don't break up!' They should have broken up. All good things must destroy themselves. Eventually. All cookies get hard."[1] Longevity, Behrle reminds us, is not necessarily the best or only measure of worth.

Yet most of us still want longevity and admire it in a magazine in part, perhaps, because we want to hang on to the illusion that our work will endure. When you visit the old URL for *can we have our ball back?*, the worst fears about online magazines come true as a site unfolds declaring, "Welcome to the love site for romantic singles." What a tragic fate, one might think, for the poems that had once lived on that site, even if many had been reprinted in the poets' books or in anthologies.

Remember, however, the power of the Wayback Machine, which provides archives of web pages preserved as they were when they were live. Here you can spend the afternoon reading the old issues of *can we have our ball back?*, discovering poems by Robert Pinksy, Anselm Berrigan, Jean Valentine, Ange Mlinko, Rebecca Wolff, and Joanna Klink, and more, all serving as a reminder that a variety of poets were being published online

1. http://jimsmonkey.blogspot.com/, July 15, 2003; accessed March 30, 2014.

early on. Even the "dead" magazines live on, while other online magazines have purposefully remained archived online at their own sites even when they have ceased publishing new issues.

Still, no one expected us to last. By us I mean both *Memorious*, as an individual magazine, and us, as in all online magazines. When a contributor complained to us that she wanted her story taken down because she couldn't have dreamed that it would stay online as long as five years, we complied, following the advice of more experienced editors whom we admired. This was a difficult and troublesome decision, because we build discrete small issues, and we see each issue as fixed content. No one would ask a print magazine to remove a story, and this is not merely because this would be logistically impossible. Print, in its own way, becomes an artifact at its conception: it is an event that has clearly occurred and is inerasable because of that temporal nature as well as its physicality. Web publishing, on the other hand, is experienced as something ongoing that is conceived as the visitor discovers it. If we conceived of our magazine as a complete made object, we needed to protect and present it as such, even if to the searcher on the web our issues are timeless. After deleting the story, I immediately changed our contract to clarify that work would remain online indefinitely. We were learning, along with everyone else, what it meant to bring work online.

We also knew that on the Wayback Machine any content we had posted would live forever. Or, well, as long of a forever as the Wayback Machine or the Internet as we know it survives. As many have learned the hard way, there are no "take backs" on the Internet. Screenshots and archives ensure that.

Subsequently, the Internet changes the narrative of our course as writers. Our juvenilia, which would perhaps have been better off burned, or kept until after death, is now on perpetual parade for the world to see. When this work, often the results of early MFA years, or even high school or college days, makes its way on to the web, it is generally there to stay, and there is no way to make an explanation for it, or to keep anyone (agents, publishers, mothers, future employers, lovers) from pulling up those poems or stories rather than the ones we want them to read. Writers submitting work to online magazines ten years ago certainly did not understand this. Some writers today are still only starting to figure this out.

The impact of this longevity has been hard for many of us to see until we have lived it. Will our work be here in a hundred years? Of course it is impossible to foresee what a hundred years will bring to our planet, much less literary culture. But will the work remain online across the course of our careers? Probably. After ten years of publishing, I have seen many poets and fiction contributors emerge and evolve in their writing careers. Over a hundred books list our journal in the acknowledgments, and our contributors have won numerous awards and published in countless journals. And every time any of those writers' names is searched on the web, *Memorious* comes up. We are part of our contributors' accessible history, their nonlinear narrative as writers.

While this new reality of permanence wrapped in an ephemeral-appearing medium may be unsettling to those of us of my generation and older, younger generations are growing used to a public life, to a lifelong record of their work and even their mistakes. None of us know what the ramifications of this will be for them or for publishing and literary history, but, meanwhile, all of us need to pay attention to what it means that the web is enduring, and that once we let something loose on the web, we lose control of it. This goes for publications as well as individuals; at ten years old, we are still learning what it means to have an easily accessible history as a magazine.

Besides misconceptions concerning the longevity of online publications, there also seems to be a popular belief that online magazines are obligated to take advantage of our medium and move beyond the limits of the printed page through multimedia work. While I very much admire the unique mission of such journals as *Born*, which published collaborative videos from 1996 to 2011, and *Linebreak*, which features poets reading the work of other poets, it seems to me that we don't all have to include multimedia work. This isn't to say that *Memorious* doesn't sometimes take advantage of the medium: we began with audio collaborations and we now publish recordings of our annual art song concert that results from our art song contest, through which we bring together poets and composers for collaboration. But I have always moved from the belief that sometimes people simply want to read a poem or story, and that I want *Memorious* to be one of the places where you can still find that as our world moves to the web. Literature can live on as literature, even while being delivered in different ways. The editors of *Electric Literature* (b. 2009) understood this when they created a platform that allows readers to choose how they want to receive the content, ranging from paperback to digital formats of ePub, Kindle, or pdf.

Another misconception online publications have faced about our medium is about quality. Along with the assumption that as an online journal we publish a certain kind of poetry can be the assumption that we only publish poor-quality or amateurish work, and that anyone can be published online. To this I respond, yes, and anyone can be published in print. This is true whether you are referring to the growing world of self-publishing, the enduring conditions in which people sometimes publish friends, or simply the amount of bad writing that someone somewhere sees fit to print. The equivalent to the claim about "anyone" being able to publish online is the idea that the printing press was the downfall of the book. The reality is that there is no inherent aesthetic affinity or quality tied to medium, and that democratic and widespread access to publishing and sharing work leads to increased diversity and a richer literary landscape.

Let's not forget that assessing the quality of online magazines is naturally a simple task: as readers we take content, process, and context into account. Is the work itself of value or interest? Is a magazine edited by someone we respect or produced by an organization we respect? Many of us felt heartbroken over the changes at *TriQuarterly* not because it was moved online, but because it was leaving behind its history and identity when it was taken from a long-standing experienced editorial leadership and passed on to students.

Our goal for *Memorious* was to create an editorial vision by publishing quality work that interested us, and to thus build an archival body that would interest readers and make them want to be part of the magazine. However, building our poetry submission base was much easier than with fiction. Poets quickly took to online publishing. Fiction writers were less responsive to solicitations from online venues and often still are. Some confess that they are looking for money, more prestige, and a place where they will be noticed by agents.

Payment aside, it seems to me to equate prestige to medium is increasingly naive. Magazines that are under a decade old cannot always compete with the long histories of the most prestigious magazines. But one of the other appealing aspects of the long-standing giants, beyond whom they have published (and of course longevity allows for the contributors' prestige to change and reflect back on the magazine), is their circulation. Perhaps the most confusing aspect of comparing print magazines to online magazines is that more people read the online magazines. According to the Council of Literary Magazines and Presses directory, on July 18, 2014, *Guernica* has 25,000 unique visitors a month, while *Blackbird* and *DIAGRAM* have 40,000. While there may be discrepancies in data and reporting, beneath the numbers is the reality that every day, hundreds of people are reading these magazines online. And of course good online magazines do get contacted by agents, who increasingly turn online to discover new authors.

Money is another issue. One of the key questions facing all publishers in the move of literature to digital platforms is that of the bottom line: do we get readers to pay for content? If yes, how so? From contributors? And if not, does the money come from advertisers? At a publishing summit I attended, a print editor from a university literary journal suggested that it was unethical and detrimental to give poetry away for free, and she questioned my choice to do so with *Memorious*. The irony was that the magazine she works for does not pay contributors for content. In other words, the ethical question for her seemed not to be about compensation on the author end, but on the editor end.

Unlike the editor working on a university publication, my work as an editor is unpaid, and like most editors, I do the work on top of my paying job. It is a labor of love, the tradition of indie literary magazines who maintain the mission of keeping an art with a small audience alive, of creating and sustaining community, of contributing to shaping the history of our art. I understand the desire to see monetary value in what we do, but I choose to embrace these other values. As for contributor payment, in the case of *Memorious*, I believe that I can support contributors more by championing their work than I can by trying to find nominal funding to pay them token amounts.

The truth is, even if we wanted to charge readers, pay walls don't work. Larger publications struggle with them, and a small magazine like ours would lose most of our readers, readers who come to us for specific pieces of content. As a society, we have become different kinds of readers online: we rarely read publications "cover to cover." The twenty-first century reader is used to picking and choosing online, like at the candy shop where you create your own mix by the pound. This doesn't mean readers don't have favorites, or brand loyalty, but readers who love us might also have another twenty or more magazines to which they feel loyalty.

The trend now at many print magazines is to turn cost over to contributors, but you rarely see this with online magazines. To me as an editor and a poet, this trend seems dangerous. It closes out writers without the privilege of disposable income. What does it mean for our literary community if poets have to pay three dollars to every journal they submit to, on top of what they are already paying in contest or reading fees, which now are creeping up toward thirty dollars, in order to try to have a book published? That the defense of fees is often to compare submission fees to "the price of a latte" reflects part of the problem.

For *Memorious*, the third financial option, advertising revenue, was always out of the question. My cofounders and I agreed early on that we didn't want any ads interrupting the look and experience of the magazine. We don't have to endure that in most print literary journals—imagine ads on the same page as poems—and we certainly won't inflict that on our readers. Where does that leave us? Scrambling and paying out of pocket just as poets and editors and patrons have done from the beginning of the printing press.

I have been using "us" and "we," but the staff behind those words has been powerfully mutable because of the flexibility of location the web allows. I have been the one constant on our staff. Rob Arnold's involvement faded after *Memorious*'s first two years because of his job at *Ploughshares*, although he continued to help with design and other occasional projects. In 2008 he officially retired to the role of contributing editor, and in 2010, he became the managing editor of *Fence*. Brian Green of Seattle,WA, has been replaced as webmaster by Heather Van Aelst of Somerville, MA., and as our fiction editor by first Jessica Murphy Moo of Seattle; Barrett Bowlin of Binghamton, NY; and now Ian Stansel of Cincinnati, OH, and Joanna Luloff of Denver, CO. The magazine has relied on the work of assistant poetry editor, Matt McBride, who has worked with us out of Ohio since 2009, as well as a rotating cast of assistants, readers, and contributing editors from all over the country, including Adam Day in Kentucky and Hadara Bar-Nadav in Missouri. The magazine has moved with me from Massachusetts to Ohio to Mississippi, but its staff continues to work from their home turfs. Being a web magazine means we aren't tied to place, although each of the three cities I have been based in has shaped the magazine in some way.

Meanwhile, the environment of the publishing world has continued to change. In 2008–9, there was a dramatic shift in the reception of online magazines. The economy tanked and even university print magazines were struggling, with some of them getting pressure to move entirely online. Facebook moved out of the dorm room and into the offices of the literary world. It was a new world, one in which people grew open to taking online publishers more seriously. Social networking helped level the playing field: suddenly magazines like *Memorious* had more ways of broadening our readership without a marketing budget. With the help of then assistant editor Laura van den Berg, we grew a presence on Twitter and Facebook and in the blogosphere.

In 2009, AWP approved our Fifth Anniversary Panel—one of the first anniversary readings of an online magazine at the conference. In 2012, Rick Barot's poem in our magazine was selected by Mark Doty for *Best American Poetry*, and as I looked at the table of contents, where *Memorious* was sandwiched between *Southern Review* and *New England Review* in a lineup that included the *New Yorker* and the *Nation*, where we were in the company of those journals we had first admired, I noticed that there was only one other online-only journal in that particular table of contents. Does this stasis in representation mean something? Maybe, or maybe not, for another way of looking at it is that out of a list of almost forty journals, there were only five of us founded in the twenty-first century. Perhaps an online journal's path can now be to simply build a reputation like the print journals did before us.

Were we happy to be in print? Yes, but it wasn't the medium that mattered, it was the company *Memorious* was keeping, the confidence in our work shown by editors we admired, and the awareness of the broad readership that particular print anthology would find. Categorizing what we read by medium no longer makes sense. Most of us who are lovers of literature are conflicted in our beliefs and practices. We spend increased hours online while continuing to buy and read books; we read an array of print and online magazines. We resist or give in to the e-reader, but still rely on Project Gutenberg and Google Books for books we can't otherwise access in a timely manner. We teach using print magazines and anthologies; we teach using web links. The reality is that the Internet is an efficient, affordable, democratic means for sharing words that coexists with print. At least for now.

It wasn't clear to me ten years ago what the future of web publishing would look like, and I certainly couldn't have foreseen the platforms and forces that shaped where we are now. I did, know, however, that I wanted to be part of the possibilities of that future, because it was important that people who knew about and cared about literary culture be part of creating what it would be on the web. What did we want it to be? What kind of traditions did we want to build there? Many of us are still dedicated to figuring that out.

Failbetter's first issue has an introduction from the editors:

The fact that failbetter.com was founded by two self-proclaimed Luddites is a philosophical inconsistency we are willing to live with. Being a bunch of bookstore vagabonds, who in an era of eBooks still savor the spiritual grace and soulful texture of the printed page, we first hesitated at the prospects of putting together an e-zine. The word itself—e-zine—as if it were a sound produced by an involuntary bodily movement—annoyed us. But forced with a chronic inability to afford even a modest print run, coupled with the regrettable realization that most literary journals may soon go the way of the dodo, we at failbetter.com suddenly thought better of the e-zine option.[2]

The word "e-zine" has fizzled out, but *failbetter* remains. In 2010, I put together a panel at AWP on online magazines, for which *Memorious* was joined by the editors of *Guernica, Blackbird, failbetter*, and *Drunken Boat*, and the most memorable moment to me was when *failbetter* editor Thom Didato said something to the effect of "we are having the wrong conversation by talking about computers." He was right: along came a variety

2. "From the Editors," failbetter.com 1.1 (Fall/Winter 2000): http://www.failbetter .com/01/FromTheEditors.htm; accessed March 28, 2014.

of mobile devices, e-readers, and iPads; what we read on is continually changing. And clearly he, like me, is no longer a Luddite.

Ten years ago, we couldn't sell people on the idea of an inevitable future in which online publishing dominated. Now, more and more of all of our lives has moved to the web. When the *Huffington Post* asked me to respond to the question of whether online magazines have "come of age," I wrote: "Yes, online journals have 'come of age': we've evolved from being the medium that people did not take seriously, and considered ephemeral, to being an enduring medium that models innovation in the important work of keeping literature relevant and accessible to readers. Online and print journals are essentially doing the same work: bringing together writers and readers. The practices of readers are now closing the assumed gap between these mediums."[3] I still believe that it is the readers who will lead us into the future of publishing.

What will the future bring? The mediums may prove to be ones we can hardly imagine now. Will we all read poems on Google glasses? I can't imagine even fifty years ahead for publishing based on technology alone. But when I look at the next ten, I look forward to seeing innovations for online magazines, innovations which I hope are in the areas of design and usability, in the areas of aesthetic movements and new writers we have yet to discover. Meanwhile, the poems we have published live on in pixels and in the pages of the writers' books; they live on in our lived experience of having read them.

Many magazine editors and book publishers say that they had no idea what they were getting into when they founded their magazine or press. It is impossible, I think, to imagine what will become of these ventures that begin in bars and living rooms and take on lives of their own. There are moments when I wonder what it would have been like for my own writing or my personal life if I had never started *Memorious*, or if I had not kept it going for so many years. But the richest part of the experience, the part that keeps me going and makes me love what I do, is the people. Every single poem that has been published in the magazine has been selected by me, and I have personally corresponded with all of our poets, and nearly all of our contributors. I take a continued interest in our contributors because they create the sort of work I want to see in the world. Just as with so many of the magazines that are our predecessors, a community was born around the magazine regardless of the medium.

Long ago, you waited for a bard to come through town. Now, a lover of poetry can sit down at an electronic device and summon a bard, in print or

3. Anis Shivani, "Online Literary Journals Come of Age: 15 Top Online Journal Editors Speak," *Huff Post Books*, November 21, 2010; accessed March 30, 2014.

video or audio, wherever he or she goes. To someone who grew up traveling the world through books from a small town, this seems like an extension of everything I love the most. A magazine, though born from the ideas of a person or two, is made up by all of the communities it touches and draws from. In some ways, nothing has changed.

The Future of the Gatekeepers

JANE FRIEDMAN

From 2005 until 2011, the poet Billy Jones ran an online contest called "The Poet Laureate of the Blogosphere," annually awarded to an actively blogging poet. Jones wrote that it "was a means to make relatively un-known poets better known and to prove there are still great poets who don't make the rounds of the university circuits."[1] The award was given to a nominated poet who received the most votes, making it something of an online popularity contest.

During the 2010 nomination and voting process, poet Robert Brewer, who actively blogs for his employer (a commercial publisher) and on his personal website, scored the most votes. But the competition had become so contentious by that point that Jones decided to call it a tie between Brewer and the runner-up. Brewer's affiliation with a corporate interest was viewed as a discredit; because Brewer was paid to blog, some argued, and had the backing of a publisher, he shouldn't win. What was not stated, but implied, is that a poet of lesser means, or a starving artist, was a more authentic and deserving choice. Brewer's image didn't match the long-standing avant-garde culture of poetry—that exists even in on-line communities—that assumes one cannot pursue profits and a higher purpose simultaneously. Even Dana Gioia, a well-known critic of the con-temporary poetry community, has said that the most important quality of a poet is that he can't sell his poetry, because this frees the poet to do his art for love. The possibility that the pursuit of both money and art might enhance each other is rejected.

What is most intriguing here—and will serve as a stepping-off point for exploring the future of the little magazine—is that an online popularity contest for poetry would validate the currency of author "platform" (the ability for an independent writer to directly reach and spur his audience to

1. Jason Boog, "Help Choose the 2010 Poet Laureate of the Blogosphere," GalleyCat blog / MediaBistro, April 7, 2010, http://www.mediabistro.com/galleycat/help-choose-the-2010-poet-laureate-of-the-blogosphere_b11466; accessed October 1, 2013.

action—in this case, to vote), but place moral qualifications on how that currency is achieved. This case reflects several challenges ahead for literary journals specifically and the literary culture more broadly.

The three elements I plan to explore in this essay are as follows:

1. The purpose of gatekeeping;
2. The evolution of the little magazine outside of the gatekeeping function; and
3. How writers and their work get discovered now and in the future.

The Purpose of Gatekeeping

While Brewer was initially criticized for being a poet with a corporate patron, another argument soon surfaced: quality. One anonymous person wrote: "[His] blog is NOT representative of good poetry.... The others are actually respected and talented poets."[2]

This raises the ineffable question: Who determines what is good or who is talented? In this particular contest, the point was to honor someone not already anointed by the usual gatekeepers, and to determine quality by popular vote. But this goes against the grain of the literary establishment mindset, which, by and large, only recognizes writers as having "made it" when they publish in specific outlets or pass muster with a particular set of gatekeepers. If we haven't heard of a particular author before, a reliable method of judging their quality has been to look at their credits. The gatekeepers are hyperaware of this role and responsibility, and well-known literary journals and publishers aren't shy about publicizing an acceptance rate of 1 percent or less. Scarcity is the assumed rule; many must be rejected and only a few can be accepted. If getting published is not difficult, how do we know who or what really matters, or that quality is being represented?

This phenomenon is more important than it might seem on the surface; indeed, it is the whole engine that has kept the little magazine alive since the very beginning. If a publication only reaches a few thousand people at best, then its influence and prestige must far outpace its actual reach to matter to writers and the broader culture. Even if very few read the publication, and it is a failure in commercial respects, people need to have heard of it and equate its name to respectability and exclusivity.

That game is starting to fall apart because, in the digital age, literary

---

2. Robert Brewer, "Blogging Poets," Poetic Asides Blog / *Writer's Digest*, April 26, 2010, http://www.writersdigest.com/editor-blogs/poetic-asides/personal-updates/blogging -poets-poet-laureate-of-the-blogosphere; accessed October 1, 2013.

journals premised on great literature must now play the exclusivity game *even harder*, to the point of absurdity, and manufacture what is ultimately a false scarcity. The number of places and opportunities to get published has never been greater; the cost of distributing and publishing work is falling to zero; most writers can get read more widely by publishing themselves online than in print. Literary journals, even if they don't acknowledge it themselves, are often protected far more by legacy and long-standing reputation than by somehow producing the "best quality" literature.

In Spring 2013, Richard Nash wrote an essay for the *Virginia Quarterly Review* on the disruption of publishing's business model, arguing that the gatekeeping function was never that effective in the first place. While he is speaking of book publishers, the same principles apply to any publisher or editor of literature:

The skill that is commonly associated with the pinnacle of editorial talent—picking the right book—is, frankly, nonsense. Success, in terms of picking things, is a hybrid of luck with the non-self-evident and money with the self-evident, and even the self-evident often requires luck. . . . The advent of self-publishing has rendered this ever more visible. . . . Publishing has no particular ability to discern what is good or not, what is successful or not. This is true not just at the level of predicting commercial success, but also at predicting critical success. . . . This is not a knock on publishing. There's no evidence that stockbrokers can pick good stocks, or touts good horses.[3]

Nash doesn't see this as evidence that publishing will die—quite the contrary. But he does call for publishers, if they are to survive the disruption to their business, to focus on other valued functions. One of the most important of these, from the publisher's perspective, is likely to be editing. But this doesn't go far enough.

Moving beyond the Gatekeeping Function

Few literary journals have responded to the new publishing environment by setting aside or de-emphasizing their gatekeeping function. If they were to do so, this is what it would entail:

1. Instead of limiting the number of opportunities to write and publish with the publication, offer more.
2. Interact with the readership—which is likely to be populated largely

3. "The Business of Literature," *Virginia Quarterly Review* 89, no. 2 (Spring 2013), http://www.vqronline.org/articles/2013/spring/nash-business-literature/; accessed October 1, 2013.

by writers—and foster a community. Use the reader-writer community to help identify what gets published.
3. Curate more. Point to work elsewhere that exemplifies the qualities
and values of the publication's editors.
1. Focus less on the print publication artifact, and more on activities
that embody the publication's values or brand.

Let's start with the last point first, since it drives everything else: the publication's values or brand. The power and necessity of brand was starting
to be understood more than fifty years ago by the founding editors of the
Paris Review. Travis Kurowski observed, in his essay "In Exile and Against
Criticism: *The Paris Review* and the Branding of Contemporary Literature":

> The editors saw that, in order for any readers in America or abroad to notice it
> during a time both color television and the hydrogen bomb came to fruition, when
> advertising had begun its stranglehold on culture, they had to work hard to de-
> velop interest and trust in the magazine through the magazine's content, image,
> and overall concept.... For the majority of literary magazine editors, the content
> *itself* was supposed to be significant enough. And for the early *Paris Review*, the
> content of the magazine was still primary, but to get that content into the minds
> and hands of readers they had to do various things to make the magazine a mar-
> ketable venue ... [and] make new and experimental literature a part of the culture.[4]

Today's literary journals must go one step further. The content—or print
artifact—should *not* be primary, especially since it's likely to transform.
Instead, the mission or purpose behind the publication ought to be primary. People may or may not consume print journals in the future; they
may or may not have time to read their content. But a person is likely to
be continually invested in the deeper philosophy or driving force behind
the journal's brand, and may be interested in events, digital media, communities, curated content, and membership opportunities spun from that
brand.

Put another way: Most people are looking for meaning and identity, not
more paper to put on their shelf, more things to read, or another subscription to buy. Most of us are overwhelmed with to-read piles and media to
consume. But one literary journal that has mastered the delivery of meaning and identity, specifically through the purchase of paper-based products, is *McSweeney's*. Has there ever been a more widely known and loved
journal, seen across so many bookshelves, that has so often remained un-
read? That's not to say the content doesn't live up to its mission or its

4. Travis Kurowski, "In Exile and Against Criticism: *The Paris Review* and the Branding
of Contemporary Literature," in *Paper Dreams: Writers and Editors on the American Literary
Magazine*, edited by Travis Kurowski (Madison, NJ: Atticus Books, 2013).

packaging, but that the purpose behind the publishing, and the special, tactile qualities reflected in the product have become just as important as the writing itself. One cannot separate out those qualities when talking about *McSweeney's*; it is part of its very essence.

Let's go back to the first point—that literary journals should offer more opportunities to publish. This might seem potentially destructive rather than redeeming. Given that just about anything can and will get published in a digital environment, doesn't it make more sense for a literary journal to take an opposing stand, and to selectively publish what is deemed to be of superlative quality? If Nash's earlier argument on the nonsense of gatekeeping remains unconvincing, then publishing might do well to learn from a long-standing nemesis, Jeff Bezos, the founder and CEO of Amazon. In a 2011 letter to shareholders, titled "The Power of Invention," Bezos wrote:

Invention comes in many forms and at many scales. The most radical and trans-formative of inventions are often those that empower others to unleash their cre-ativity—to pursue their dreams.... We are creating powerful self-service platforms that allow thousands of people to boldly experiment and accomplish things that would otherwise be impossible or impractical.... I am emphasizing the self-service nature of these platforms because it's important for a reason I think is somewhat non-obvious: even well-meaning gatekeepers slow innovation. When a platform is self-service, even the improbable ideas can get tried, because there's no expert gatekeeper ready to say "that will never work!" And guess what—many of those improbable ideas do work, and society is the beneficiary of that diversity.[5]

The self-service platform—and the circumvention of the gatekeeper—is not unique to Amazon. Forbes opened up its brand to thousands of blog-gers. Wattpad, the biggest community publishing site in the world, al-lows writers to experiment and test their work with early readers, and has attracted established authors such as Margaret Atwood. And Nash—to put his money where his mouth is—started Cursor, a publishing platform that combines traditional editorial discrimination with the wisdom of the crowd.

This is not to say that the crowd is a better way of determining qual-ity (though Amazon might argue for it, since their definition of quality is sales). But if a literary journal has collected an audience of readers and writers who are attuned to that journal's mission and philosophy, that is a very powerful community that will be more invested, and more valuable to the publication, when they have opportunities to be involved. Involve-

5. Jeff Bezos, "2011 Letter to Shareholders: The Power of Invention," US Security and Exchange Commission Archives, http://www.sec.gov/Archives/edgar/data/1018724 /000119312512161812/d329990dex991.htm; accessed March 28, 2014.

ment takes many different forms, including selection of the work that's produced, communicating with the authors and editors of that work, and interacting with the brand in the physical world. Not everyone may participate—in fact, studies of such communities show that only a small percentage will—but inviting conversation, access, and collaboration is a quality of digital-age publishing and communication that literary journals aren't exempt from.

Underpinning this idea, the one that very editor or gatekeeper must understand, is that "publishing" is no longer a specialized or important process. It is a button on a screen, it is a self-service approach that has produced an avalanche of the written word, and very little of it worth reading. David Foster Wallace said, "There are four trillion bits coming at you, 99 percent of them are shit, and it's too much work to do triage to decide."[6] So we have a fire hose of media, the average person can never consume everything she is interested in, and most literary journals are likely to be lost in that fire hose of content unless they offer something more—something that *means* more—than just announcing, "Here's our latest issue!"

This avalanche of content also brings us to point #3, or the value and function of curation. "Curation" has become an overused and sometimes despised term in publishing, since it has been applied to everything from what a person decides to tweet to lowbrow Buzzfeed slideshows. Yet the underlying principle is sound: we need trusted filters to help save our time and introduce us to stories and media we might not have encountered on our own. When people or institutions provide such a service, and help cut through the noise, they are often perceived as more invaluable than the original content providers themselves.

When done well, the act of curation furthers the values and principles of the publication's brand, and builds a community of people invested in it—people who believe what the publication believes—which is of far greater long-term value than simply producing a finite publication that people either subscribe to or not.

The Age of Disaggregation and Discoverability

In the days before social media and blogging, a website's primary method of getting traffic was to get indexed by search engines, secure links from

6. "Excerpts from a Conversation with David Foster Wallace," *New Inquiry*, July 18, 2010, http://thenewinquiry.com/features/excerpts-from-a-conversation-with-david-foster -wallace/; accessed October 1, 2013.

other popular websites, and publicize the website off-line. The home-page design was considered a top priority and served as the front door for visitors.

Today, most content-driven websites see only 30 percent of their traffic coming in through the home page. This simple statistic belies a staggering shift in content consumption, which is that the majority of online readers consume content piecemeal, and usually outside the context it originally appeared in. Readers may never go any further into a publication than a specific piece they discovered through a friend's e-mail, a social media link, or quick Google search. In industry terminology, this is called the disaggregation of content.

This is why specialization and reliance on selling a cover-to-cover read-ing experience is risky; disaggregation of content has only increased over time for just about all media outlets, especially newspapers, magazines, and television. Read-it-later services such as Pocket and Instapaper al-low people to consume content on their own terms, at a time of their own choosing, and in a context and environment they have created for themselves. An editor's work and intentions in creating an "experience" in a specific issue largely go unrecognized online—and have little impor-tance or relevance—when that content is more often accessed and read on a one-off basis.

In recognition of this shift, a range of new publishing start-ups have focused on selling "singles," and publishing outside of an issue-based schema. Byliner, Atavist, and Matter are just a few examples of such mod-els in 2013. (It seems a new one is announced every day.) Yet few, if any, print-based literary journals have changed how and what they publish in response to the trend of disaggregation.

Complicating matters is the necessity—in the age of content abun-dance—of "discoverability." A magazine's archive of published work, if even available in a digital environment, is often not discoverable (easily found or meaningfully searched by people who would be interested in it), or given context. Yet readers are more often turning to search engines, community sites, and social media for discovering what they want to read, in part because of the decline of physical bookstores and libraries in the United States. Digitally native publications, and some commer-cial print-based publications, already understand the importance of SEO (search-engine optimization) and are far more successful in marketing and promoting their content—and making it discoverable to readers— because it has been carefully tagged and categorized with keywords or metadata that describe the content and its context to search engines and other aggregators.

Literary journals (and print-based publishers in general) have been so slow to improve the discoverability of their content that it's not unusual for individual writers to reach more readers on their own, through online means, than through publication and distribution in a print journal. In fact, a journal can often benefit greatly from publishing a highly recognizable online writer who then publicizes to their readership that their new piece is available.

And so we come back to our story about Robert Brewer and the Poet Laureate of the Blogosphere. Since the purpose of the contest was to recognize poets who were not on the usual, traditional path—the one controlled by the gatekeepers—the question of quality had to be determined in some other way: by popular vote, which is of course directly impacted by a poet's online reach to his readers.

Because the community was not pleased with the direction of the voting, they reverted back to the argument gatekeepers have always employed to protect their existence: We need to select and support the poet who is good and talented. But what means do we have to measure (assuming we *can* gather evidence for quality) aside from looking at (1) wide popularity and reach to a readership or (2) what influential people say? There *is* a third option. We can also look at whether the person in question is able to make money off the work they're producing, and paradoxically, this was the very thing that made Brewer's win upsetting to a segment of the community. Brewer had found a business model that supported his art, which involved working for a commercial publisher. Other writers do it in a variety of ways, whether that involves securing grants and fellowships, crowd funding, freelancing, teaching, or speaking.

One of the final challenges facing the literary publishing community is to reject the starving-artist myth, the assumption taught to just about every creative writing student that financial sustainability isn't possible if you're making good art. In the current environment, as futurist Kevin Kelly has argued, any artist with 1,000 true fans can conceivably make a living doing exactly what he loves to do.

What is paradoxical, however, is how the literary culture continues to place primary value on print-based publication, which carries far more cost, time, and long-term financial investment and sustainability to be done well (exactly why it is prized, since there is a hard limit to what can appear in print), yet puts a very low value on writers who publish and distribute own their own—through blogs, social media, and digital media. These are the writers who have found they are free to do their art for love. Shouldn't *they* embody the ideal writer, the one not seeking payment from a publisher, or the status that comes from the artificial scarcity and cost of print publication, but who is instead producing art, reaching his readers, and possibly being paid directly by them?

Literary journals have long perpetuated a great deal of pretense to sustain themselves. That is not to say they haven't been important to the culture or that they have ceased being meaningful to the literary community. But they are destined for irrelevance, and may ultimately have to cede way to other online-born publications that do not act superior to their readers and contributors or fetishize the print artifact and print legacy, but instead serve as supporters and partners of writers. Is that not the very definition of what a little magazine is supposed to do? Find and support great writing? Literary journals would do well to focus their attention on less-popular art and long-term projects that require funding. Since the Internet has always favored content that is *the* most popular, art that's more challenging or takes longer to be appreciated is a wellspring of opportunity for journals. So is the book or long-form writing project that an author may be unable to successfully sell to commercial publishers, who are more risk-averse than ever. If the literary journals think well of their ability to gatekeep, edit, curate, and be tastemakers, then they should focus their energies on finding and funding those worthwhile authors (especially the digitally unsavvy) who get lost in the noise, because the one thing you can't count on any longer is having the cream rise to the top without someone actively pushing it there. It's time for the little magazine to work much harder, and much more transparently in partnership with their community, for the values they believe in, instead of focusing on the fading reputation and the place of print.

Poetry Magazine: On Making It New

DON SHARE

I've received some letters asking me to state publicly my editorial position ...

Ezra Pound's injunction to "make it new" seems not to apply to the question of what an incoming editor of *Poetry* magazine intends. Though Harriet Monroe clearly established *Poetry*'s vision in an editorial in her first issue[1] and in the famous "Open Door" policy published in the second,[2] the question gets asked anew when there's a change at the top of our masthead. In 1949, for example, when Hayden Carruth became the editor, one of the magazine's long-standing guarantors posed it, commenting that though *Poetry*'s policy may have been clear to the staff, it certainly wasn't to her. ("You don't seem to get enough important names," she complained.) Called upon to make a definitive statement, Carruth wrote that though he thought the answer was inherent in the magazine's pages, it was "we aim to publish good poems."[3] Sensible as this seems, he only lasted a year in the job. When Karl Shapiro took over from him in 1950, *Time* magazine sent a reporter to ask what *his* editorial "policy" would be. Shapiro was "horrified," he later said, because—either ignoring or embodying the "Open Door" doctrine—he'd "never thought of a literary magazine having a policy." Nevertheless, in his third issue, he wrote that the explanation for the "persistence" of *Poetry* magazine was threefold: it discovered and encouraged "new talent," presented the new work of known poets, and preserved a month-to-month record of American poetry. No surprises there, in spite of which Shapiro lasted but five years. Understandably, the succeeding run of editors, from Henry Rago and Daryl Hine to John Frederick Nims and Joseph Parisi, published no introductory statements on the subject, and let the poems speak for themselves.

    Then ten years ago an editorial, less than two pages long, by *Poetry*'s

1. Harriet Monroe, "The Motive of the Magazine," *Poetry* (October 1912), 26–28.
2. Harriet Monroe, "The Open Door," *Poetry* (November 1912), 62–64.
3. Hayden Carruth, "Intramural," *Poetry* (May 1949), 93.

new editor, Christian Wiman, appeared. It began calmly enough, with the neutral-sounding words quoted in the epigraph to this essay. But that first sentence was a ruse, for Wiman memorably inaugurated his tenure by indicating a distaste for poets who have a poetics ("bores"), describing an office under attack by submissions from "a horde of iambic zombies," admitting a suspicion "that 'editor' and 'idiot' are synonyms"—and imagining ruthless future readers who "will look at all these poems into which we've poured the wounded truths of our hearts, all the fraught splendor and terror of these lives we suffered and sang" ... and *giggle*. All he wanted, he announced, was "poems from poets whose aim is way beyond *Poetry* magazine, indeed, beyond all magazines."

I don't see how any post-Wiman editor could top that.

I'm recounting this history in order to let myself more or less off the hook. Changes will surely come as I take over from Chris, with whom I worked for six years—years that proved him to be one of the magazine's canniest and most stalwart stewards. Though editors, like poets, must avoid cliché, I'm very happy to admit up front that his are hard footsteps to follow. It's an honor, but an even greater responsibility, for me to see the magazine into its second century. And I hope in the issues to come readers feel that the vision of the magazine is being refreshed, though without disruption to its proven record. The "motive" of the magazine, as Harriet put it, remains what it always has been: "to keep free of entangling alliances with any single class or school," to be, that is, eclectic.

In thinking about my predecessors' work, and wondering how to live up to it, I've asked myself why Harriet Monroe's original and originating policy has endured so well. It's fascinating to note that Harriet knew her own mind, but when it came to poetry she had a sixth sense that guided her in spite of herself. Her own taste was for a poetics that, though she called it "new," was rooted, like modernism itself, firmly in the late nineteenth century. She liked, and wrote herself, poems that seem hopelessly dated now. Fortunately, that countervailing sixth sense allowed her make literary history. She invented a box, you could say—and promptly set to work thinking outside it. And so her magazine was, therefore, like she was: unpredictable, difficult, and infuriating. As a consequence of these traits, we can now take for granted that poets such as T. S. Eliot, William Carlos Williams, Wallace Stevens, Ezra Pound, H. D., Hart Crane, Marianne Moore, Langston Hughes, and many more, are part of the pantheon of English-language poetry. Their poems, confounding and aggravating to readers when they first appeared in our pages, exemplify what Peter Quartermain has called "stubborn poetries"—opaque at first, this was work that became clearer and dearer to us over time.

Of necessity, then, but also by inclination, I'm going to take the long

view, which means taking risks with unpredictable, difficult, and infuriating work—just as all my predecessors have. The value of "stubborn"
poems, apart from the considerable pleasure of thinking about what
they're up to, is that they get us to focus our attention and sharpen our
critical skills, something we need more than ever in an age, like ours, of
distraction. As it happens, poems teach us how to read other poems, so I'll
always be looking over my shoulder as I move forward: a bad way to walk
or drive, but a time-tested way of editing *Poetry*. The composer Van Dyke
Parks, when asked about the tension between eclecticism and tradition-
alism, said that it was wonderful when somebody called him a "futuristic
traditionalist." I hope to be called that someday, too.

A glance all the way back to 1914 fortifies and emboldens me. Quartermain, in an essay I published in my first solo issue of the magazine ("Reading the Difficult," October 2013) takes as an epigraph these lines from William Carlos Williams's "At Dawn":

O marvelous! what new configuration will come next?
I am bewildered with multiplicity.

Nearly a century later, *Poetry* receives about 120,000 poems a year. At the
dawn of my tenure as editor, I share Williams's exuberance: it's a joy to be
bewildered with poetry's multiplicity. Faced with the new, poems from
the past still accompany us. So let me issue an invitation to readers with
a stanza from the dawn of the era of little magazines, Robert Frost's "The
Pasture":

I'm going out to clean the pasture spring;
I'll only stop to rake the leaves away
(And wait to watch the water clear, I may):
I sha'n't be gone long.—You come too.

Some serendipitous lines from Alice Fulton's "Make It New," also published
in my first issue, may suffice as well:

... It will be new

whether you make it new
or not. It will be full of neo-

shadows. Full of *then*—both past and next,
iridescent with suspense.

Editors of literary magazines have for at least a century inexorably expressed their commitment to discovery, to doing something, or finding
something, or embodying something new. This is one part of Ezra Pound's

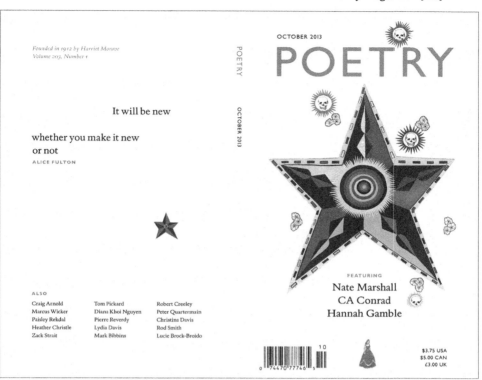

Founded in 1912 by Harriet Monroe
Volume 203, Number 1

OCTOBER 2013

POETRY

OCTOBER 2013

It will be new

whether you make it new
or not

ALICE FULTON

ALSO

Craig Arnold
Marcus Wicker
Paisley Rekdal
Heather Christle
Zack Strait

Tom Pickard
Diana Khoi Nguyen
Pierre Reverdy
Lydia Davis
Mark Bibbins

Robert Creeley
Peter Quartermain
Christina Davis
Rod Smith
Lucie Brock-Broido

FEATURING

Nate Marshall
CA Conrad
Hannah Gamble

$3.75 USA
$5.00 CAN
£3.00 UK

FIGURE 6. Cover of *Poetry* 203, no. 1 (October 2013). Source: The Poetry Foundation.

considerable influence that shows no sign of abating. Yet everyone knows that Pound didn't originate the modernist mandate to "make it new." As Michael North explains, "The crucial fact to begin with is that the phrase is not originally Pound's at all. The source is a historical anecdote concerning Ch'eng T'ang (Tching-thang, Tching Tang), first king of the Shang dynasty (1766–1753 BC), who was said to have had a washbasin inscribed with this inspirational slogan."[4] Pound's interest in Confucian texts, it's worth noting, coincides with the moment of *Poetry*'s founding. Working from a French translation of the *Da Xue*, a text on good government, he found the story of King Ch'eng T'ang, who supposedly had a bathtub

4. Michael North, "The Making of 'Make It New,'" *Guernica: A Magazine of Art and Politics* (August 15, 2013), online at http://www.guernicamag.com/features/the-making-of-making-it-new; accessed October 1, 2013. All of the following translations, and Pound's quotes, are from North's essay as well.

or washbasin with an inscription engraved on it that goes like this in French:

Renouvelle-toi complétement chaque jour; fais-le de nouveau, encore de nouveau, et tou-jours de nouveau.

In James Legge's translation, which Pound knew, it reads:

If you can one day renovate yourself, do so from day to day. Yea, let there be daily renovation.

Pound's rendering into "American" first went like this:

Renovate, dod gast you, renovate!

The better-sounding phrase "make it new" became the title of a book of Pound's essays later on, in 1934; and he recycled the idea further in his 1935 book *Jefferson and/or Mussolini*, where this version of his translated line appears: "Make it new, make it new as the young grass shoot." As North points out, Pound's recycling (which he calls "recombinant") "was not itself new, nor was it ever meant to be." Instead,

the complex nature of the new—its debt, even as revolution, to the past, and the way in which new works are often just recombinations of traditional elements—is not just confessed by this practice but insisted on. This is what makes the slogan exemplary of the larger modernist project, that by insisting on the new it brings to the surface all the latent difficulties in what seems such a simple and simplifying concept.

This digression on Pound is important not only because *Poetry* was a crucial part of the "modernist project" (and he such a part of the magazine's history), but because we now take for granted that literature and literary magazines survive through transformation of (or even distortion of) the past. As it happens, the oddest transformation of *Poetry* magazine came near the end of the tenure of Joseph Parisi, who contributed to the previous incarnation of this book in 1978. His essay, "The Care and Funding of Pegasus," detailed the magazine's financial difficulties; but as every reader of this present book will know, *Poetry*'s money troubles came to a final and resounding end with Ruth Lilly's famous bequest in 2003. And here the magazine began to renew itself more dramatically than ever.

That year the Poetry Foundation was established, under the rubric of which the magazine found new company in such successful programs as Poetry Out Loud, a national recitation contest cocreated with the National Endowment for the Arts; and the Harriet Monroe Poetry Institute, a forum for fresh thinking about poetry, in both its intellectual and its practical needs.[5] With Christian Wiman as Parisi's new young successor, a major redesign for the magazine was accomplished, working with the Winterhouse design studio and William Drentel. Retaining elements of its iconic, book-like feel, and with a nod to the artist and typographer Eric Gill, who created the 1932 version of the Pegasus logo still in use today, *Poetry* took on a clean and contemporary appearance. Editorially, Wiman took many risks, publishing daring critical work and letters to the editor in an expanded back-of-the-book section, which he considered as important as the poems he published.

By the time I arrived at the magazine in 2007 as *Poetry*'s senior editor, there was a also a website that featured a monthly table of contents, a few links to full poems or articles, and the occasional "web exclusive." Just about the first thing I convinced my colleagues to do was to put *all* of the magazine's content online for free (dovetailing with the Open Access movement), which was done despite fears that this would cannibalize subscriptions, though this never happened. In fact, we were able to triple print subscriptions to a peak of about 30,000, a number we've stayed close to ever since, even through a recession. In addition, and thanks to the foundation's talented digital programs staff, headed first by Emily Warn and then Catherine Halley, the magazine's reach broadened into new dimensions with a monthly podcast, a poetry app for handheld devices, and digital subscriptions to the magazine, supplemented by a freely available digital back run of the entire magazine. We also established a presence on such social networking platforms as Facebook, Twitter, Tumblr, and Pinterest. In 2011, we were recognized with two National Magazine Awards from the American Society of Magazine Editors for General Excellence in the category of Literary, Political, and Professional Magazines, as well as for Podcasting, beating impressive competitors from the world of mass-market magazines.

As the magazine's centennial approached—and after a century with no permanent office space of its own—the magazine at last found a home in John Ronan's new Poetry Foundation building in downtown Chicago. This space—designed to unfold like a poem—is open to the public, offers a 30,000-volume poetry library with free Wi-Fi, a performance space for its many events, gallery space for exhibitions, and of course good working conditions for magazine and foundation staff.

Just following the magazine's one-hundredth birthday in October 2012,

---

5. The institute convenes leading poets, scholars, publishers, educators, and other thinkers from inside and outside the poetry world to address issues of importance to the art form of poetry and to identify and champion solutions for the benefit of the art.

there was further change. Wiman and I coedited an anthology, *The Open Door: 100 Poems, 100 Years of Poetry Magazine,* which became an unexpected best seller, quickly going through four hardcover printings and appearing as well in paperback and e-book formats. And as we began our second century in 2013, Christian Wiman announced his resignation; after a five-month international search, I became his successor. At the time of this writing, the masthead now includes Fred Sasaki as art director, Valerie Jean Johnson as managing editor, Lindsay Garbutt as assistant editor, Christina Pugh as consulting editor, and Holly Amos at editorial assistant. The Poetry Foundation itself found a new president, on John Barr's retirement, the poet, scholar, and teacher, Robert Polito, who has said that his goal is "to move our national cultural conversation about poetry beyond life enrichment to include the vital close reading skills and other critically alert habits of mind that come from reading and writing."

The way we do our reading and writing has changed dramatically since Harriet Monroe published her first issue. As I write this, print culture really is alive and quite well; at the same time, one in three Americans now owns a tablet, and each day hundreds of thousands of individual issues of magazines are downloaded through apps on phones and other devices. Most of the poems we publish are born digital, and presumably will live long lives that way. How will literary magazines like *Poetry* fare in the years to come?

In 1930, Ezra Pound began his famous essay "Small Magazines" by claiming that "the active phase of the small magazine in America" began with *Poetry* magazine; he ended the piece, which is still worth reading today, by saying—just as you would expect—that "the new thing that is durable does not spring up without roots."[6] In his ending is our beginning. Pound's portrait hangs right across from my desk now, and as I work he seems to be staring right at me. Technological and editorial changes are in the works for *Poetry,* no longer quite a "little" magazine; but serving as Harriet Monroe's successor, the key to keeping the magazine "durable" remains what Pound always said it was: to "maintain a species of open-mindedness toward the possible and the plausible."

6. "Small Magazines," *English Journal* 19, no. 9 (November 1930).

Contributors

CARA BLUE ADAMS spent five years on the editorial staff of the *Southern Review*, where she served as managing editor and editor. Work she edited has appeared in national anthologies, including *The Best American Short Stories*, *The Best American Essays*, and the PEN/O. Henry Prize Stories. Her fiction and nonfiction have appeared in *Narrative*, the *Missouri Review*, the *Sun*, the *Kenyon Review*, and *Ploughshares*, and she has been named one of *Narrative*'s 15 Below 30 and given support from the Bread Loaf Writers' Conference, the Sewanee Writers' Conference, and the Virginia Center for the Creative Arts. She is assistant professor at Coastal Carolina University.

BRUCE ANDREWS is an experimental poet and performance writer, literary theorist, and music/sound designer for Sally Silvers & Dancers, and has just retired from thirty-eight years as a left-wing political science professor. Most recent of a dozen big books is *You Can't Have Everything … Where Would You Put It!*, followed by a chapbook, *Yessified (Sally's Edit)*, celebrating the Andrews Symposium and its expanded archive still online at http://www.fordhamenglish.com/bruce-andrews, with links to interviews, performance texts, poetry, collaborations, and critical essays on his work. Another online archive (and interactive project) materialized on April 1, 2014, as a curated twenty-five-hour "twitter sculpture" [Twitter .com @BruceAndrews25h], a 300-poem sequence.

ANDREI CODRESCU was born in Sibiu, Romania. He came to the United States at the age of nineteen, and has been writing poetry, essays, and novels. He is a commentator on NPR, an emeritus professor of English at Louisiana State University, and the editor of *Exquisite Corpse: A Journal of Books and Ideas*, in print from 1983 until 1996, then online from 1996 and ongoing at www.corpse.org. Codrescu won the Peabody Award for his film *Road Scholar*, and the Ovidius Prize for poetry. His recent books include *So Recently Rent a World: New and Selected Poems, 1968–2012, The Poetry Lesson*, and *Whatever Gets You through the Night: A Story of Sheherezade and the*

Arabian Entertainments. He is living in the Ozarks near the Buffalo River National Park.

LAWRENCE-MINH BÙI DAVIS is founding director of the Washington, DC–based literary arts nonprofit the *Asian American Literary Review* and serves as coeditor in chief of its critically acclaimed literary journal. A consultant with the Smithsonian Asian Pacific American Center, he oversaw development of the Smithsonian's first nationally touring pan-Asian Pacific American exhibition, "I Want the Wide American Earth: An Asian Pacific American Story." Since 2006 he has taught for the Asian American Studies Program at the University of Maryland. His fiction, poetry, and creative nonfiction have appeared in *Gastronomica, McSweeney's Quarterly Concern, Kenyon Review, AGNI* online, and *Fiction International,* among other publications.

DAVE EGGERS is the author of eight books, most recently *The Circle.* Eggers is the founder and editor of *McSweeney's,* an independent publishing house based in San Francisco, and cofounder of 826 National, a network of nonprofit writing and tutoring centers for youth.

JONATHAN FARMER is the editor in chief and poetry editor of *At Length* and the poetry critic for the *Slate* Book Review. He teaches middle and high school English and writing in Saxapahaw, NC, and lives in Durham.

REBECCA MORGAN FRANK is the author of one collection of poems, *Little Murders Everywhere,* a finalist for the Kate Tufts Discovery Award, and her work has appeared in such places as the *New England Review, Ploughshares, Guernica, 32 Poems, Blackbird,* and the *Los Angeles Review of Books.* She received the Poetry Society of America's Alice Fay di Castagnola Award for her new manuscript-in-progress. She is the cofounder and editor in chief of the online magazine *Memorious: A Journal of New Verse and Fiction* and an assistant professor at the University of Southern Mississippi's Center for Writers.

JANE FRIEDMAN served as web editor of the *Virginia Quarterly Review* and is also the cofounder and editor of *Scratch,* a digital magazine that focuses on the intersection of writing and money. Before joining *VQR,* she was the publisher of *Writer's Digest* and an e-media professor at the University of Cincinnati. Her expertise on the publishing industry has been featured throughout many events and media, including NPR's *Morning Edition, Publishers Weekly,* South by Southwest, AWP, and Nieman Journalism Lab. Her award-winning blog for writers can be found at JaneFriedman.com.

KEITH GESSEN is a founding editor of *n+1*. He is the author of *All the Sad Young Literary Men* and the editor or translator of *Voices from Chernobyl*; *There Once Was a Woman Who Tried to Kill Her Neighbor's Baby*; *Diary of a Very Bad Year: Confessions of an Anonymous Hedge Fund Manager*; and *It's No Good: Poems, Essays, Manifestos*.

LEE GUTKIND, recognized by *Vanity Fair* as "the Godfather behind creative nonfiction," is founder and editor of *Creative Nonfiction*, the first and largest literary magazine to publish narrative nonfiction exclusively. He is distinguished writer in residence in the Consortium for Science, Policy and Outcomes at Arizona State University and a professor in the Hugh Downs School of Human Communication. A prolific author and editor of more than thirty narrative nonfiction books, about baseball, health care, robotics, and the motorcycle subculture, among other subjects—and two memoirs—Gutkind has appeared on many national radio and television shows, including *The Daily Show with Jon Stewart* (Comedy Central) and *Good Morning America*.

AMY HOFFMAN is the author of the memoirs *Lies about My Family* (University of Massachusetts Press, 2013); *An Army of Ex-Lovers: My Life at the Gay Community News* (University of Massachusetts Press, 2007); and *Hospital Time* (Duke University Press, 1997). She is editor of *Women's Review of Books* and teaches creative nonfiction in the Solstice MFA Program at Pine Manor College. Hoffman has an MFA in creative writing from the University of Massachusetts and has received several fellowships from the Virginia Center for the Creative Arts. She lives in Boston with her wife, Roberta Stone, and she is working on a novel set in Provincetown.

LISA JERVIS is the founding editor and publisher of *Bitch: Feminist Response to Pop Culture*. In addition to her work for *Bitch*, she has been published in many outlets both little (*Hues, LiP,* the *Women's Review of Books, Punk Planet*) and not so little (*Mother Jones, Utne, Ms.,* the *San Francisco Chronicle*). She has contributed to many anthologies and is the author of *Cook Food: A Manualfesto for Easy, Healthy, Local Eating* (PM Press) and the coeditor of *Young Wives Tales* (Seal Press) and *BITCHFest: Ten Years of Cultural Criticism from the Pages of* Bitch *Magazine* (Farrar, Straus and Giroux).

GREG JOHNSON has published two novels and five collections of short stories, including the critically praised novel *Pagan Babies* (Dutton/Plume) and the collection *Last Encounter with the Enemy* (Johns Hopkins University Press), in addition to five books of nonfiction. His more than seventy-five short stories have appeared in the nation's most prestigious literary magazines, including the *Southern Review, Virginia Quarterly Review,* and *TriQuarterly,* and have won places in such anthologies as *Prize Stories: The O. Henry Awards* and *New Stories from the South: The Year's Best.* Also the author of *Invisible Writer: A Biography of Joyce Carol Oates* (Dutton/Plume), he has won awards from PEN and from the National Endowment for the Humanities. He lives in Atlanta.

CAROLYN KUEBLER is the editor of the *New England Review.* Before coming to *NER* as managing editor in 2004, she was an associate book reviews editor at *Library Journal* and founding editor of *Rain Taxi.* She has published fiction and criticism in various magazines, and has degrees from Middlebury and Bard College. A native of Allentown, Pennsylvania, she now lives in Vermont.

JEFFREY LEPENDORF serves as the shared executive director of America's two organizations serving independent literary publishers: Small Press Distribution (SPD) and the Council of Literary Magazines and Presses (CLMP). He previously served as development director to the Creative Capital Foundation and the Poetry Society of America. He received his masters and doctorate from Columbia University and his undergraduate degree from Oberlin Conservatory. He remains active as a composer and performer, and is a certified master player of the Japanese *shakuhachi* flute. His "Masterpieces of Western Music" audio course, part of Barnes and Noble's "Portable Professor" series, can be downloaded at audible.com.

GERALD MAA is editor in chief of the *Asian American Literary Review.* His poetry, translation, and criticism have appeared in places like *American Poetry Review, Common Knowledge, Studies in Romanticism,* and *Push Open the Window: Contemporary Poetry from China.* He has earned fellowships to and grants from the Bread Loaf Writers' Conference, Vermont Studio Center, and the Library of Congress Asian Reading Room. He currently resides in LA, where he is an editorial committee member for Kaya Press and a PhD student at the University of California, Irvine, who studies British Romanticism.

ANDER MONSON is the author of a number of paraphernalia including a website, a decoder wheel, several chapbooks, and six books, including *Letter to a Future Lover* (Graywolf Press). He lives in Tucson where he teaches in the MFA program at the University of Arizona and is the founding editor of the journal *DIAGRAM* (thediagram.com) and the New Michigan Press.

CHARLES HENRY ROWELL, a native of Auburn, Alabama, is editor and founder of *Callaloo*, the premier literary and cultural journal of the African Diaspora. A professor of English at Texas A&M University, Rowell has spent the majority of his career editing the quarterly journal and a number of other publications, including *Ancestral House: The Black Short Story in the Americas and Europe* (Westview, 1995), *Making* Callaloo: *25 Years of Black Literature* (St. Martin's, 2002), and *Angles of Ascent: A Norton Anthology of Contemporary African American Poetry* (Norton, 2013). *Callaloo* is currently sponsored by Texas A&M University and published by the Johns Hopkins University Press. He lives in College Station, Texas.

DON SHARE is editor of *Poetry* magazine. His most recent books are *Wishbone* (Black Sparrow), *Union* (Eyewear Publishing), and *Bunting's Persia* (Flood Editions); he has also edited a critical edition of Bunting's poems for Faber and Faber. His translations of Miguel Hernández were awarded the *Times Literary Supplement* Translation Prize and Premio Valle Inclán, and were recently republished in a revised and expanded edition by *New York Review Books*. His other books include *Seneca in English* (Penguin Classics), and *The Open Door: 100 Poems, 100 Years of* Poetry *Magazine* (University of Chicago Press), edited with Christian Wiman.

RONALD SPATZ is cofounder and editor in chief of *Alaska Quarterly Review*. A former National Endowment for the Arts Fellow in fiction, he is the founding dean of the Honors College and a professor of creative writing at the University of Alaska–Anchorage (UAA). He is the recipient of two Alaska Governor's Awards (Arts and Humanities), a Contribution to Literacy Award from the Alaska Center for the Book, five UAA Chancellor's Awards, a UAA Alumni Association Distinguished Teaching Award, and the University of Alaska Foundation's Edith R. Bullock Prize for Excellence. He holds an MFA degree from the University of Iowa Writer's Workshop.

Editor in chief BETSY SUSSLER cofounded BOMB Magazine in 1981. Under her stewardship, BOMB has grown from a quarterly publication with an audience of 3,000 to a multiplatform publishing enterprise—in print and online—with an audience of over a million annual readers. BOMB's material archive is housed at Columbia University's Rare Book and Manuscript Collection. Sussler is a 1991 NYFA (New York Foundation for the Arts) fellow in playwriting and is currently completing a novel based on stories involving her paternal grandfather. Sussler has also edited *BOMB Interviews* (City Lights, 1992), *Speak Art!* (1997), *Speak Fiction and Poetry!* (1998), and *Speak Theater and Film!* (1999). Soho Press is publishing the anthology, *BOMB Literary Interview, Between Authors*, edited by Sussler, in 2015.

REBECCA WOLFF is the author of three books of poems, most recently *The King* (Norton, 2009). A chapbook called *Warden* is forthcoming from Ugly Duckling Presse in 2014. Her novel *The Beginners* came out from River-head in 2011; occasional prose appears in many collections and anthologies. Wolff is the founding editor of *Fence* and Fence Books and the *Constant Critic*. A fellow at the University at Albany's New York State Writers Institute, Wolff lives in Hudson, New York.

ANDI ZEISLER is the cofounder of *Bitch: Feminist Response to Pop Culture* and the editorial/creative director of Bitch Media. She is the coeditor of *BITCHFest: Ten Years of Cultural Criticism from the Pages of* Bitch *Magazine* (Farrar, Straus and Giroux) and the author of *Feminism and Pop Culture* (Seal Press.) She lives with her family in Portland, Oregon.

Index

African diaspora. See *Callaloo*

Alaska Quarterly Review: audience for, 166; book series, 167–68; distribution of, 169; editorial staff of, 170; financial constraints of, 170; focus on Alaskan native cultures in, 167; fostering of literary talent in, 172; fundraising for, 166–67; Jim Liszka, cofounder of, 167; origins of, 167; recognition of, 169–70; relationship between University of Alaska and, 169, 170

Alaskan native cultures. See *Alaska Quarterly Review*

Allen, Charles. See *Little Magazine, The: A History and Bibliography*

American Society of Magazine Editors. See *Poetry*

Anderson, Elliott. See *Little Magazine in America, The: A Modern Documentary History*

Anderson, Margaret. See *Little Review, The*

Archer, Michael. See *Guernica*, 12

Asian American Literary Review: Asian diaspora and, 90; classroom use of, 87; introduction of international authors in, 91; mission statement for, 86; mixed race issue of, 87; origins of, 85; readership of, 88; title for, 85–86; US Census Form and, 83–84, 83f, 84f

Asian diaspora. See *Asian American Literary Review*

Atavist. *See* online magazines

At Length: audience for, 195–96; Dan Kois and, 189; editorial staff of, 192, 193; first print issue of, 190; fundraising for, 195; publication schedule for, 192; relation-

ship between editors and contributors to, 193

avant-garde: accessibility of, 116; critiques of power in, 115; disdain for mainstream in, 104, 108; elision of generic boundaries in, 133; importance of the internet to, 122; procedural constraints of, 108; resistance to transparency, referentiality, and formal unity in, 108, 110. See also *DIAGRAM*; *Exquisite Corpse*; *Fence*; *L=A=N=G=U=A=G=E*

AWP (Association of Writers & Writing Programs). See *Creative Nonfiction*

Baldwin, James: "Color," 84–85; "The Price of the Ticket," 84

Barr, John. See *Poetry* Foundation

Beat Poets. *See* language poetry

Behrle, Jim. *See can we have our ball back?*

Believer, The. See *Memorious*

Best American Essays series. See *DIAGRAM*

Best American Poetry series. See *DIAGRAM* and *Memorious*

Bezos, Jeff, 213

Bitch: advertising and, 80–81; circulation of, 73, 75; cover art for, 75; distribution of, 75; donor cultivation for, 75; editorial process for, 78–79; merchandise for, 81; origins of, 70; reader feedback and, 74; *Sassy* as inspiration for, 71; social media and, 82; US Postal Service and, 79; web presence of, 81

Black Arts movement. See *Callaloo*

Blackbird, 199, 203, 206

Black Mountain Poets. *See* language poetry